IMAGES
of America

CLARK COUNTY

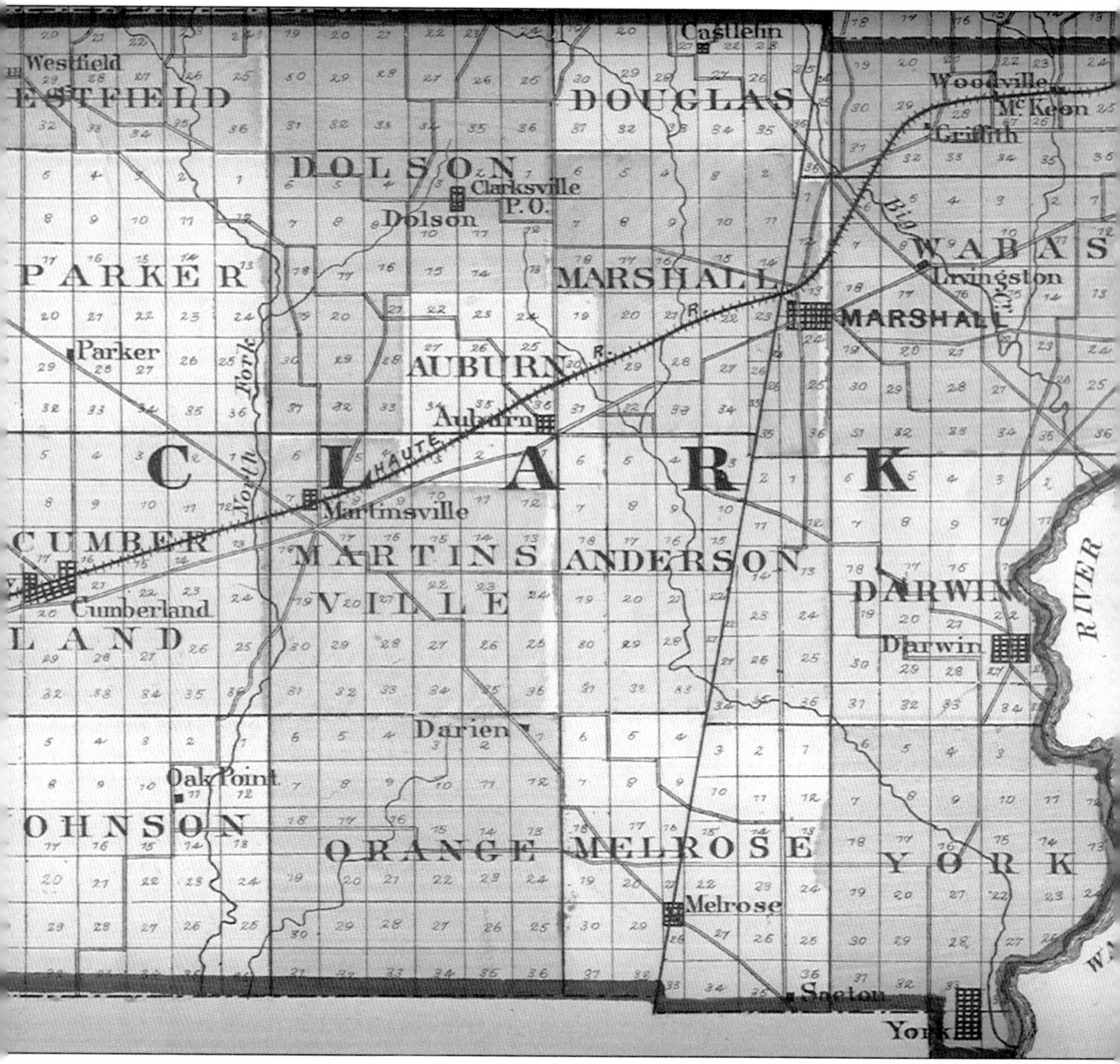

This map shows Clark County, Illinois, in 1875. (Courtesy of Pat Rhoads and the Millcreek Restaurant.)

ON THE COVER: The J and W Tire Shop in Marshall makes use of a military theme to sell tires. (Courtesy of the Clark County Historical Society.)

IMAGES
of America

CLARK COUNTY

Dwight Connelly
and the Clark County Historical Society

ARCADIA
PUBLISHING

ISBN 978-0-7385-6025-0

Published by Arcadia Publishing
Charleston, South Carolina

Printed in the United States of America

Library of Congress Control Number: 2008942894

For all general information contact Arcadia Publishing at:
Telephone 843-853-2070
Fax 843-853-0044
E-mail sales@arcadiapublishing.com
For customer service and orders:
Toll-Free 1-888-313-2665

Visit us on the Internet at www.arcadiapublishing.com

CONTENTS

Acknowledgments

This capsule history of Clark County would not have been possible without the help of many individuals and resources. The excellent pictorial history *Casey: The Early Years, From the 1830's to 2003* by Joyce Van Dyke Skinner and Loistel Summerville was of particular help in telling Casey's story. It is an incredibly impressive work. Loistel has also been particularly helpful in providing photographs and guidance. The Martinsville sesquicentennial book *History of Martinsville, Clark County, Illinois*, edited by Ellen Rowe Zschau, was also helpful. In Marshall, Eleanor Macke has generously made available her extensive photograph collection and detailed information about Marshall buildings and businesses, and has assisted in other ways. Also in Marshall, Ron Deisher has shared his large collection of photographs and his knowledge of Marshall history. Jim Knowles of Marshall has provided several historical photos. In Effingham, Phil Lewis spent many hours copying Clark County postcards from his collection for potential use in this history. Others willing to share their photographs, whether as postcard collections or otherwise, include Sharon Carlin of Casey, Wayne and De Ann Ramsey of Casey, Police Chief Herman Davidson of Martinsville, Pat Rhoads of Clarksville, the West Union public library, the Marshall public library, the Casey public library, and the Clark County Historical Society. Because of the extensive duplication of photographs in the various collections, most individual images are not specifically credited.

INTRODUCTION

In 1671, the Illinois country had been claimed by France, which lost it to Great Britain in 1763 as a result of the French and Indian War. The British made the Illinois country part of Canada, and forbade settlement by residents of the 13 colonies, mainly to avoid contact with the Native Americans. During the Revolutionary War, Virginia governor Patrick Henry sent George Rogers Clark to Virginia's "county of Illinois" to take the largely unsettled area from the British. Clark accomplished this by capturing Vincennes, Kaskaskia, and Ft. Massac. Clark County is, of course, named after the famous general.

Virginia ceded this area, which had very few white settlers, to the new government of the United States in 1784, and it became part of the Northwest Territory in 1787. The vast area was opened to organized settlement, and the " Illinois country" was made part of the Territory of Indiana in 1800, with Vincennes as its capital. Illinois became a separate territory in 1809, and a state in 1818, with Kaskaskia as its first capital, followed by the new city of Vandalia in 1820 and Springfield (with a population of only 1,100) in 1839.

As settlers came in, the Native Americans were forced farther west, so there was only limited interaction between whites and Native Americans—mostly Kickapoo, Winnebago, and Potawatomi—in what is now Clark County. Most of the early settlements began along the Wabash River, and most new residents were farmers, although millers, storekeepers, and blacksmiths were not far behind.

The first settlers in what is now Clark County arrived around 1814 at York, Union Prairie, and Walnut Prairie. With a population of less than 1,000, Clark County was formed out of Crawford County in 1819, and extended all the way to the Canadian border. A county seat was established at a bend of the Wabash River two miles north of present-day Darwin, and named Aurora (Aurora Bend). There was a county jail, with a downstairs for those who drank too much whiskey, and an upstairs for those who could not pay their debts. However, Aurora was not a good location, so in 1823 the county seat was moved south two miles to McClure's Bluff, where John McClure ran a ferry.

McClure's Bluff was platted in 1823 by William Lockard. It was later named Darwin (after Erasmus Darwin, an English naturalist), and in its first five years the lots sold for more than those in Chicago. The initial sale of lots was enhanced when whiskey was provided by the local government to encourage bidding. With a ferry, a steamboat landing, a pork packing plant, boat building, a whiskey distillery, general stores, and county government, Darwin became a small trade center.

Settlement continued northward and westward. Fayette County was formed from Clark and Crawford in 1821, Edgar County from Clark in 1823, and Coles (including Cumberland) from Clark and Edgar in 1830. When the National Road was planned through the county—as well as talk of a railroad along the same route—many residents felt that Darwin was becoming too remote to be the county seat.

In January 1835, William Archer (now Colonel Archer, thanks to brief service in the Black Hawk Indian war in 1832) issued a circular announcing the laying out of the town of Marshall on land purchased by him and Illinois governor Joseph Duncan (1834–1838) where the old Hubbard Trace (Vincennes to Chicago state highway) crossed the new National Road. The Hubbard Trace, which connected Vincennes, Palestine, York, Darwin, Danville, and Chicago, was laid out in 1822 by fur trapper and businessman Gurdon Hubbard along an old trail. In 1827 the state had declared the portion of the road from the ferry landing opposite Vincennes through Palestine (location of the land office) and York to Darwin as a state road. The Lincolns, including Abe, passed through Clark County in 1830, apparently on this road. That same year the legislature attempted to set in motion an extension of this road from Darwin through Paris and Danville to Chicago.

In describing his new town of Marshall, which was named after Supreme Court chief justice John Marshall (1801–1835), Archer noted that "mills are convenient, this selection will be healthy, and there is sufficient timber and the best of stone for building." He added that "the people of the county may find it convenient and to their interest to place the permanent seat of justice for the county at the crossroads."

Archer had strong political ties, serving in the state general assembly (1824–1826), the state senate (1826–1834), and the house of representatives (1838–1848), part of this time with his friend Abraham Lincoln. In addition to his work in Clark County, beginning in 1836 Archer was also heavily involved in developing the Illinois and Michigan Canal, as well as in laying out the canal city of Lockport. His work with the canal resulted in a Chicago street being named for him. In the midst of all this activity, Archer's wife, Elizabeth (Harlan), died at the age of only 39, and he never remarried. They had one child, a daughter.

In 1836, the legislature selected Archer to build the state road from Darwin to a point on the new National Road where his new town of Marshall was located. The legislation also authorized him to build "a substantial wooden bridge across Big Creek where the same is now crossed by the Vincennes and Chicago Road, and also a bridge of the same kind across Mill Creek."

In March 1837, county residents did vote to remove the county seat from Darwin by a margin of 378 to 228, but Marshall did not automatically become the new county seat. Another town on the National Road, Auburn (Clark Center), which had been platted in 1836, also wanted the seat of government. Since there were no newspapers in the county at that time, the question was argued vigorously at the mills and blacksmith shops. No doubt various deals were made. The victory, in August 1837, went to Marshall, which received 453 votes to Auburn's 362, and the county seat was moved there in 1838.

However, as the western part of the county became more populous, there was again agitation to move the county seat. In 1839, Colonel Archer improved, at his own expense, the "Charleston Road," as far as its intersection with the "Darwin-Charleston road" in the northwestern part of the county. At this intersection he platted the village of Westfield, hoping to enhance Marshall's role as the key location in the county for both commerce and government. The "Charleston road" was eventually continued on to Springfield, and was known in Coles County as the "Archer Road."

Unfortunately, Archer ran into financial difficulties, and was sued in Clark County Circuit Court in 1842, with his friend Lincoln representing the plaintiffs. Archer defaulted, and the plaintiffs won damages of $6,277.33. Archer had no hard feelings against Lincoln, and nominated him for vice president in 1856.

Agitation to move the county seat from Marshall continued, and a vote was held in May 1849, for removal, but Marshall kept the seat of justice by the narrow margin of 771 to 640. Colonel Archer had prevailed, but despite his founding of Marshall and Westfield, his road building, his activities throughout the state, and his political connections, he had more debts than money when he died in Marshall on August 9, 1870. But he died with the respect of his fellow citizens, and left a legacy unmatched by any other resident of Clark County.

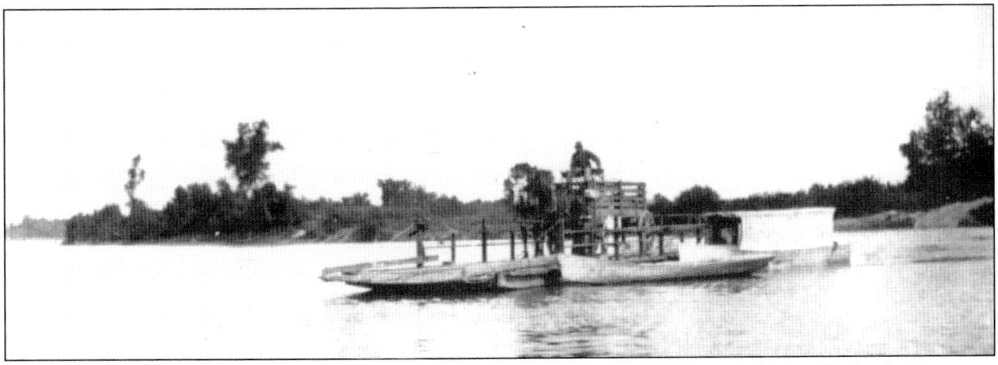

This old ferry at York was typical of the numerous ferries that crossed the Wabash River in the 1800s, including the more famous one at Darwin. But before the ferries, flatboats, horses, and wagons, there were the Native Americans, who were attracted to what would become Clark County by the temperate climate, the Wabash River, the mixture of woods and open areas, and plenty of wild game. These same characteristics also attracted European settlers.

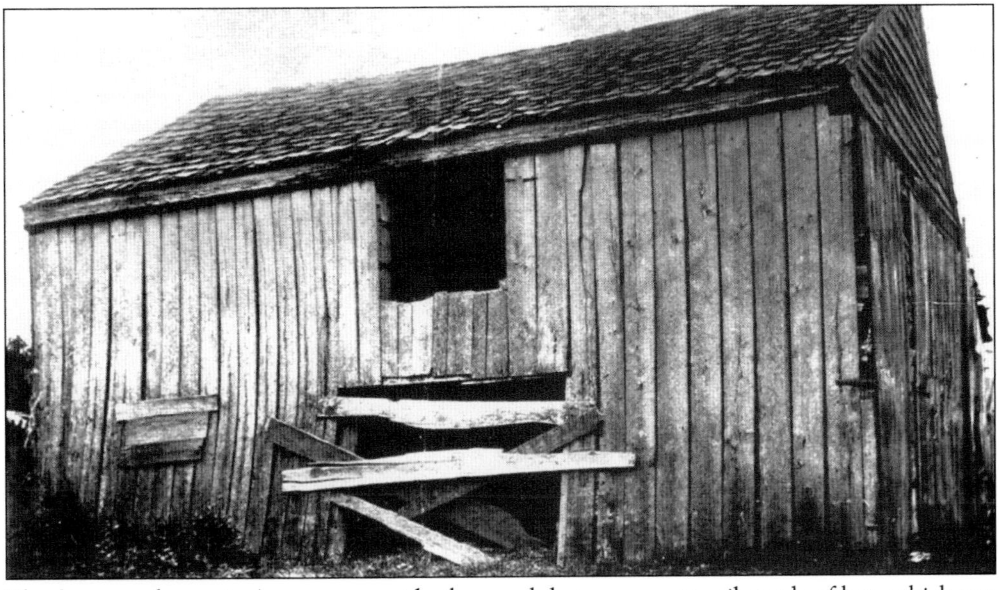

The first courthouse in Aurora was not built as such but was a corn crib made of logs, which was later sided with sawn boards.

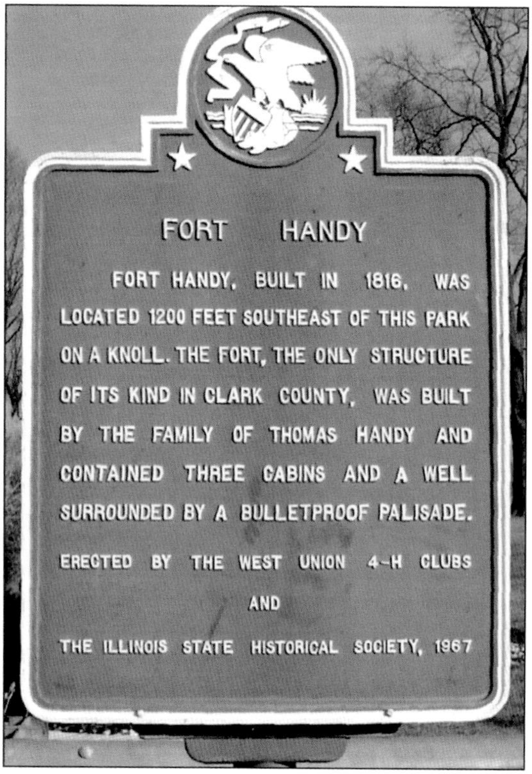

West Union has the distinction of being the location of the only "fort" built in Clark County, that being Fort Handy. The Handy family came from New York, and by 1815 had settled in Union Prairie (West Union). There were signs of Native American hostility, so in 1816 they erected a fort a half mile southeast of what is now the West Union city park.

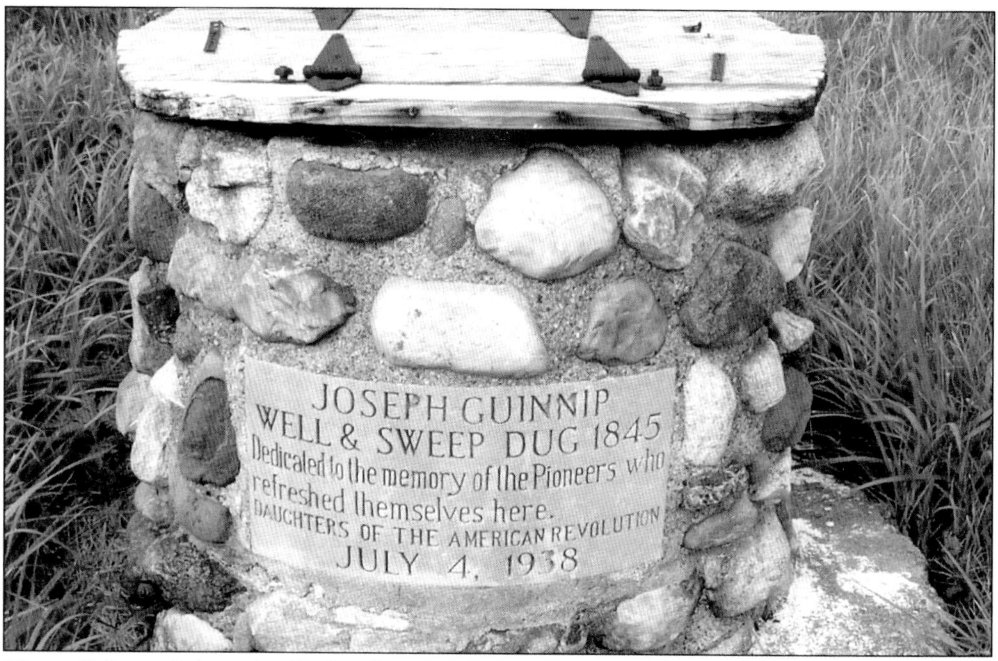

This well, located along the Clarksville Road, just north of I-70, originally featured a sweep, which is made up of a post with a fulcrum pole attached to a rope and water pail, designed to make raising the full bucket of water much easier. Abraham Lincoln reportedly used this well while a circuit-riding lawyer.

One

TRANSPORTATION

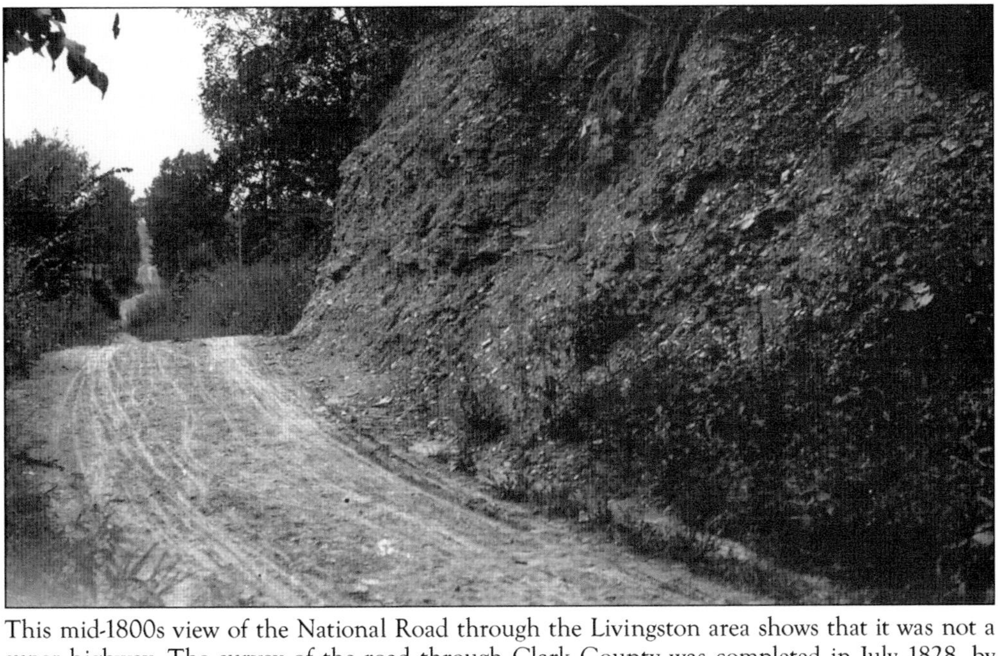

This mid-1800s view of the National Road through the Livingston area shows that it was not a super highway. The survey of the road through Clark County was completed in July 1828, by Joseph Schriver, and it was considered passable but unfinished by the time Marshall was laid out in 1835. It was officially opened to Vandalia in the summer of 1839.

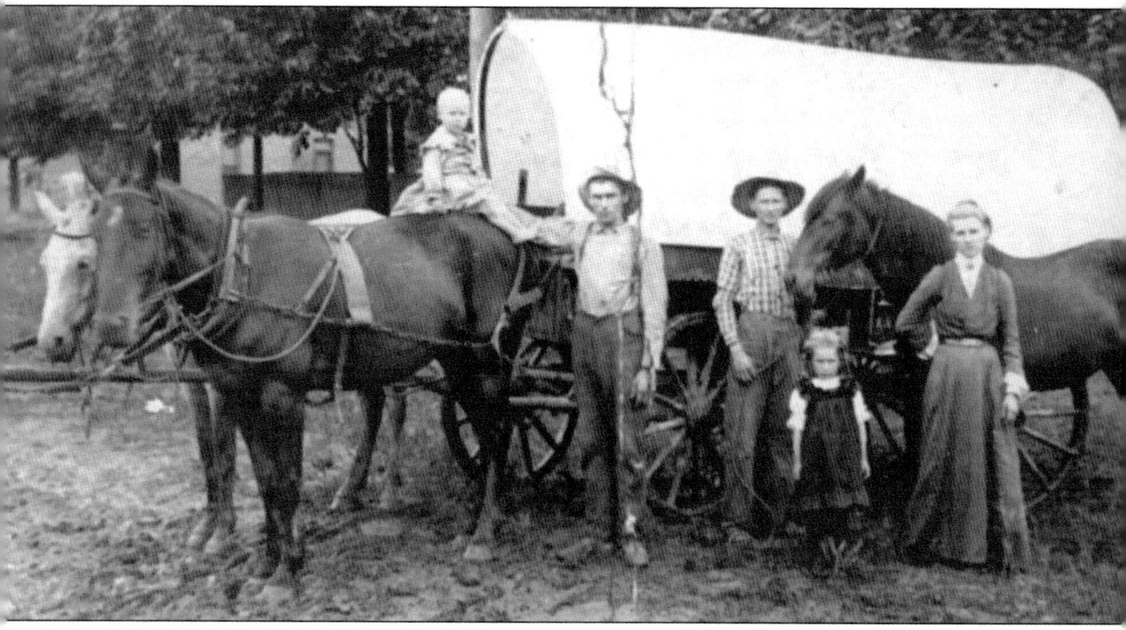

Typical of travelers along the early roads of Clark County, including the new National Road, were families in the small covered wagons pulled by horses or oxen. The high axles usually allowed the wagon to clear the frequent stumps in the road. The large Conestoga wagons drawn by six-horse teams and pulling 10,000 pounds of freight were the semi-trucks of their day, moving commerce east and west along the road. Smaller wagons, stagecoaches, single horses, oxen, and foot traffic provided plenty of business for the inns along the road, such as the Archer House (1841) at Marshall, Shaffner's Stage Coach Inn (1850s) east of Martinsville, the National Hotel (1840s) at Casey, and similar hotel-tavern businesses along the road.

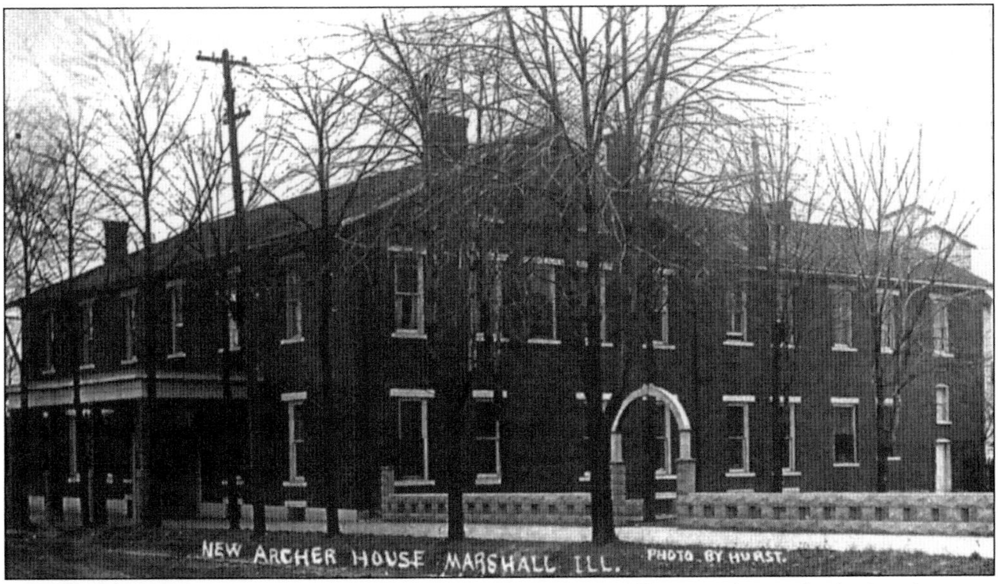

The Archer House, built in Marshall in 1841–1844 by Col. William Archer and John Bartlett, was one of the first hotels along the National Road. These views show how it originally looked with all sides exposed. The hotel stood like this until about 1918 when Frank Machlin built a garage on its west side. It is on the National Register of Historic Places, and is currently vacant.

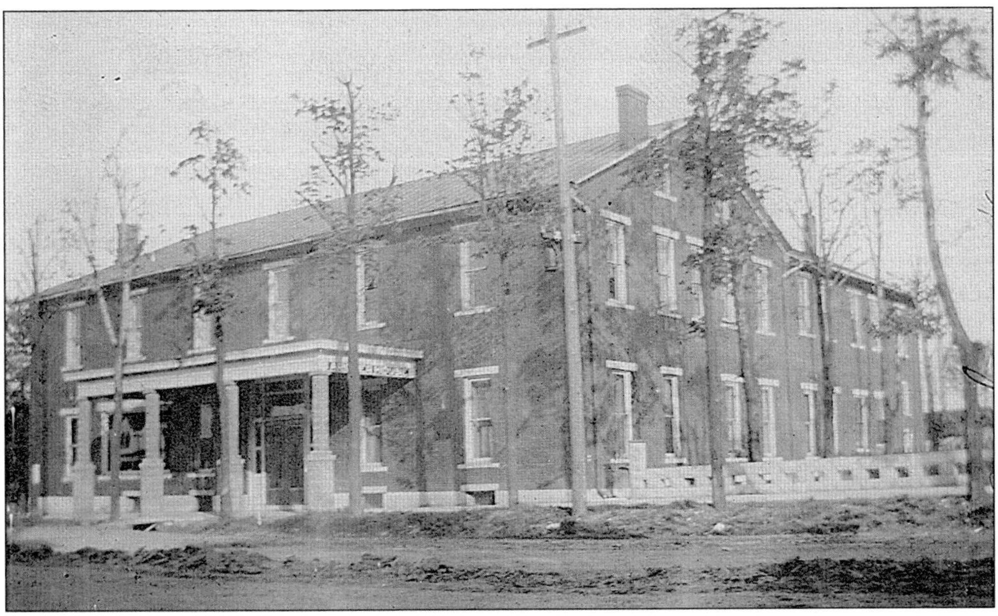

The Archer House hotel has also been called the Madison House, the National-Dixie Hotel, and the St. James Hotel. The oldest hotel and second oldest building in the state, the National Road (Archer Avenue) is on its north side and the Vincennes-Chicago Road/Dixie Highway (Michigan Avenue) on its east side. The Big Four railroad ran beside it along Michigan Avenue from 1879 to 1907. Among its guests were Abraham Lincoln and Pres. Grover Cleveland.

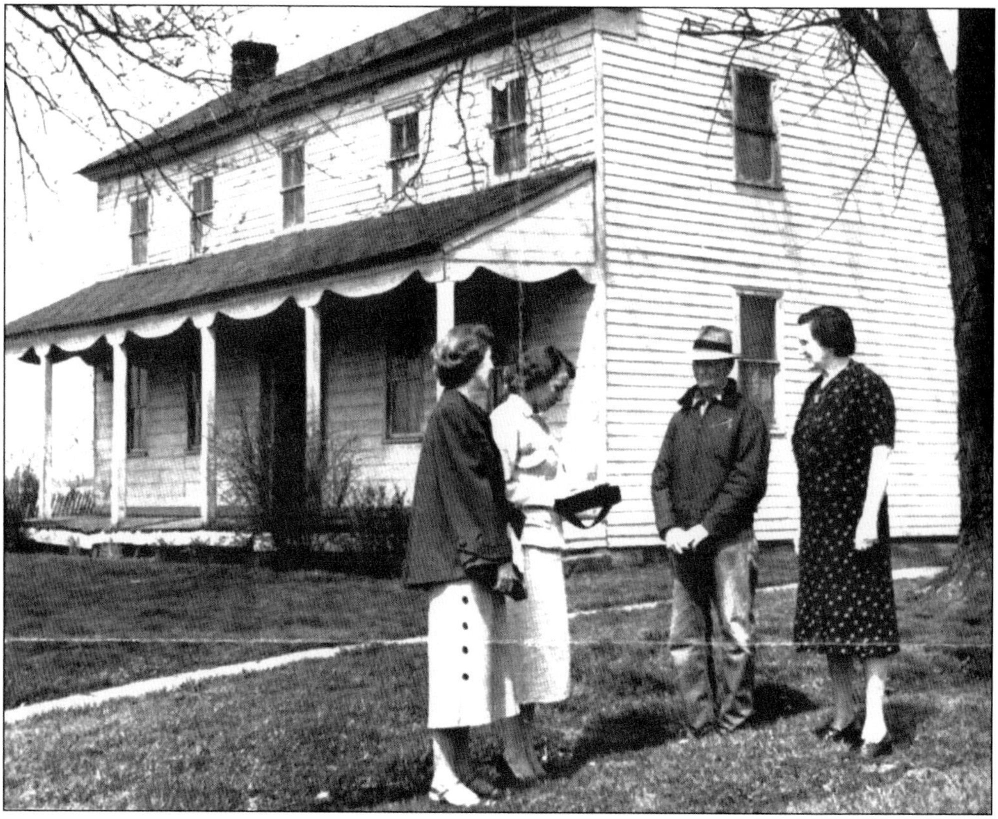

Jack and Veda Shaffner, right, explain to guests that Shaffner's Stage Coach Inn was built by John Shaffner in 1850 along the National Road just east of Martinsville. In addition to food and drink for weary travelers, there was also a barn for stagecoach horses. The inn, built of oak and poplar, had to be relocated to make way for the new Route 40, so Mr. and Mrs. Robert E. Bennett bought it and moved it in 1975 to just north of Clark Center as a family residence.

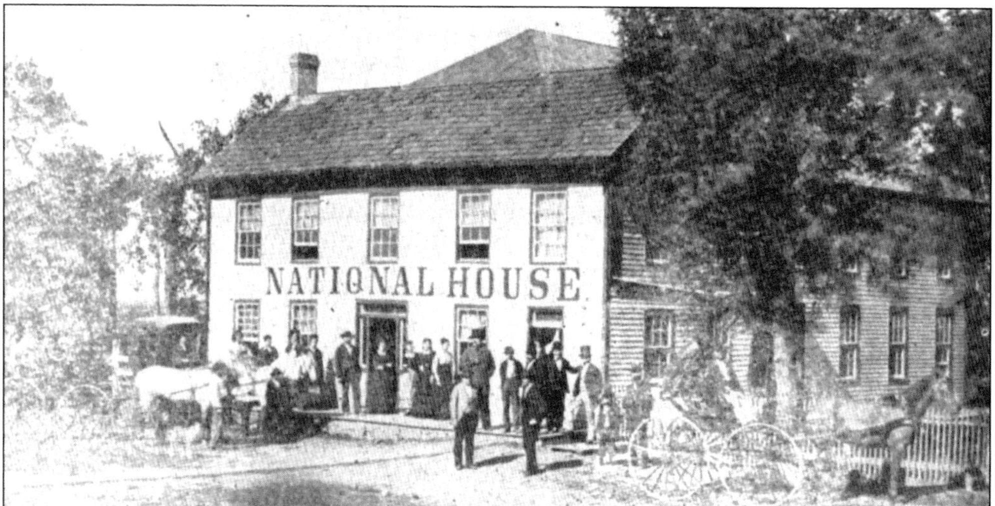

The National House was built in the 1840s by John Lang along the National Road in what is now downtown Casey. It burned in 1888.

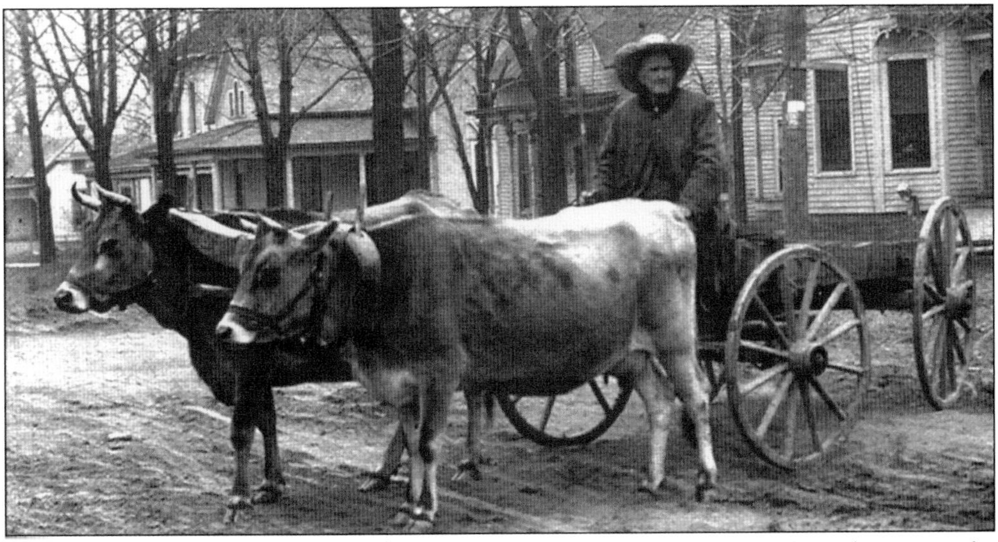

Een Cole is an example of how local people may have utilized the National Road. He is at the intersection of Ninth Street and Archer Avenue in Marshall.

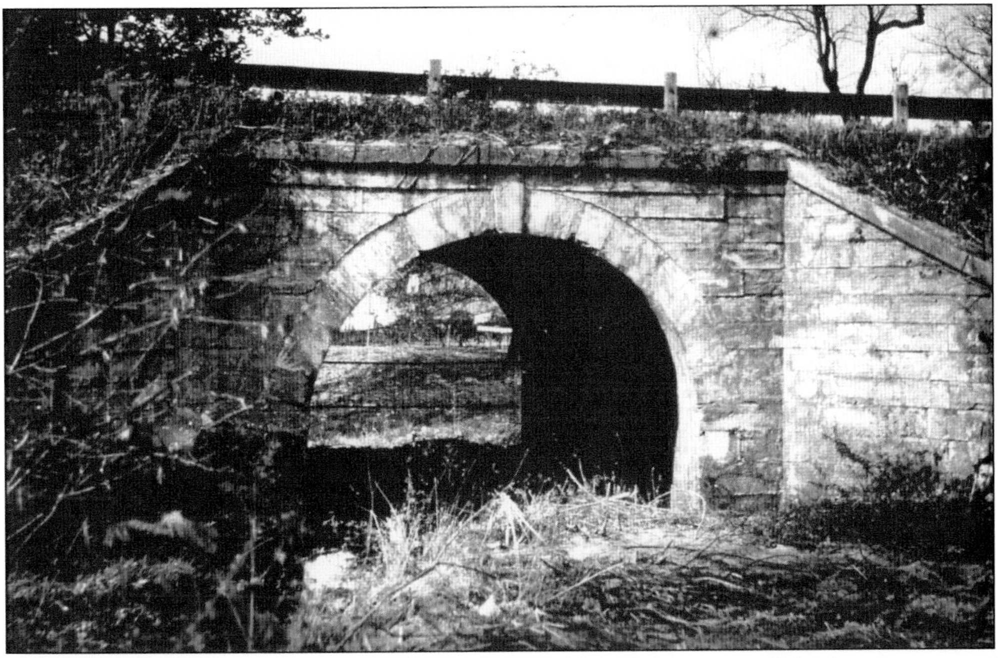

The Old Stone Bridge, or Starkey Bridge, just west of Marshall, is one of the few remnants of the original National Road. Built of local stone in 1837, the structure still handles traffic on Old Route 40. A historical marker is nearby, just outside the Oak Ridge Subdivision.

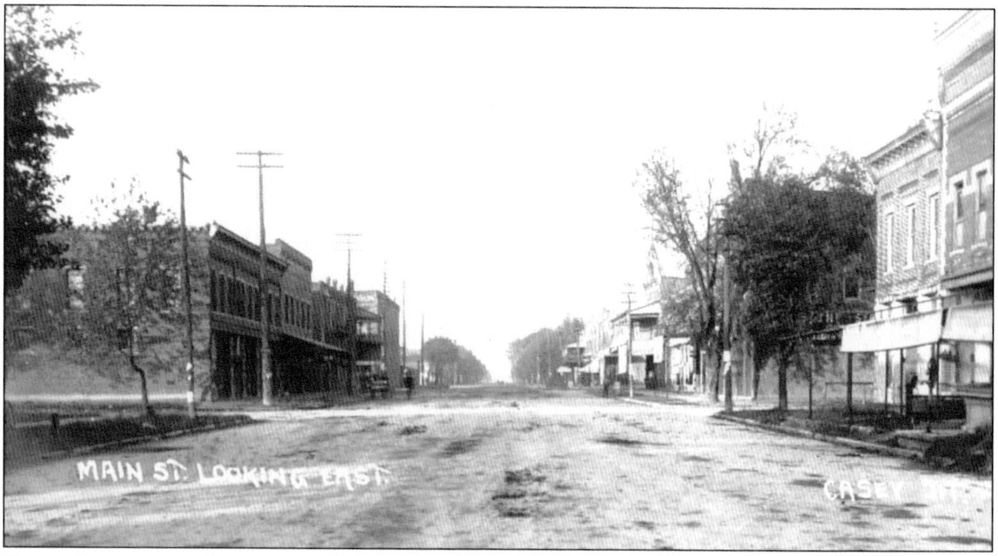

Even after cities such as Casey featured brick buildings in the downtown area the old National Road was still unpaved. A petition to pave Casey's main street was submitted in 1906. Martinsville's downtown section of the National Road was not paved until 1920.

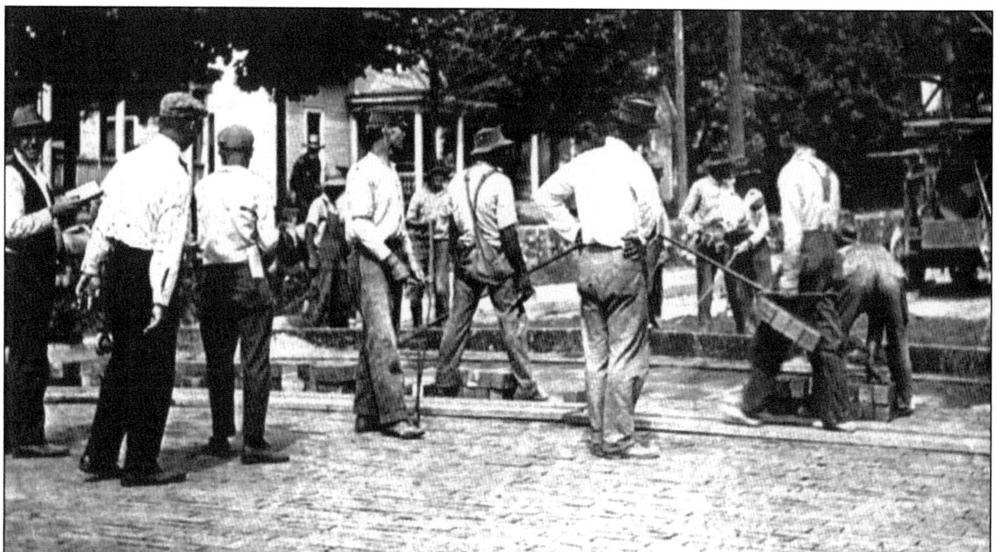

The paving of the National Road in downtown Marshall was not accomplished until 1910.

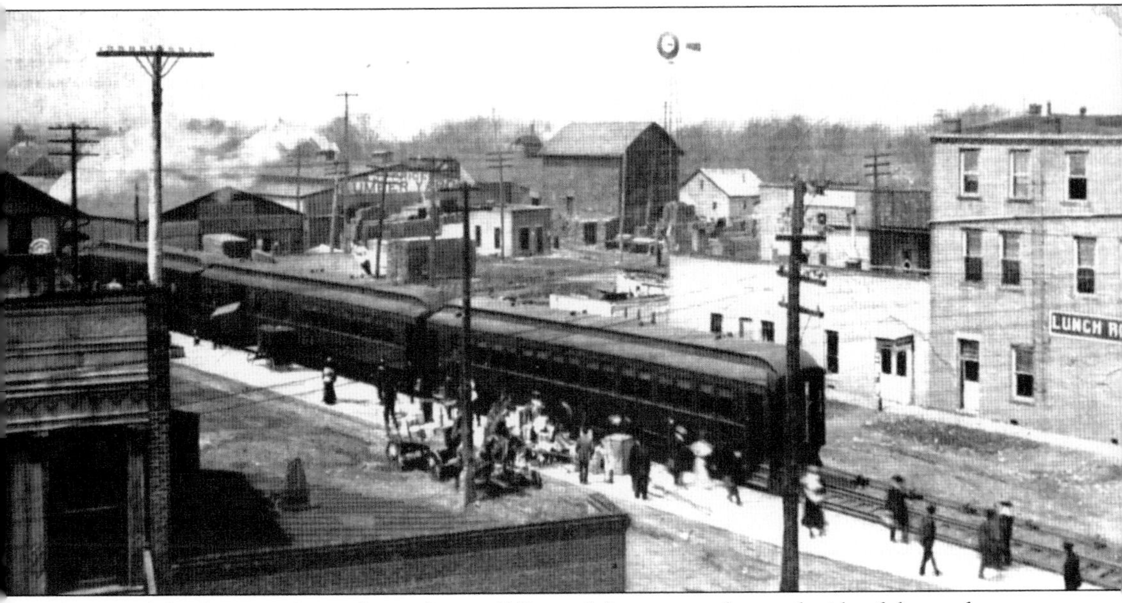

This Vandalia depot in Casey, located just off Central Avenue on the south side of the tracks, was built in 1890, the year the first passenger trains came through. Also shown are some of Casey's landmarks at the time, such as Price Lumber. When passenger train service was discontinued, the depot was torn down in the late 1970s. Other than the National Road, the most important element in the development of Clark County has been the railroad. Clark County's first railroad was the Vandalia Railroad (later called the Pennsylvania), which came through Marshall, Martinsville, and Casey in 1870. A second major railway line ran north and south through the county, beginning in 1879, with depots in Marshall and West Union. A third railway, shorter and more regional, was the Cincinnati, Hamilton, and Dayton Railway (CH&D), which operated from the late 1800s to 1935. It ran north and south with depots in Westfield and Casey, and was also known as the Doty line.

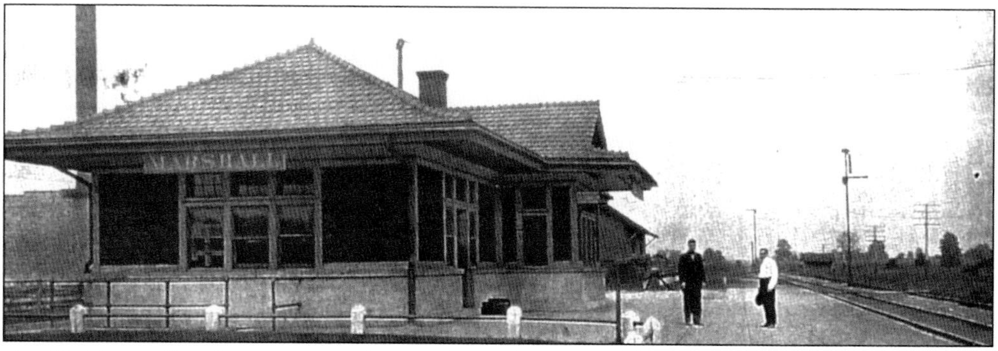

The Big Four railroad ran north and south through Marshall, beginning in 1879, along Michigan Avenue and beside the Archer House and the Newberry gristmill. The original depot was located at Michigan Avenue and Locust Street, but the track was moved a mile and a half east in 1907, and the depot was razed. The new depot, pictured above, was constructed that same year, and torn down in 1968.

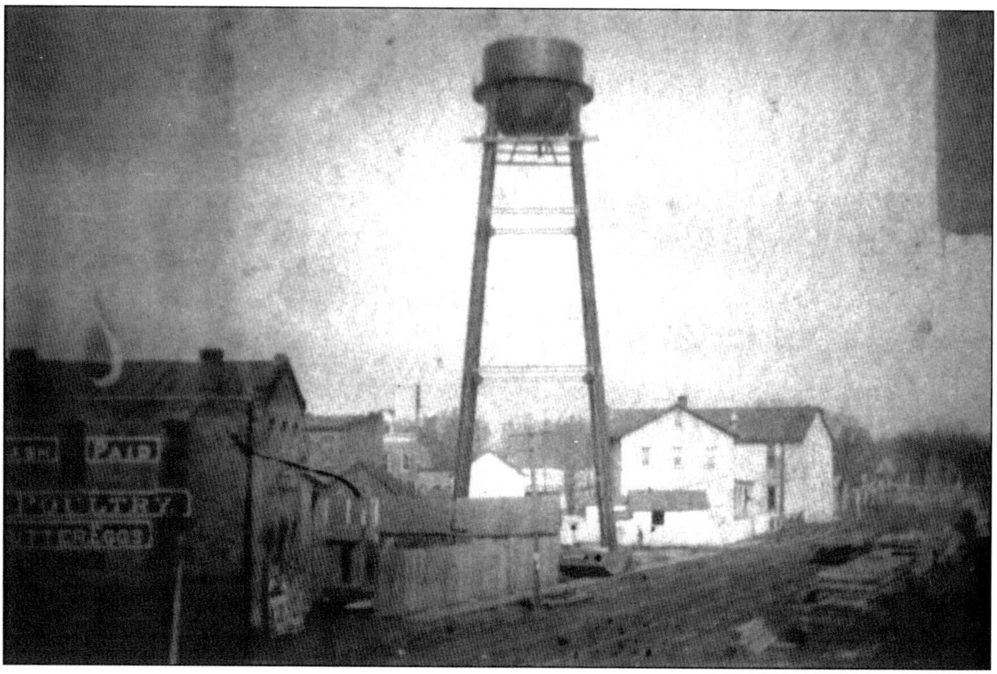

This view, looking north, shows the Big Four railroad tracks running alongside the Archer House down Michigan Avenue in Marshall. Note that the Archer House still sits independently of any attached buildings on the west. Marshall was also on the Vandalia (Pennsylvania) railway line, which ran east and west a mile north of the city, beginning in 1870.

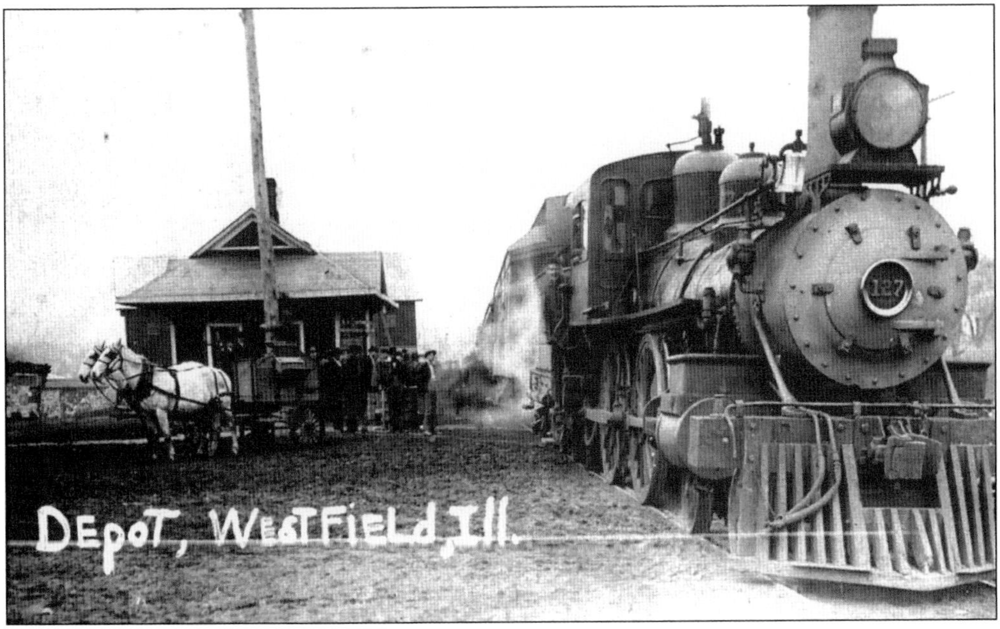

While not the biggest railroad, the CH&D, later called the Doty line, made an important contribution from its inception in the late 1800s. It was important to Casey, Westfield, Westfield College, and the booming settlement of Oilfield, as it connected all these points with cities to the north and south until it died in 1935. The above scene is at the Westfield depot.

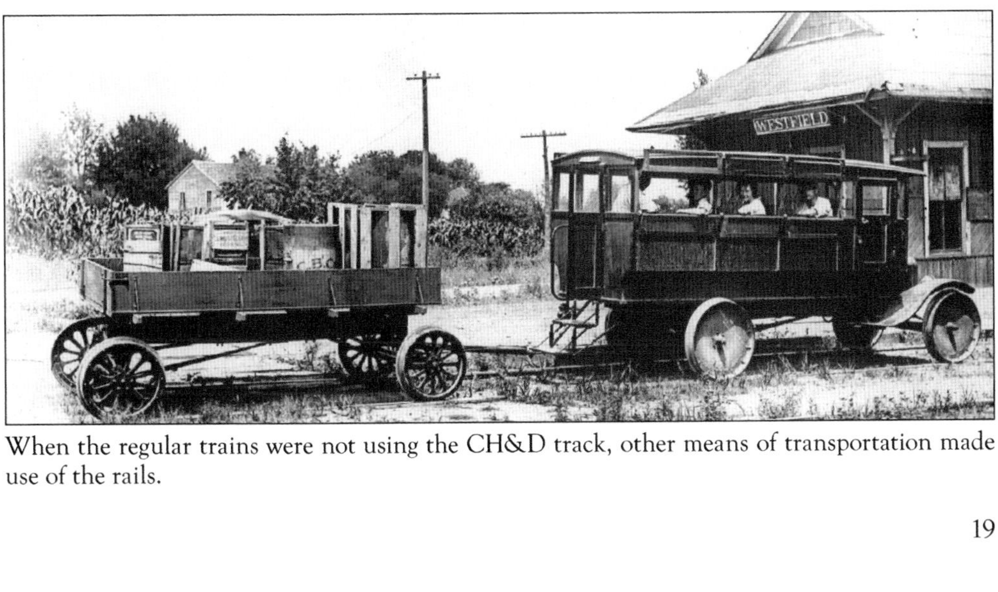

When the regular trains were not using the CH&D track, other means of transportation made use of the rails.

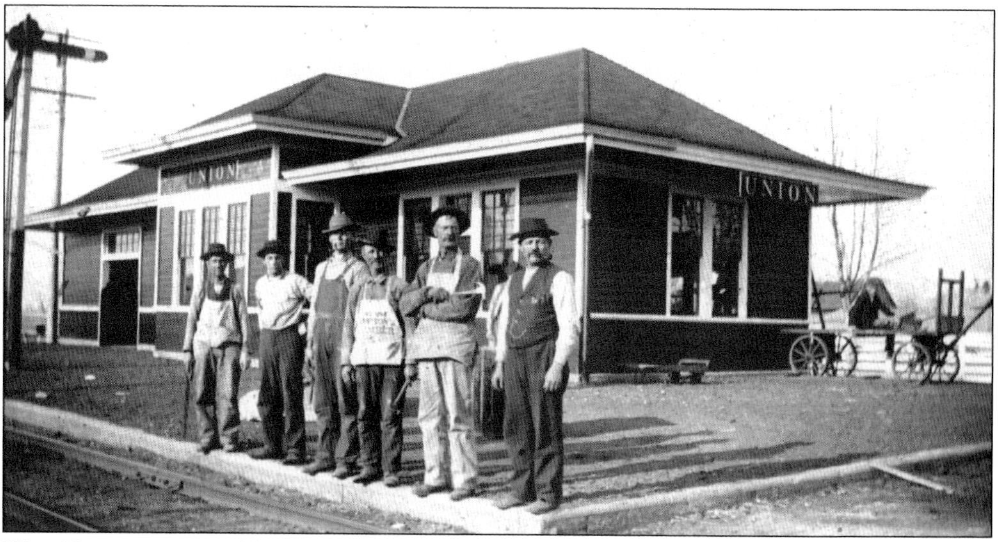

West Union was served by the Big Four railroad, running north and south. In the 1920s, there were four passenger trains through each day. Gordon Coryell met the 4:00 a.m. train and hauled the mail to the post office in a four-wheel cart. Freight trains moved commerce in and out of West Union.

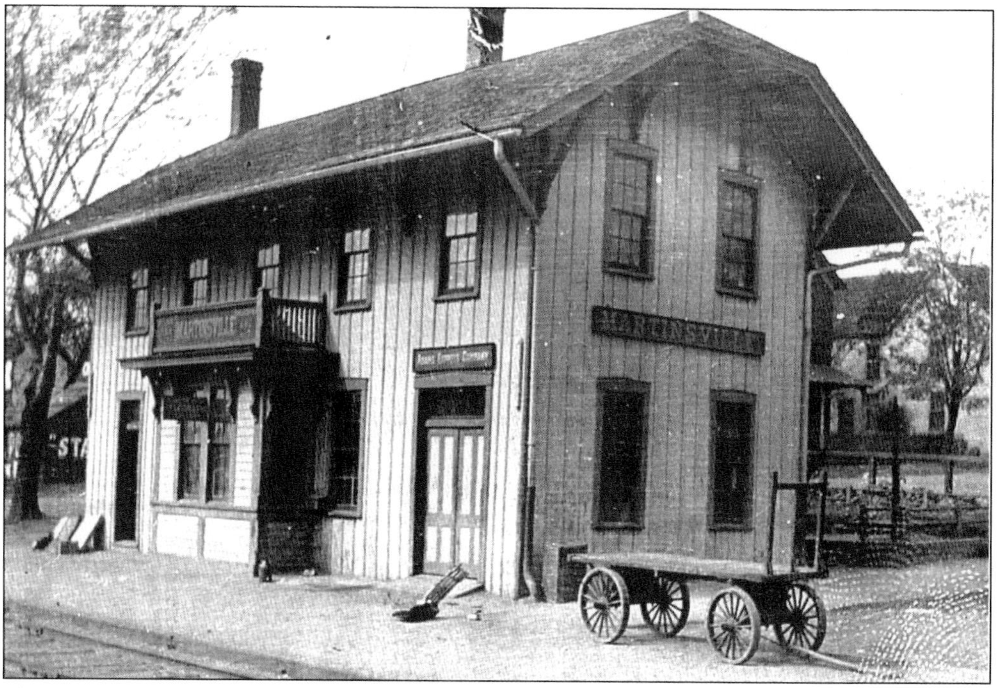

The freight, mail, and passenger stops at Martinsville helped the city prosper, and hotels were built near the depot to accommodate travelers.

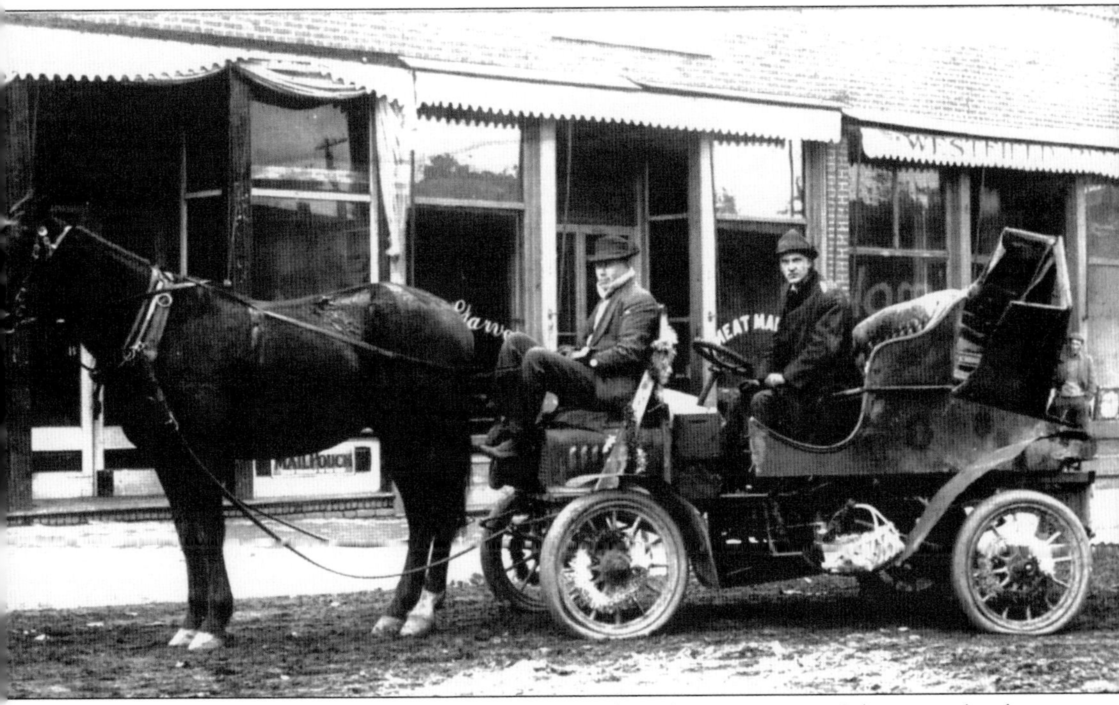

While this photograph could illustrate the transition from horse to automobile, it may be that these Westfield drivers just ran out of gas or had mechanical troubles. The *Westfield Review* newspaper office is in the background. In view of today's interest in developing automobiles that use less gasoline, it is interesting that in 1900, 25 percent of cars ran on batteries alone. Then Henry Ford came along in 1908 with his inexpensive Model T, just in time to make a new oil industry boom. Over the years, nearly every domestic brand of automobile has been sold in Clark County, including Ford, Chevrolet, Dodge, Studebaker, Maxwell, and Nash.

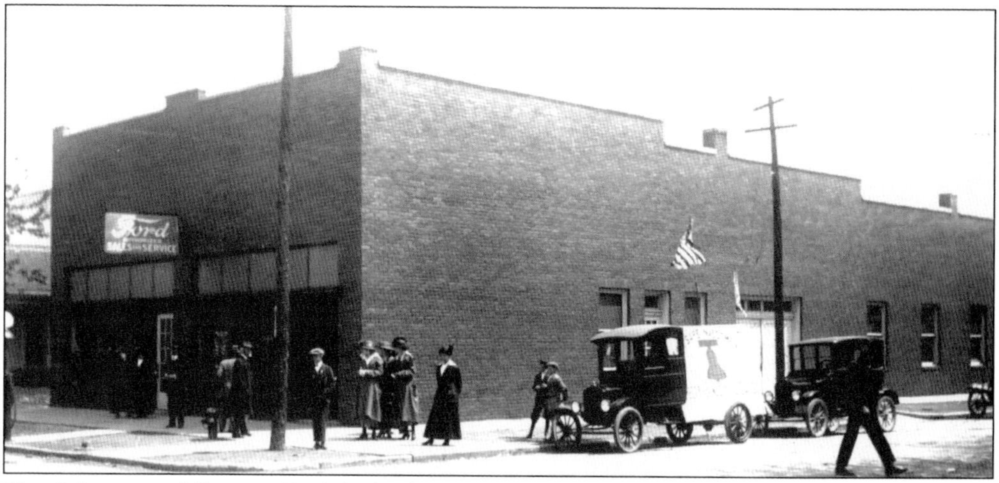

This Johnson and Pierson Ford dealership in Casey was set up at the southeast corner of Main Street and First Street in 1917. In 1928, the building was rented to the Ettelbrick Shoe Company as a manufacturing site, and the Ford dealership moved to 17 West Main Street, then to Indiana. Dwight Moody opened another Ford dealership in the West Main building in 1933, selling it in 1949 to C. M . Johnson Motor Sales. In 1959, Moody and son-in-law Don Elliott bought the business from Johnson, and Moody-Elliott Ford operated on West Main Street until 1998.

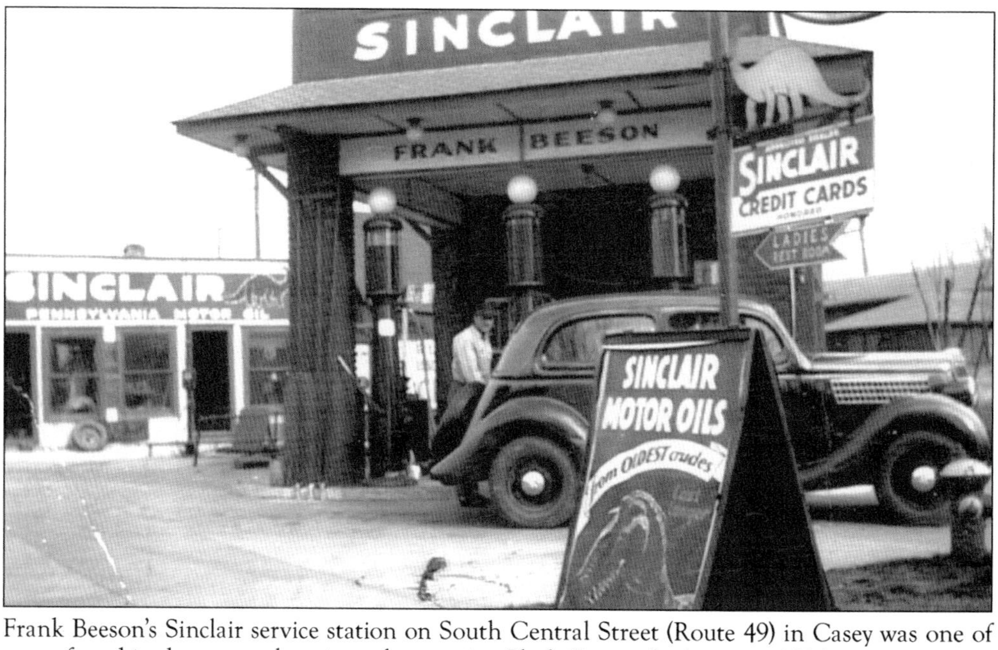

Frank Beeson's Sinclair service station on South Central Street (Route 49) in Casey was one of many found in downtown locations along major Clark County highways in 1936.

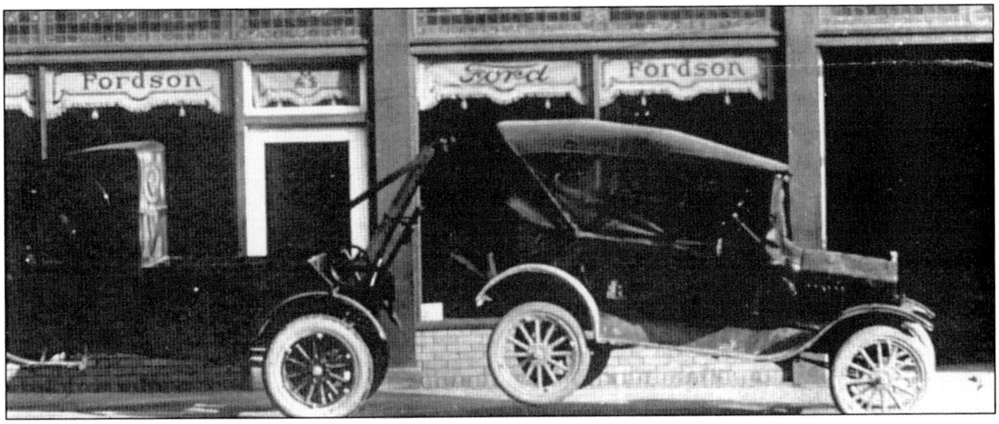

Even Fords need an occasional tow. The tow truck is also a Ford, of course, since this is a Marshall Auto Sales advertisement.

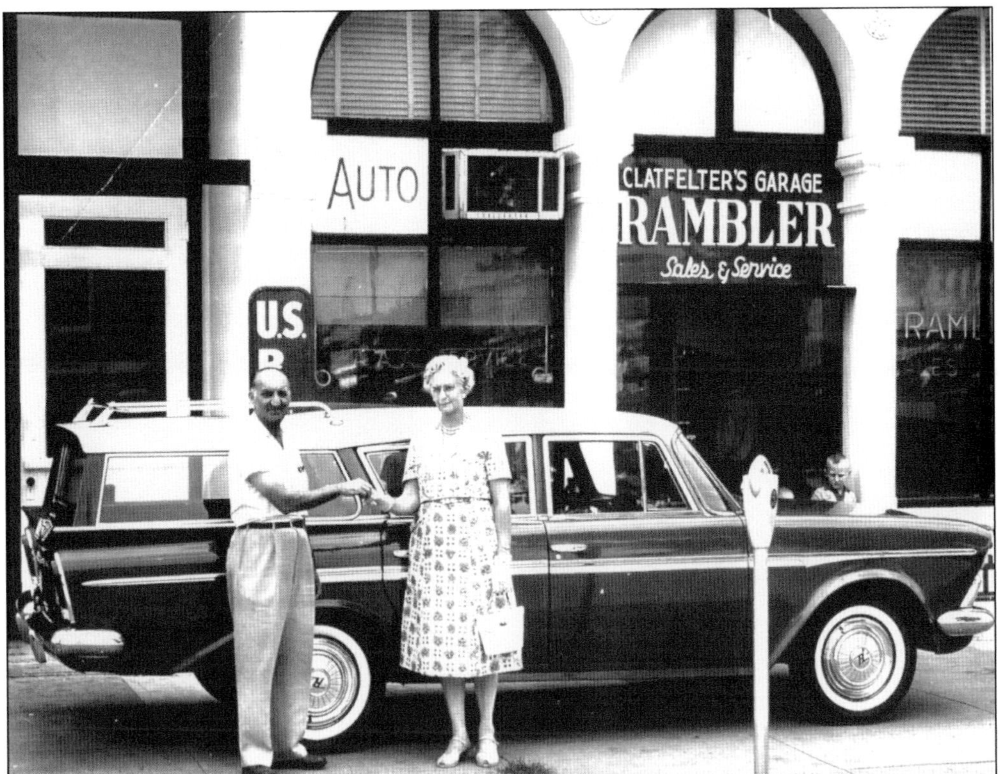

Wayne Clatfelter gives keys to a Nash Rambler to Mrs. Claude McDaniel, who won the car. The dealership was on South Fifth Street in Marshall, opposite the courthouse. Dulaney Bank now occupies the site. Note the parking meter, which came to Marshall in 1949.

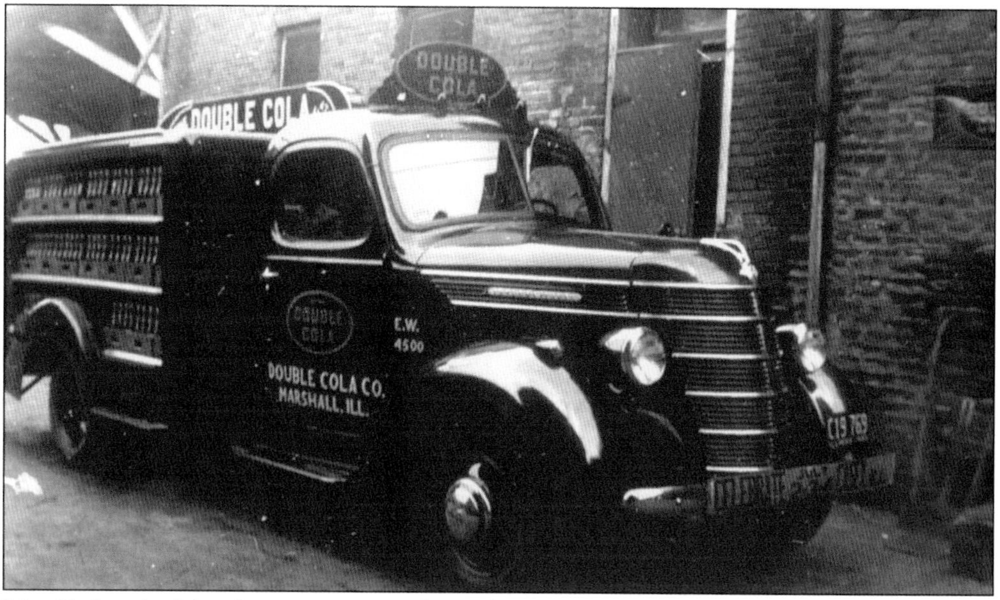

John Rademaker's bottling company was located at 115 South Sixth Street in Marshall with alley access. His early delivery vehicle was a horse and wagon, rather than this sleek truck. In addition to Double Cola, he produced other drinks in custom manufactured bottles.

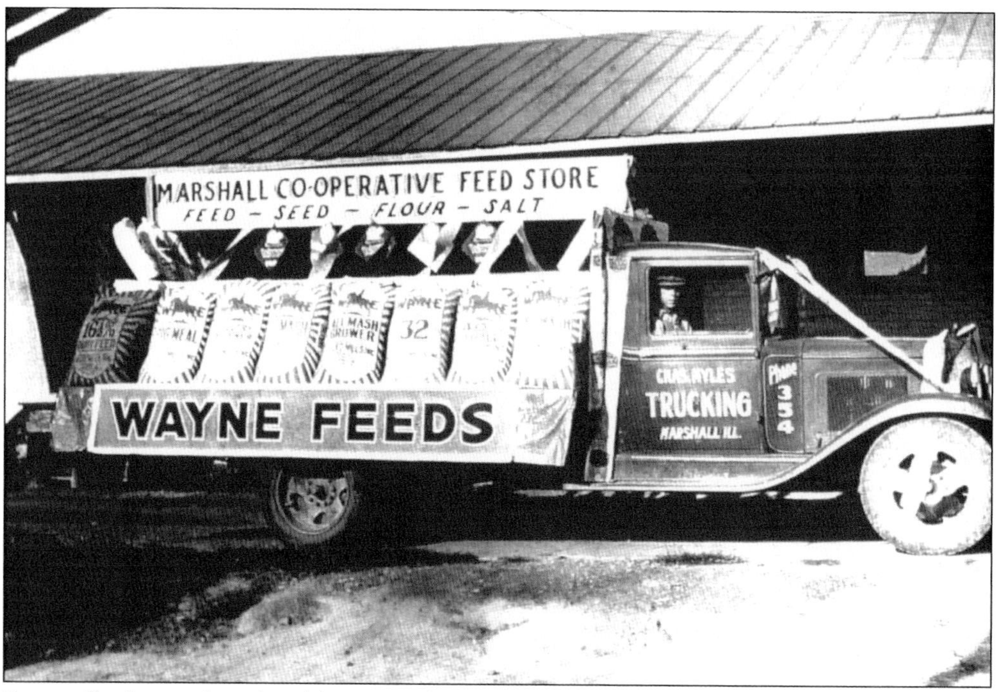

Eventually the truck replaced horses and oxen as farmers and merchants moved their goods. Farmers also began to see a need to cooperate in forming their own business operations. This truck belongs to Charlie Myles.

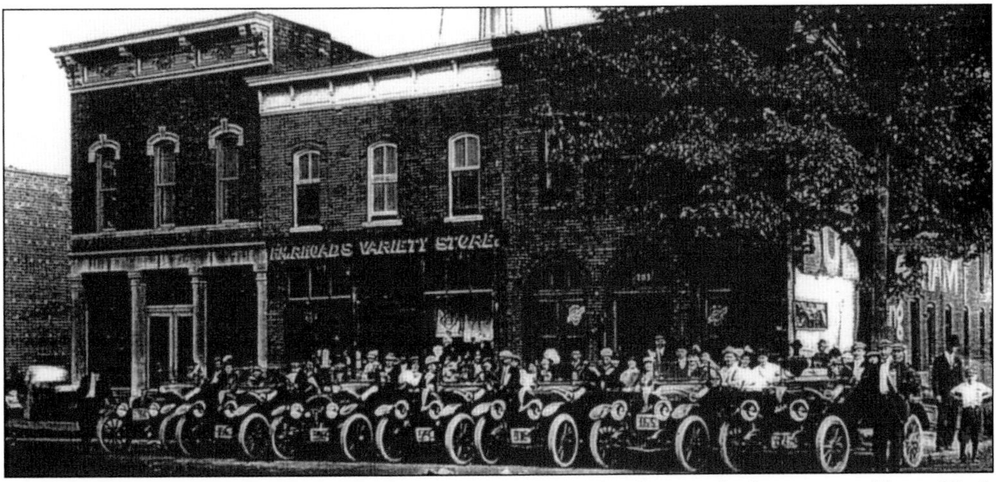

The Maxwell automobile has disappeared, but 13 of the large vehicles were sold in Clark County in 1914. Charles Brandenstein's Implement and Harness Shop evolved into the Maxwell dealership, operating where the Marshall Family Restaurant is now located. To the left of Brandenstein's shop is the Rhoads Variety Store, which had earlier been Rhoads Groceries, and an empty building which had been a bowling alley and Blundell's Restaurant. Farther east, the vacant lot would eventually hold Frank Machlin's garage, Bryant's Garage, and Rhoads Garage.

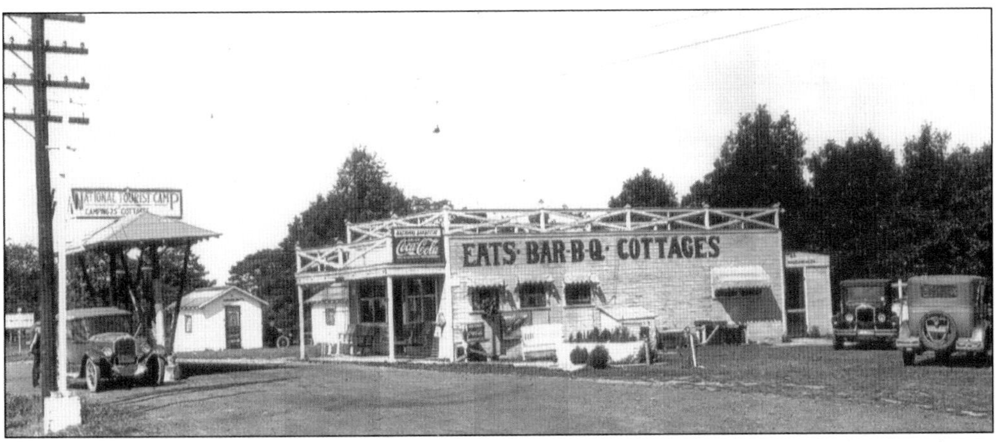

The National Tourist Camp, located a mile west of Marshall on the National Road (Route 40), was typical of overnight facilities which lined major highways as the number of auto travelers increased. Other such campgrounds included the Noyes Park Grocery and camp at Michigan Avenue (Route 1) and Mulberry Street in Marshall, the Husted camping facility just east of Martinsville, and the Oak Grove Lodge west of Casey.

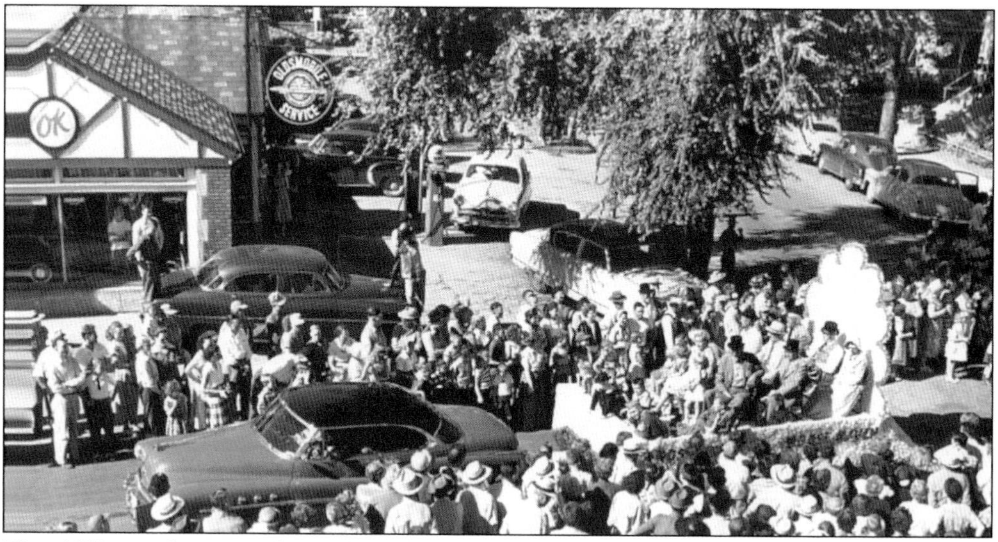

This 1953 parade past Robert Chevrolet at Main and Alabama Streets was one of the many activities celebrating Casey's centennial.

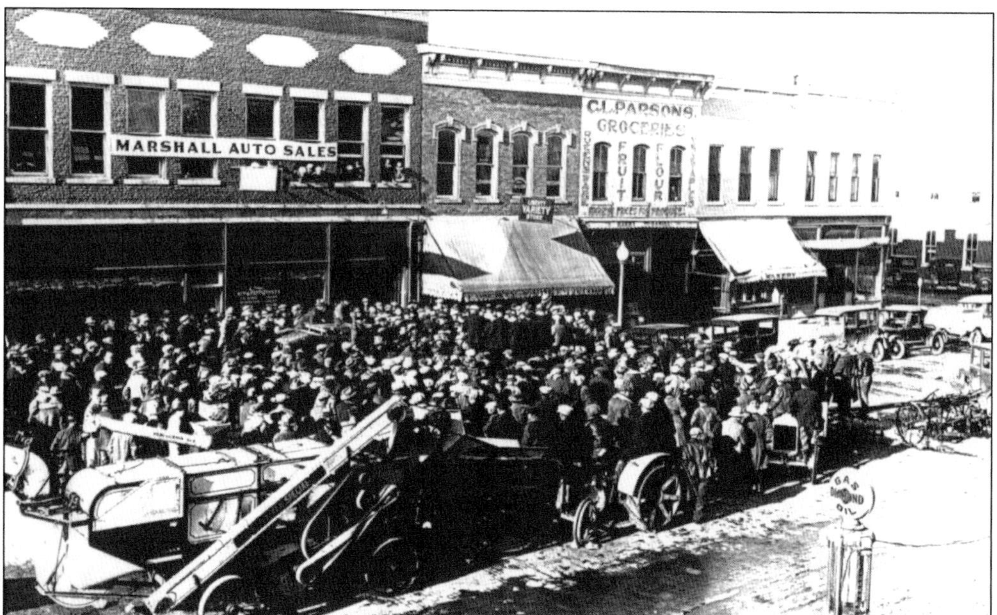

Marshall Auto Sales was one of the most successful dealerships in the county, selling Ford cars, Fordson tractors, and farm machinery at 614–616 Archer Avenue, the current home of the Marshall library. To the east are the Liberty Variety Store, Parsons Grocery, and Elite Bakery.

Two

AGRICULTURE

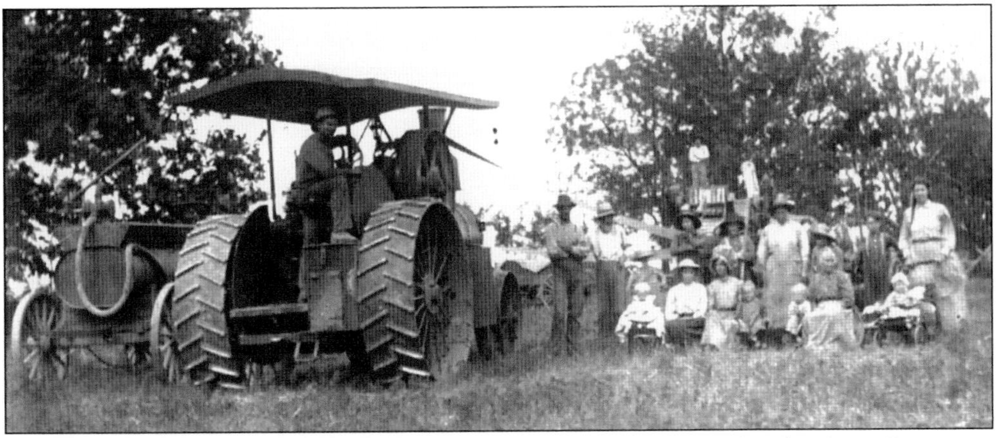

Charlie Maxwell of rural Martinsville made use of his steam tractor for threshing. During an especially cold winter, he took it across the frozen Wabash River by laying down planks and carefully driving across them. One of the earliest farm machines in Clark County was the steam tractor, which was large, heavy, and not very maneuverable, but it had plenty of power to turn large belts, which in turn operated harvesting equipment.

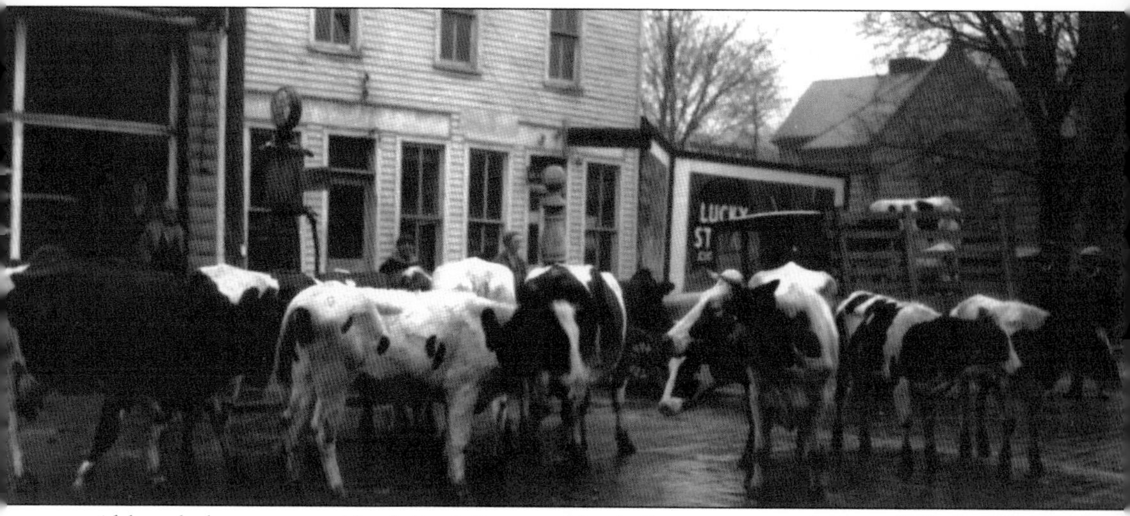

Although these cows on North Sixth Street in Marshall are not strays, farmers did have a problem with strays in the early 1800s, as fences were few and inadequate. Several farmers marked, or branded, their animals and registered their marks with Clark County officials. Following are two examples: "Be it known that on the eighteenth day of March in the year of our Lord one thousand eight hundred and twenty came William B. Archer and ordered his mark of hogs, cattle, etc. which is 'an underbit out of the underside of the right ear.'" and "Be it remembered that on this 3rd day of May A.D. 1839 came Josiah Connelly and ordered his mark on cattle, sheep and hogs to be recorded which is 'an under bit in right ear.'" Fortunately these two similar markings belonged to farmers who lived far apart. Between 1819 and 1861, a total of 304 such marks were recorded in Clark County. In some instances the same individual would later record a different mark.

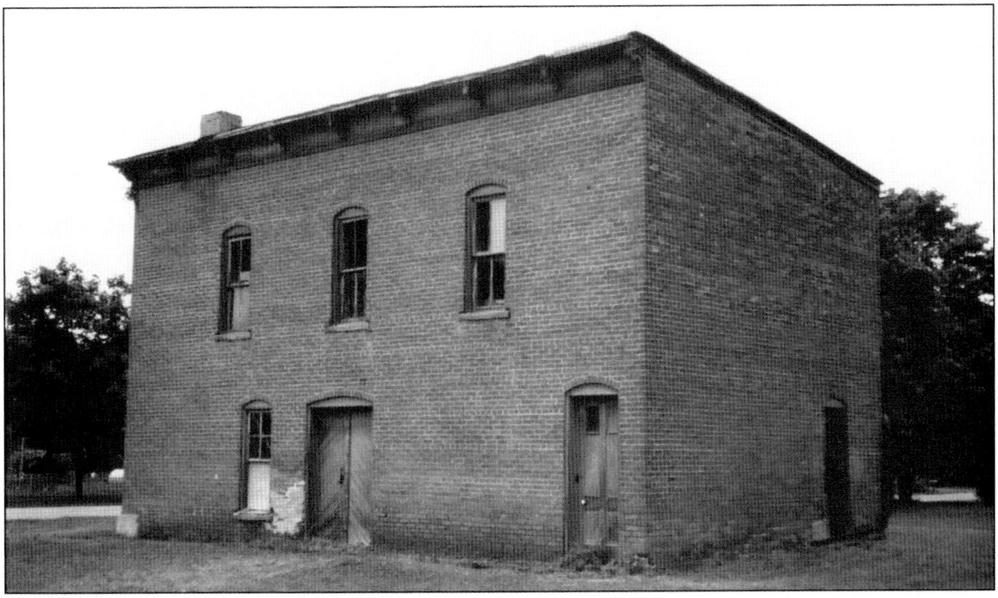

Among the earliest businesses in Clark County was the blacksmith shop, which not only kept horses shod but made and repaired all sorts of metal utensils and equipment. The Wes Millhouse blacksmith shop in Clarksville, built in the 1860s, was one of these. An attempt was made to save this historic building, but preservation funds were unavailable, and it has been torn down.

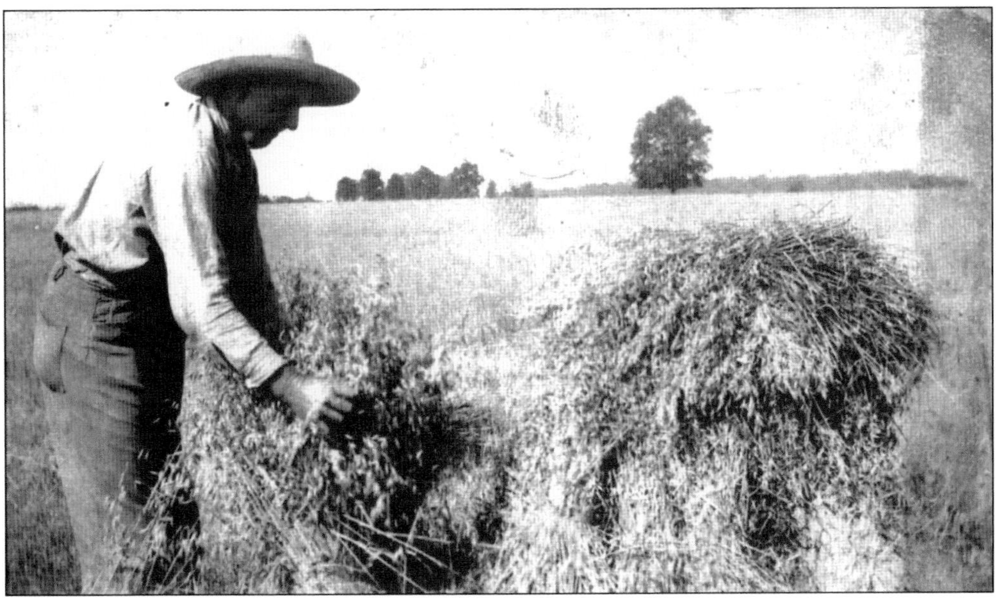

Robert Stricker of Clarksville harvests wheat by hand.

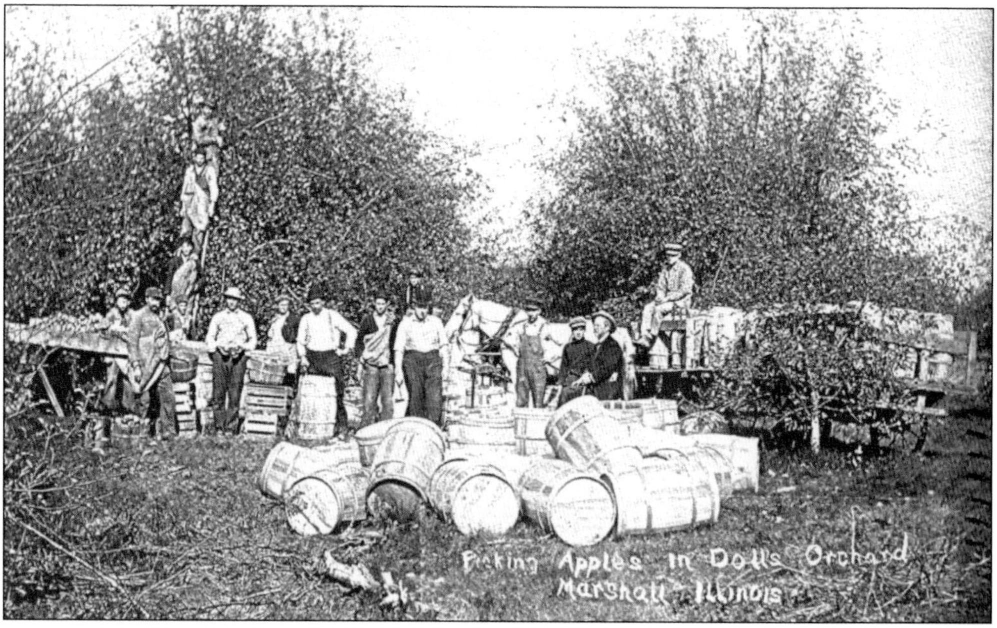

Apple orchards have been an important crop in Clark County in past years, with sales outside the county. This photograph was taken at Doll's Orchards northeast of Marshall, but there was also Cline Orchard just east of Martinsville, Newman Orchard northeast of Martinsville, and an orchard south of Martinsville opposite the Needmore Store. None of these has survived.

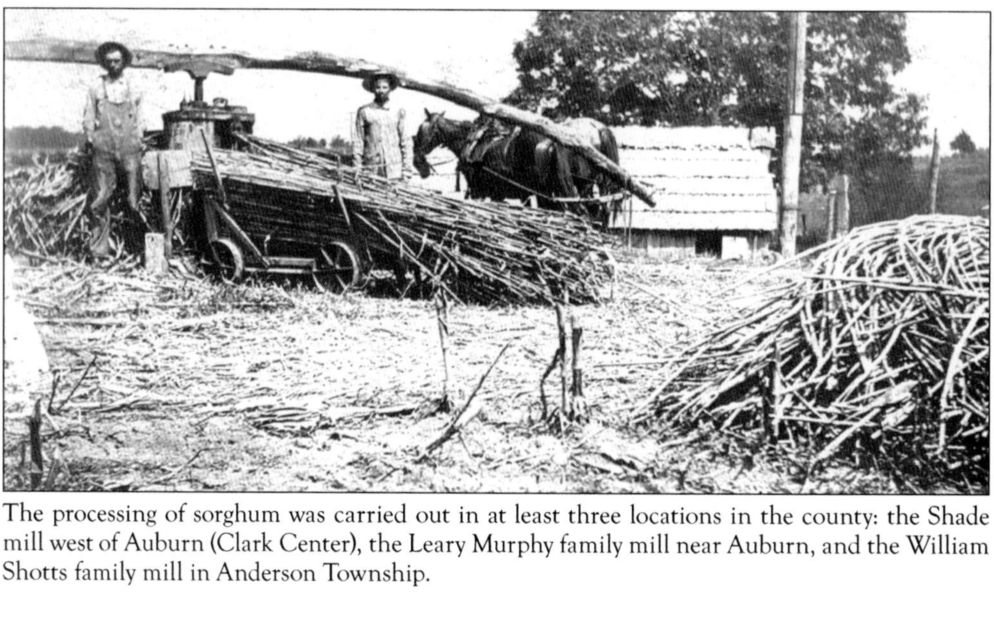

The processing of sorghum was carried out in at least three locations in the county: the Shade mill west of Auburn (Clark Center), the Leary Murphy family mill near Auburn, and the William Shotts family mill in Anderson Township.

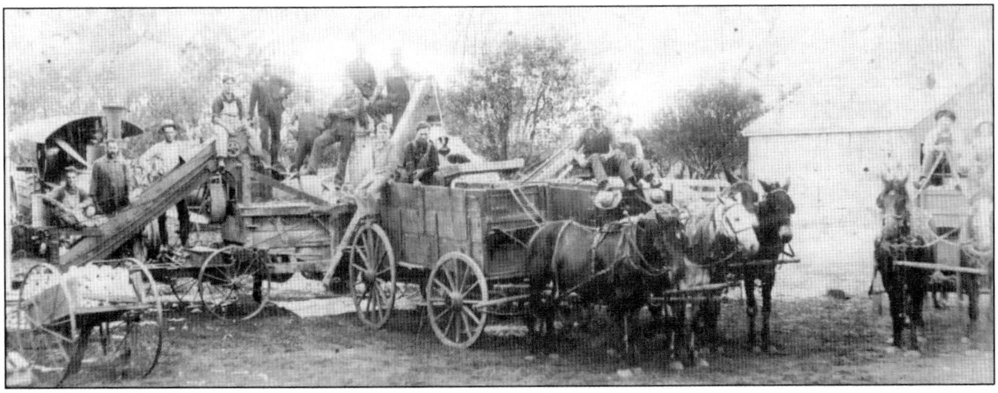

Changes taking place in farming are indicated in these two scenes. In the above photograph, from the West Union area, mules and horses seem the dominant power force. In the lower photograph, also from the West Union area, steam is providing the power. Steam, of course, eventually gave way to gasoline and diesel, and farm equipment keeps getting bigger.

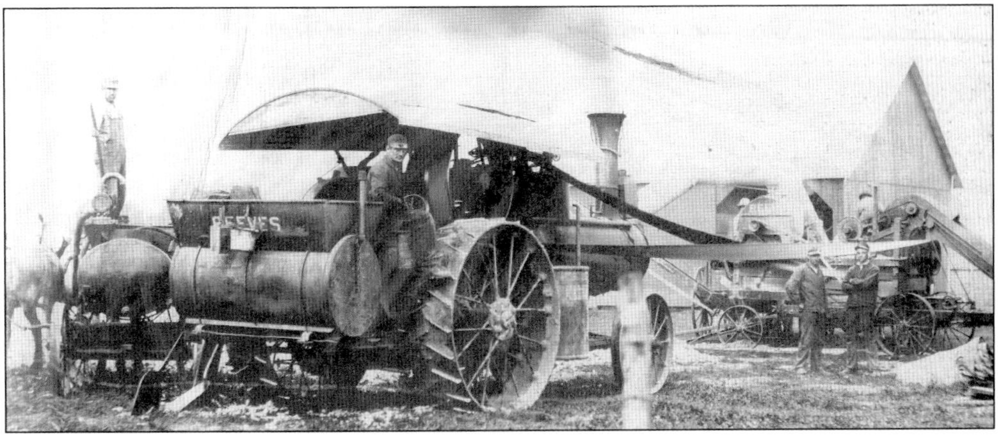

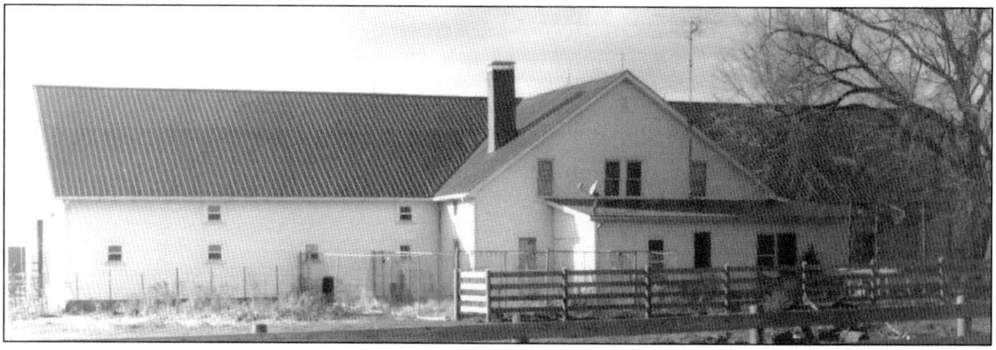

Farmers in Clark County have varied needs for barns. The above structure, south of Marshall on Route 1, for example, is based on the European model of a combination house and barn, which was also common in the horse country of Kentucky. It was built in 1938 by G. O. Frazier, and the living area in the center of the barn was completed in 1943.

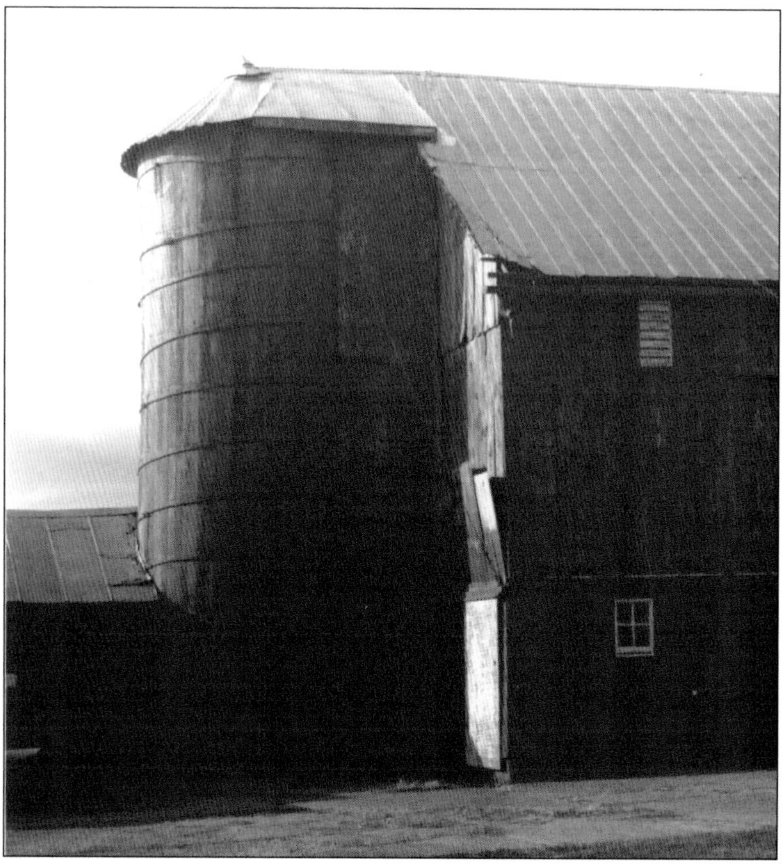

Wooden silos were not uncommon in the early 1900s, but few are left in Clark County. This one is located southeast of Marshall on the 1350 Road.

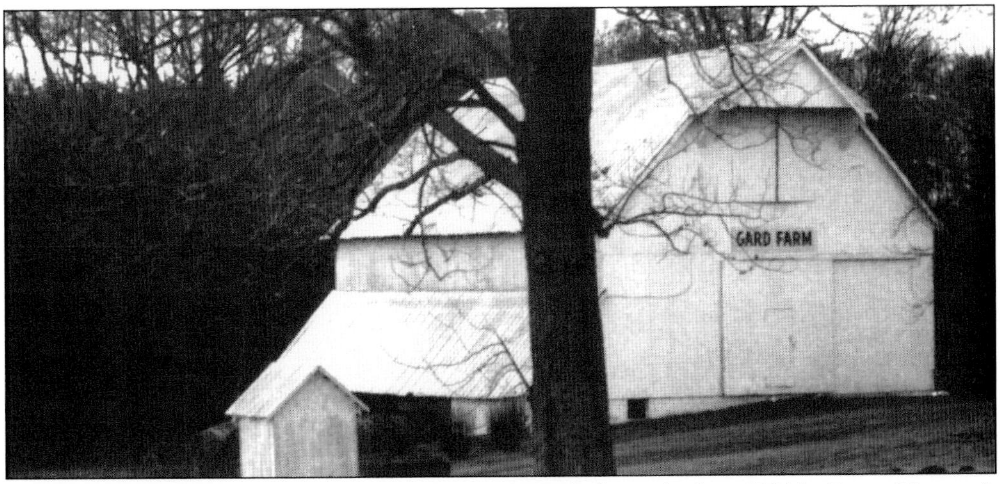

This barn, located on the Ernst Road southeast of Marshall, was built in 1936 by Percey Hasten. It is a three-story bank barn, making use of the hill to create a walkout basement. The Gards milked dairy cows and sent the milk to the Kraft Cheese factory in Marshall.

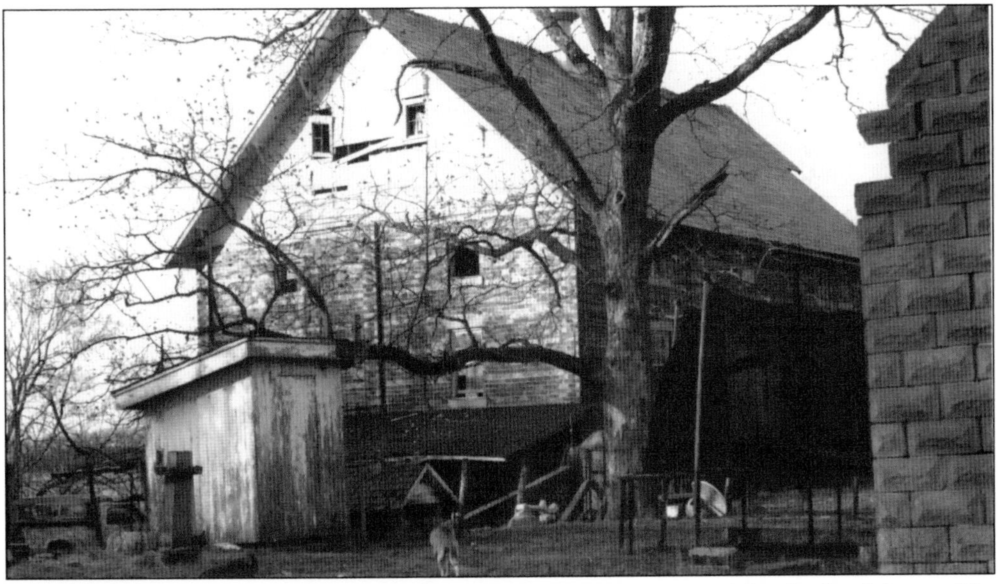

The Baughman barn, built in 1916 by W. D. Baughman Sr., is one of the few brick barns. The bricks came from Terre Haute, and the oak lumber was cut locally by a steam sawmill. Located on the 2250 Road south of Darwin, it is a bank barn, and was used for livestock, hay, and machinery storage.

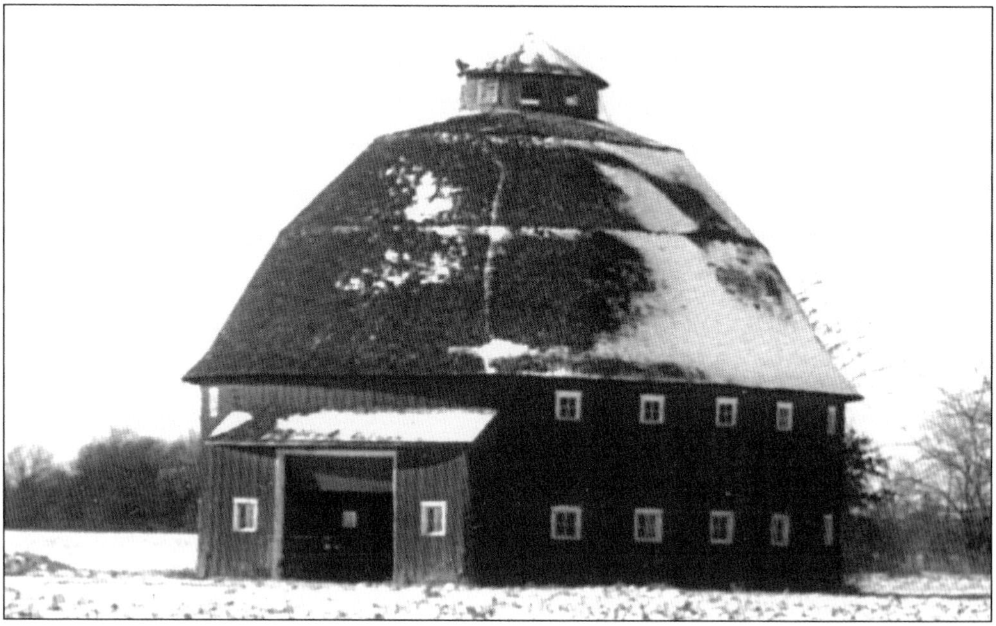

This barn was built in the early 1900s by Charles Weaver, a cattle feeder, on his 100-acre farm just north of new Route 40 in Casey. It was the only round barn in Clark County. After storm damage, it was torn down in the 1980s.

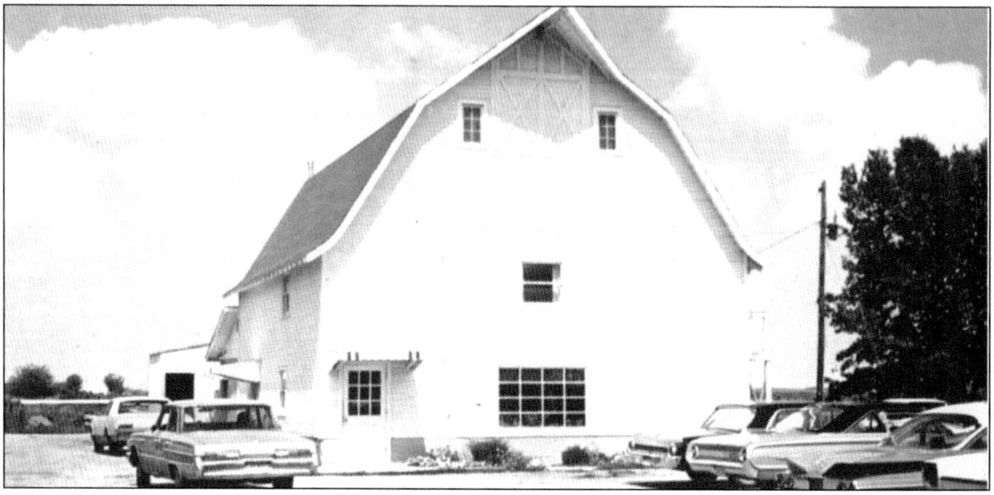

This dairy barn on East Main Street in Casey was built in 1924 by Glen Jones and was converted to the White Barn Tea Room in 1964 by Edith Jones and daughter Lois Ellen Biggs. Two silos in back were torn down, and the lumber was used inside. It is now an apartment building.

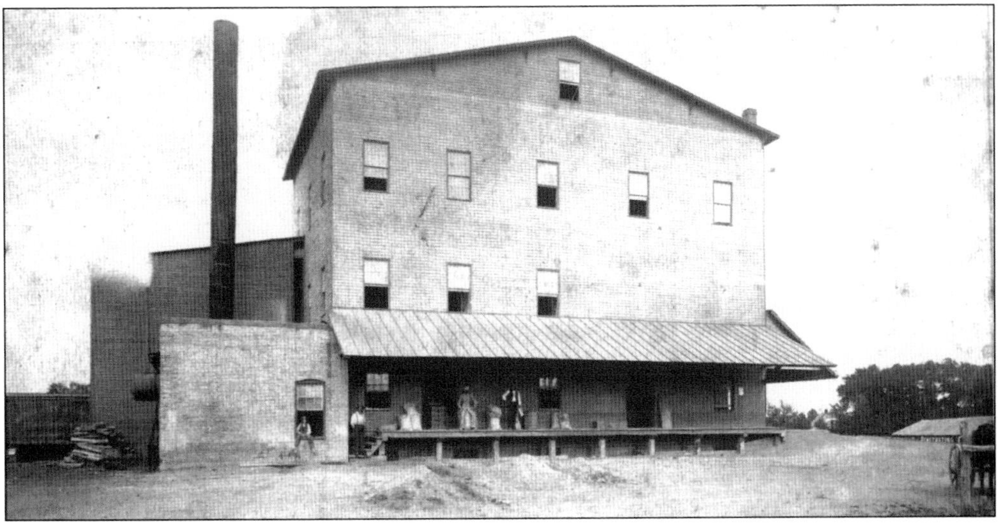

The Marvin Mill in Marshall was located at the northeast corner of Sixth and Maple Streets, where the Kirchner Building Center is now located.

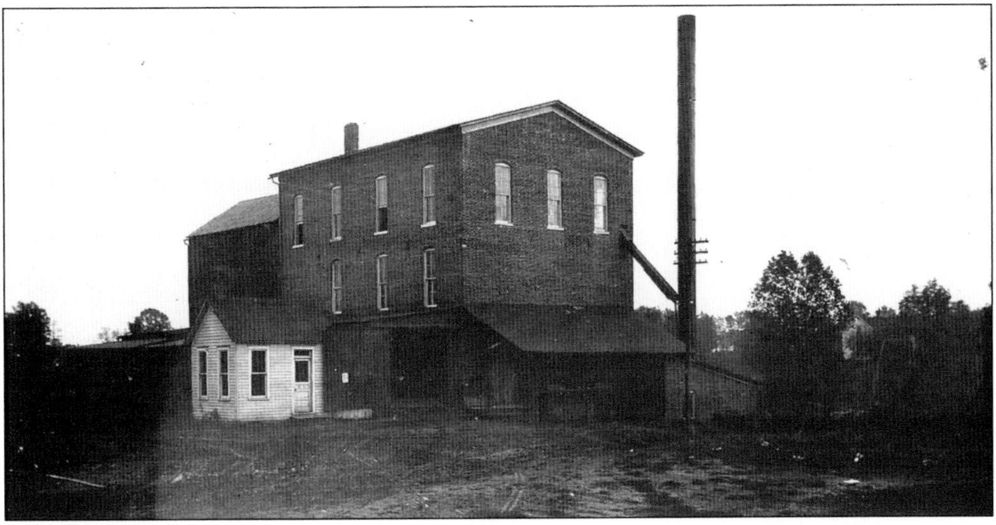

This gristmill in Martinsville was built in 1854, a block north of the National Road. It was bought by G. W. Cooper in 1856 and enlarged in 1859. One of the largest and busiest mills in the area, it was connected with the Vandalia Railroad by a special side track that crossed the National Road. It sat next to a millpond, which has since been drained. One of the Littlejohn grain operations is still active at the site, having survived and rebuilt after a disastrous fire in 1975.

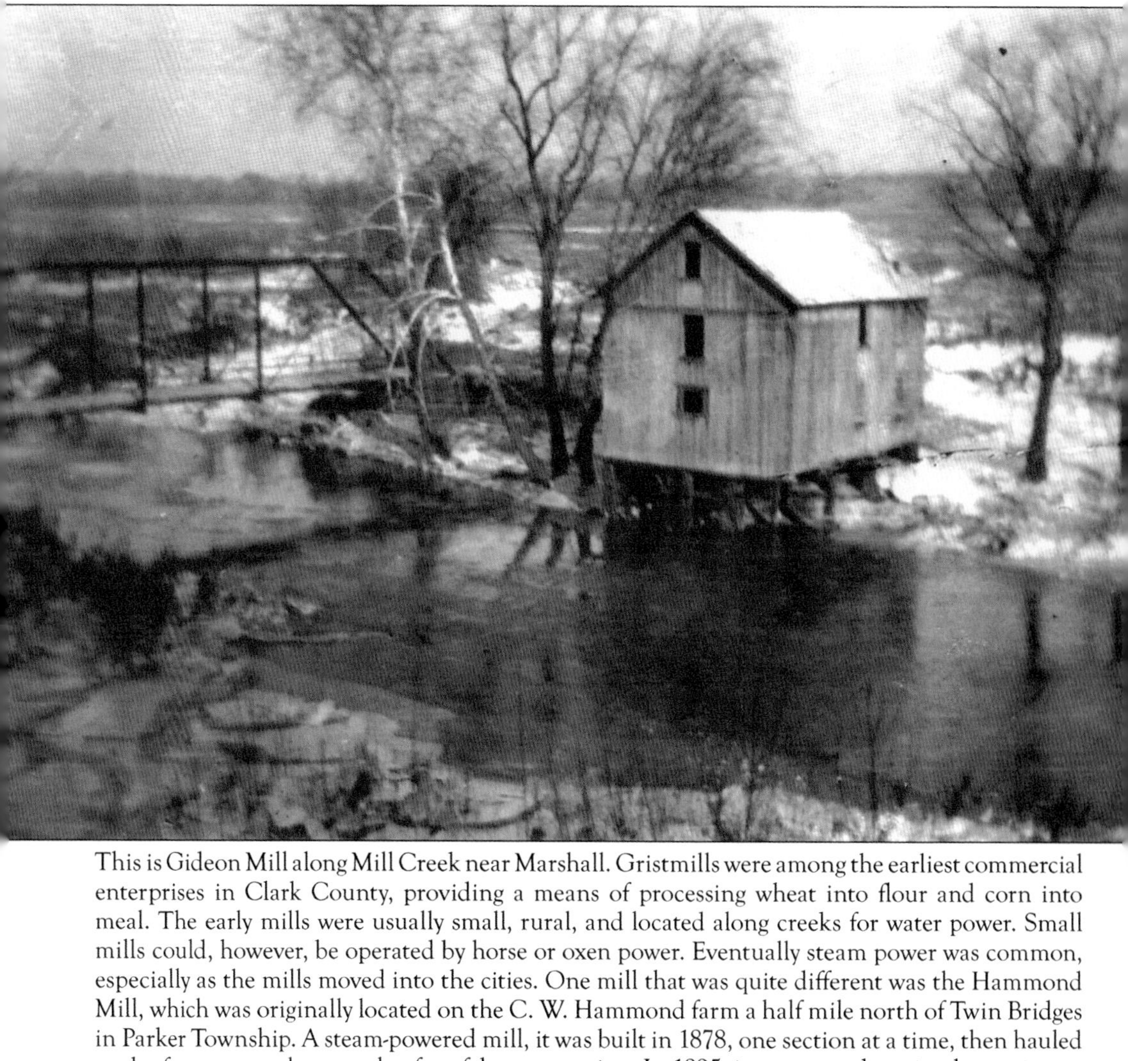

This is Gideon Mill along Mill Creek near Marshall. Gristmills were among the earliest commercial enterprises in Clark County, providing a means of processing wheat into flour and corn into meal. The early mills were usually small, rural, and located along creeks for water power. Small mills could, however, be operated by horse or oxen power. Eventually steam power was common, especially as the mills moved into the cities. One mill that was quite different was the Hammond Mill, which was originally located on the C. W. Hammond farm a half mile north of Twin Bridges in Parker Township. A steam-powered mill, it was built in 1878, one section at a time, then hauled to the farm—an early example of prefab construction. In 1895, it was moved section by section to Casey, using a team of 100 horses, and located across the road from the current Kirchner Lumber Company. The operation of gristmills was hazardous because of the explosive nature of grain, and mill fires were common.

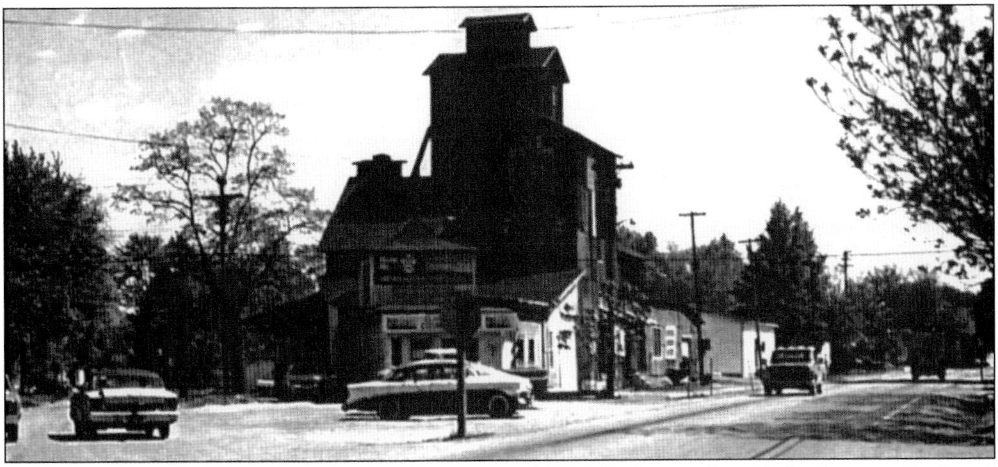

Typical of the mills that grew large in the towns (then died) was the Clark County Coal and Feed Company in Marshall, formerly owned by the Newberrys. Established in the 1850s at the south intersection of Michigan and Archer Avenues and Eighth Street, at one time, the Big Four railroad ran beside it. This structure and the former Black Hotel across the street to the east were torn down, and Eighth Street was closed in 1973 for expansion by Stanfield Motors, later Ashley Chevrolet-Buick. Today it is the site of a service station and parking lot.

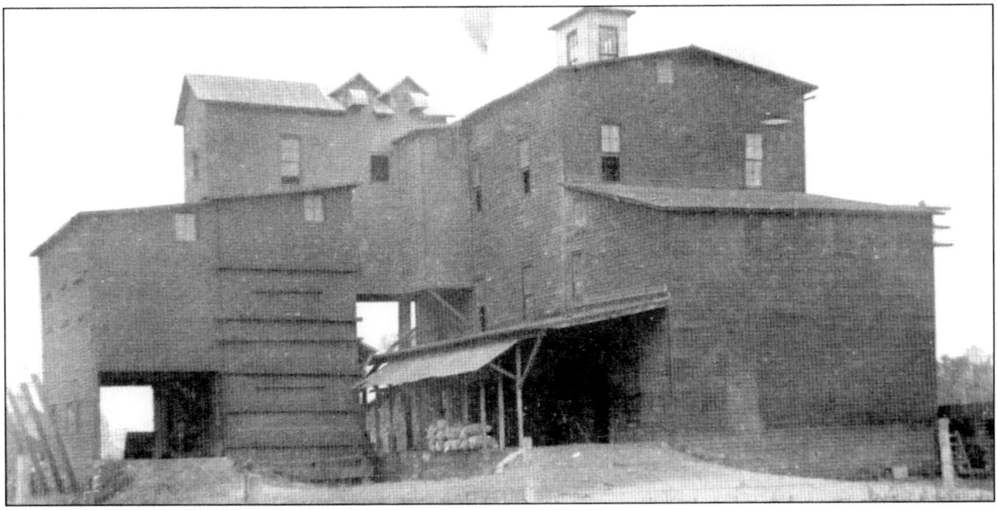

Poorman's gristmill in West Union was built in 1890 by Ben Poorman and managed by his son Will. Another son, Russell, operated the mill from 1912 to 1924. The mill burned in the early 1920s but was rebuilt. In later years, it was used for storage rather than as a gristmill.

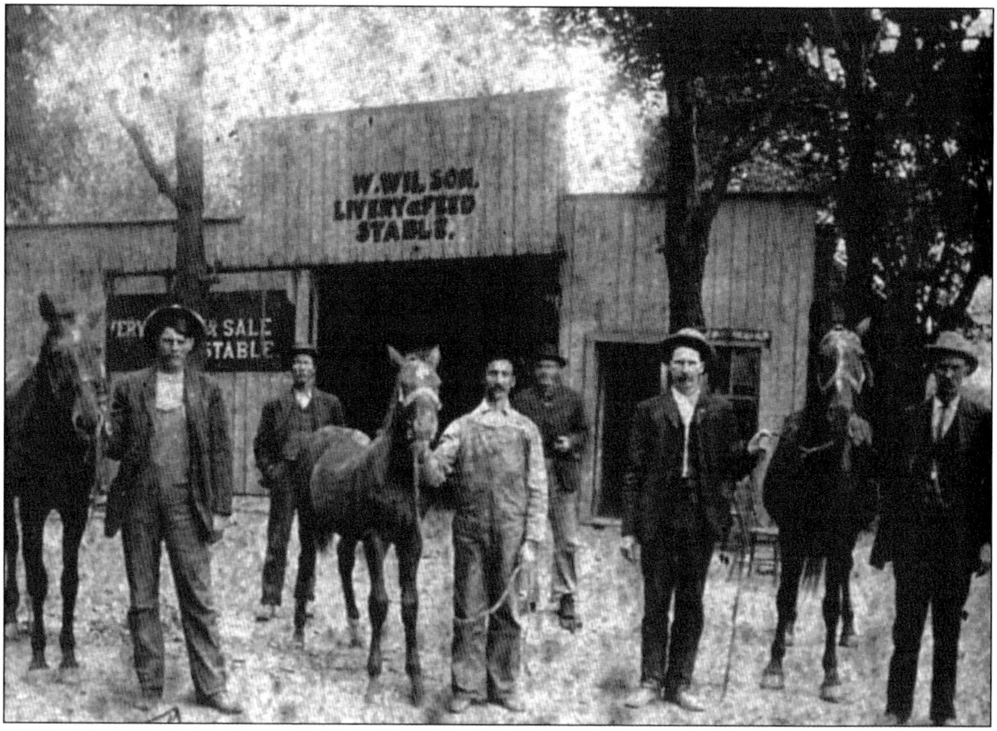

The Wilson Livery and Feed Stable was located at the corner of Seventh and Plum Streets. Following the livery stable at this site was the Rector barn and the Rector Jitney Bus headquarters. It is currently the location of the post office.

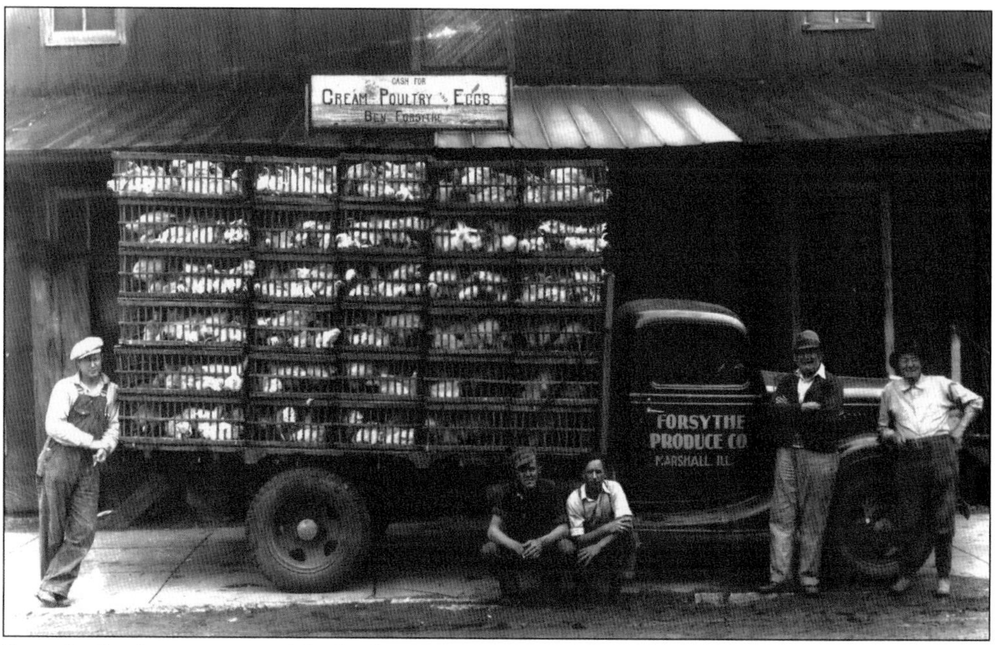

Forsythe Produce was one of the leading businesses in Marshall.

Three

Government and Schools

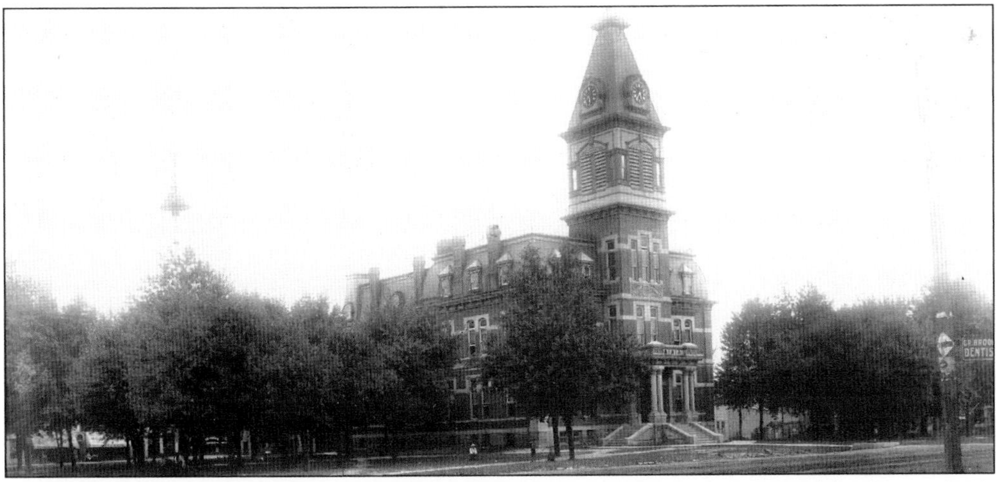

This magnificent Clark County courthouse was built in 1888 and destroyed by fire in 1902. Although county government was important to the early settlers, city government was less important. Marshall was platted in 1835, but did not set up a city government until 1855. Casey was platted in 1851–1853, but did not become an official city until 1871. Westfield was platted in 1839, but was not incorporated until 1866.

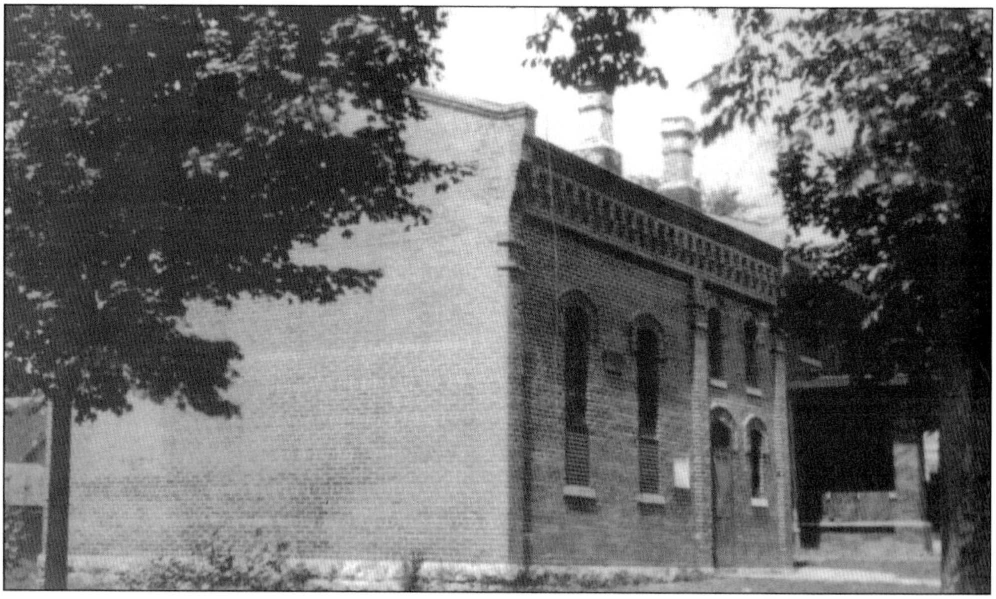

This 1895 county jail in Marshall was torn down in 1982, and the current jail was built in 1984. Now this jail is too small. A sales tax was approved for building another jail, but officials indicate that remodeling and expanding the present structure may be preferable.

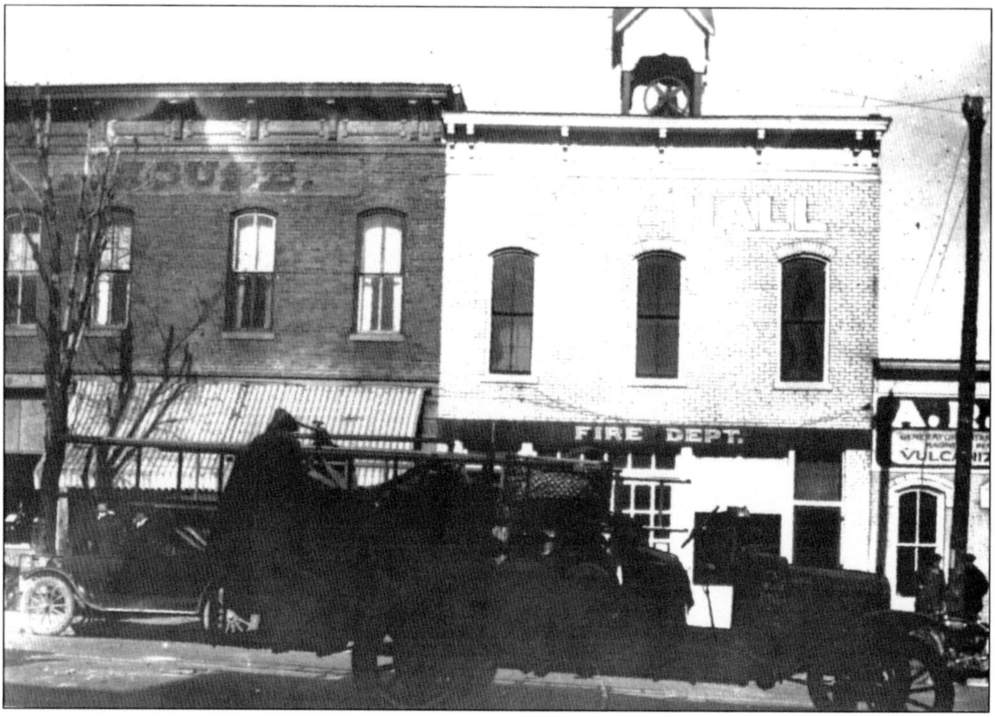

Marshall's former city hall, fire department, police station, and jail are pictured on Archer Avenue next to the Wright House Hotel. The library was on the second floor at one time.

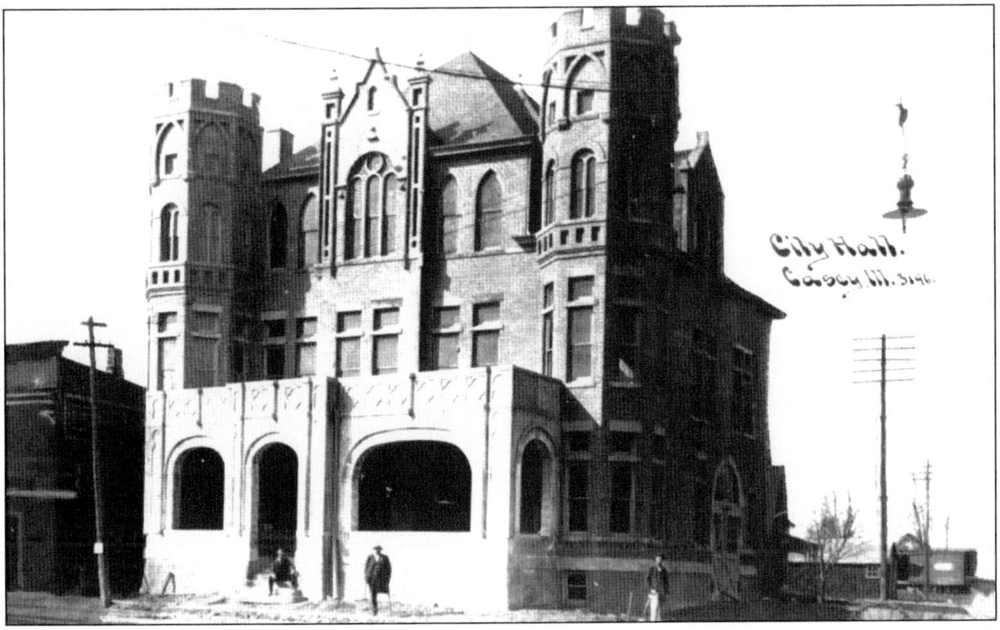

Casey's old city hall was an impressive structure worthy of being a county courthouse. It was built during the oil boom in 1907 at the corner of North Central Avenue and Alabama Street and demolished in 1973. Note the Doty railway line in back.

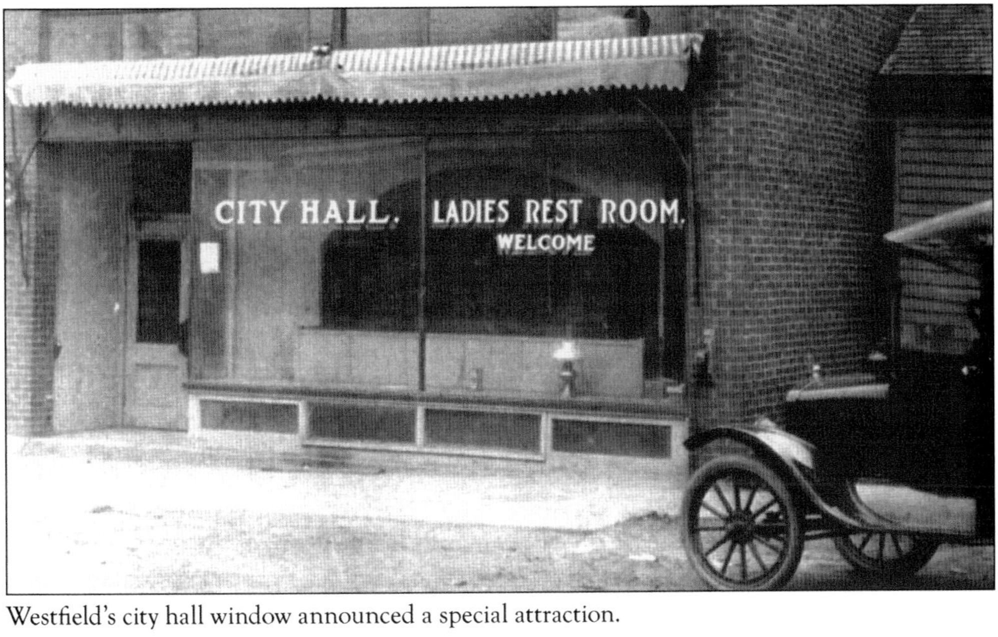

Westfield's city hall window announced a special attraction.

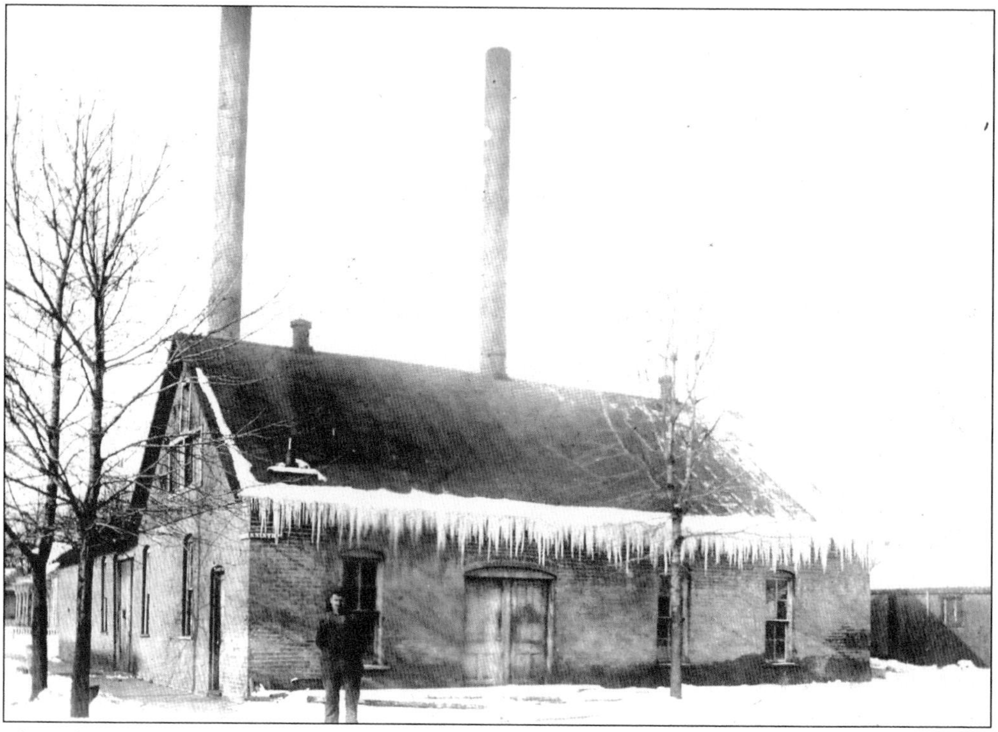

This electric plant at Marshall was built in 1892 at 201 North Michigan Avenue where Entertainment Tonight Video is now located. Marshall furnished electricity to Martinsville in 1913. Casey had electricity in 1902, and Westfield had it in 1913.

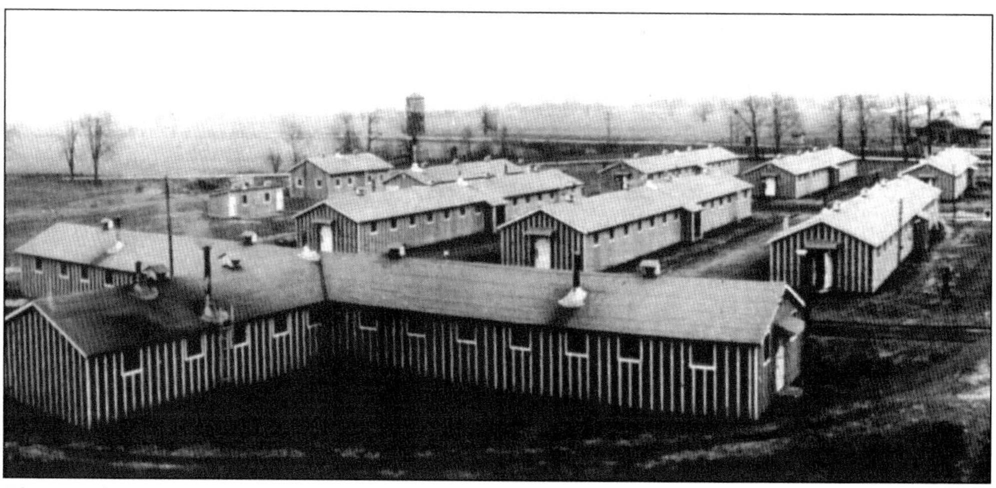

This Civilian Conservation Corps barracks north of Marshall was one of many locations that housed men seeking jobs during the Great Depression.

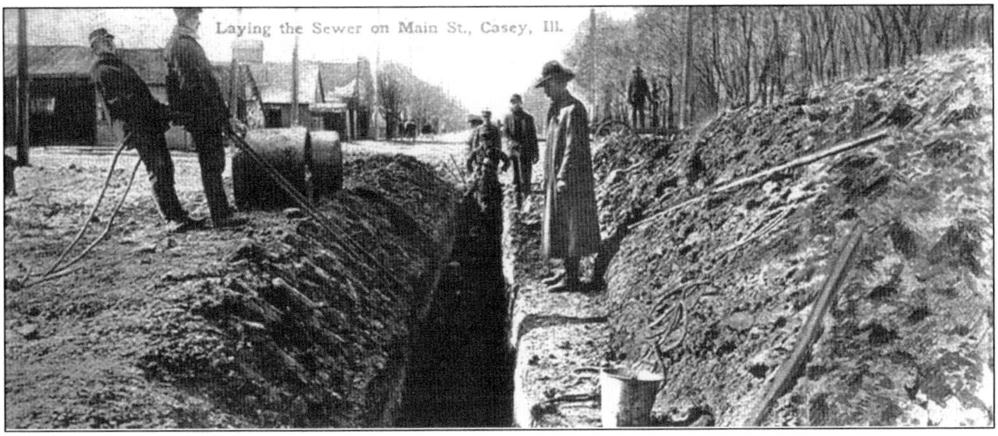

Casey's sewer line on Main Street was laid in 1907, the same year the 186-foot water tower was built at a cost of $6,600.

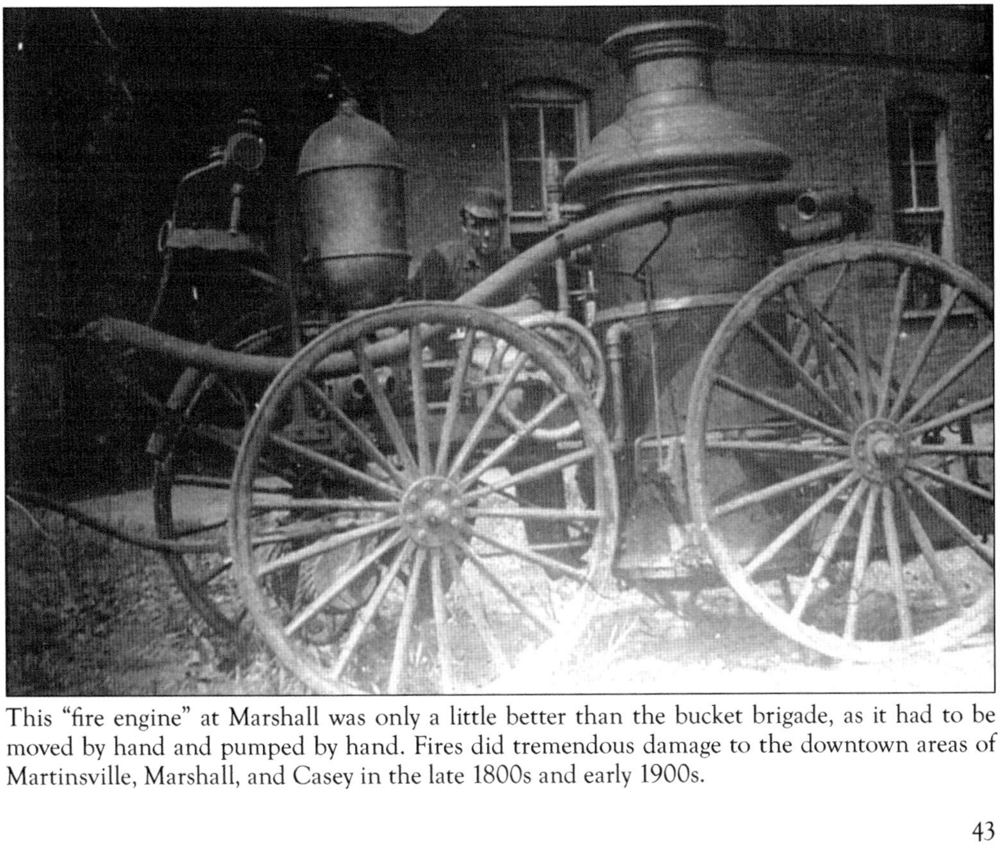

This "fire engine" at Marshall was only a little better than the bucket brigade, as it had to be moved by hand and pumped by hand. Fires did tremendous damage to the downtown areas of Martinsville, Marshall, and Casey in the late 1800s and early 1900s.

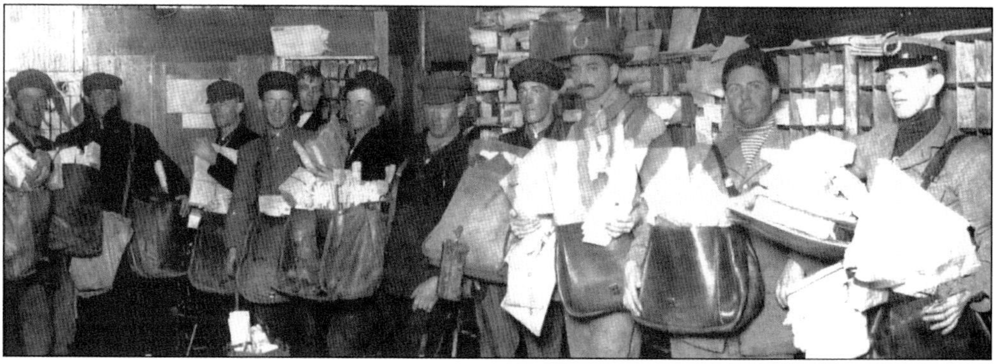

By 1838, mail was coming through Clark County three times a week, and by 1842, there was daily mail service. These Marshall men began home delivery in 1909. Rural mail service was established in 1903 in some communities.

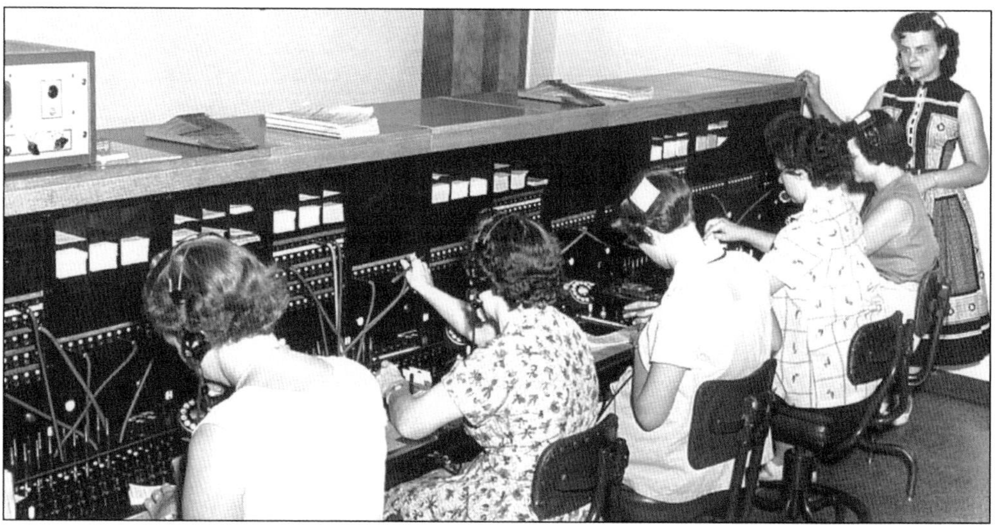

These Casey telephone switchboard operators are, from left to right, Helen Davis, Eileen Faulkner, Bernie Shawver, Janet Freeman, Norma Gains, and chief operator Martha June Perry. Residential service was initiated in Casey around 1898 with 32 subscribers. Long distance service followed in the early 1900s, and the first telephone directory was published in 1903 with 254 listings. Rural "party" lines came later, with each family having a distinctive ring, such as two longs and a short.

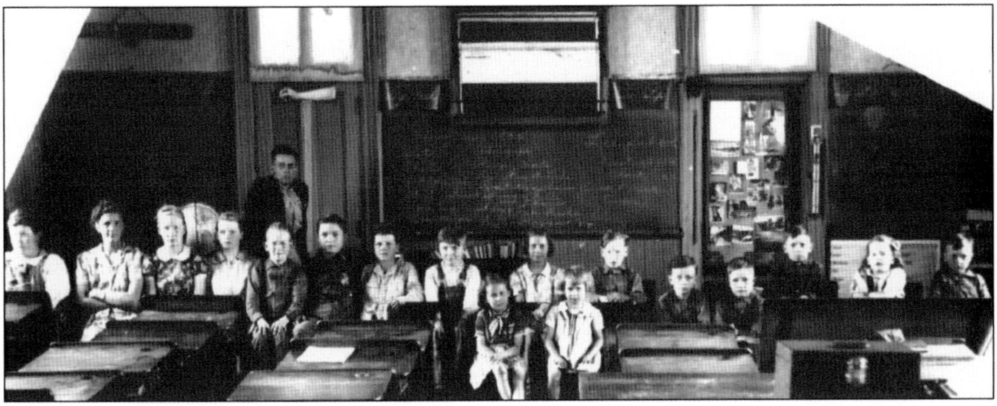

The above photograph was taken in 1935 at the Lee School, a mile east of Westfield. The building was used as a private home after the school was abandoned. The photograph below of Hall School in Darwin Township shows what has happened to most of the county's one-room schools. The earliest schools, like the early churches, were often conducted in homes. The first schools were "by subscription," meaning each student had to pay a tuition, but it was not long before free public schools sprouted up all over the county. The subjects were reading, writing, arithmetic, and social studies. The one-room schools included all grades, eventually up to grade eight. There was only one teacher, often with limited education, who was also responsible for making sure there was wood or coal for heat and drinking water from the outdoor pump.

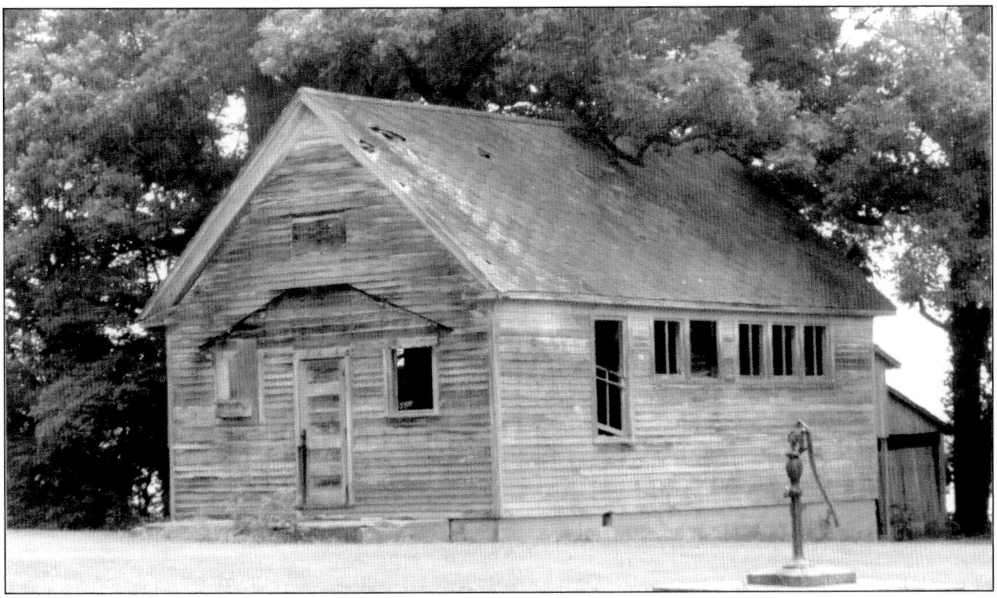

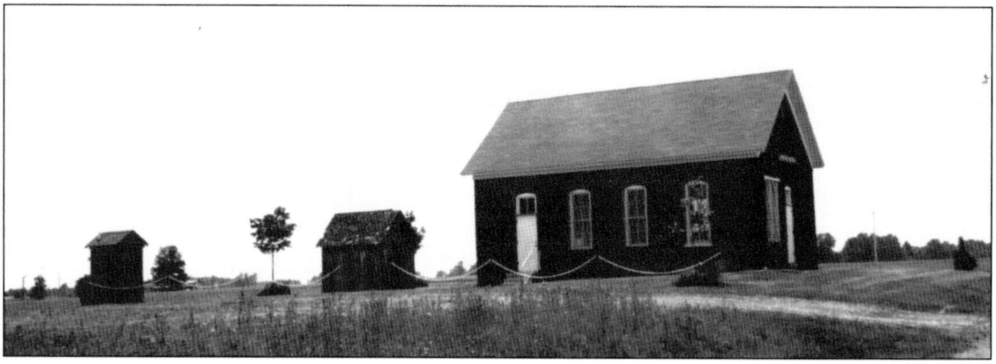

The Lincoln School, north of Martinsville, has been restored through the efforts of the City of Martinsville, Lynn Kelly, and others, and is now a museum open to visitors. This brick structure is typical of how the one-room schools looked and functioned.

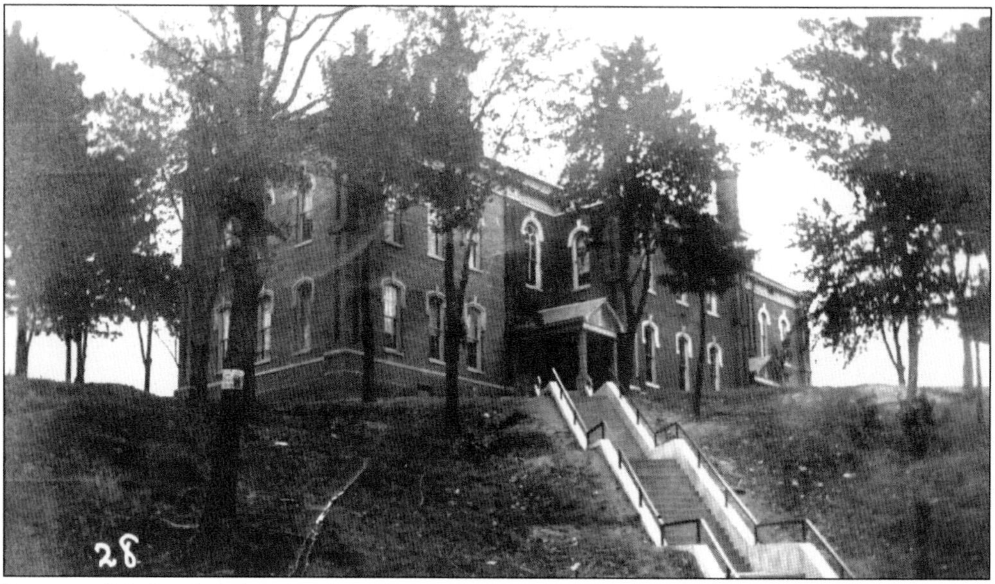

Martinsville's South Side School, built in 1870 to 1872, sat on a high bluff south of the railroad tracks. Initially there were four rooms, two down and two up. High school classes were added in 1885, and the first class graduated in 1887. Additions in 1891, 1900, and 1910 accommodated an increased enrollment. High school classes were moved to the new high school in 1921, and elementary classes were moved out in 1935. The building was torn down in 1950.

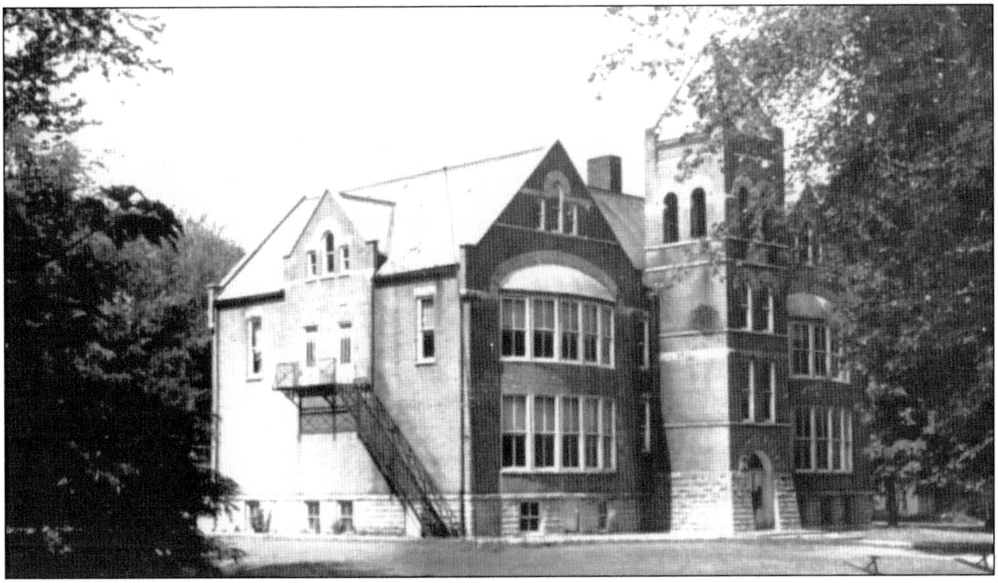

Pictured here is Marshall's old North Side School.

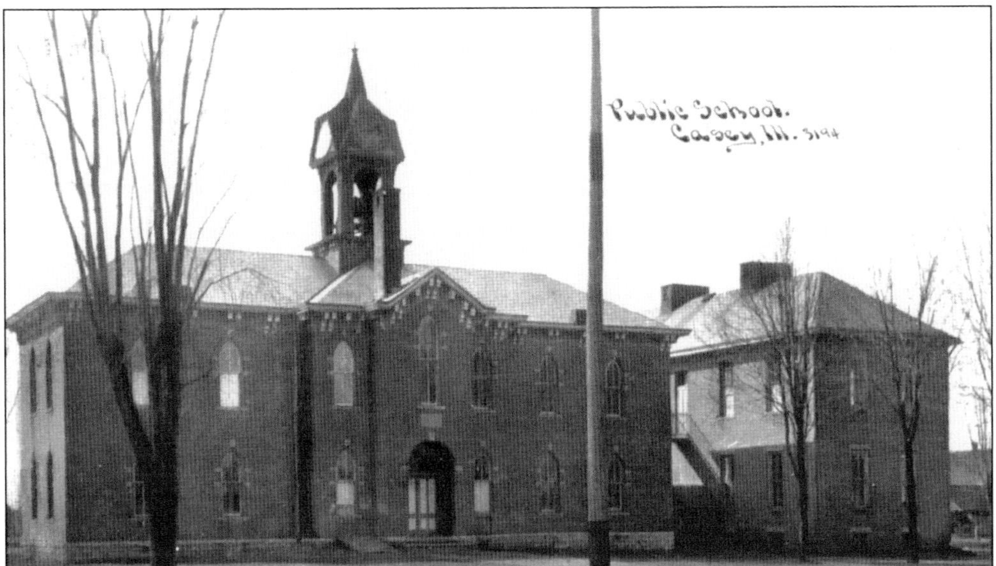

A two-room school building was erected in 1860 on this site in Casey and was replaced by the first brick school building in 1870, featuring four rooms. It was condemned and replaced by the above building in 1881. This building, in turn, was torn down in 1928 and replaced with Roosevelt School.

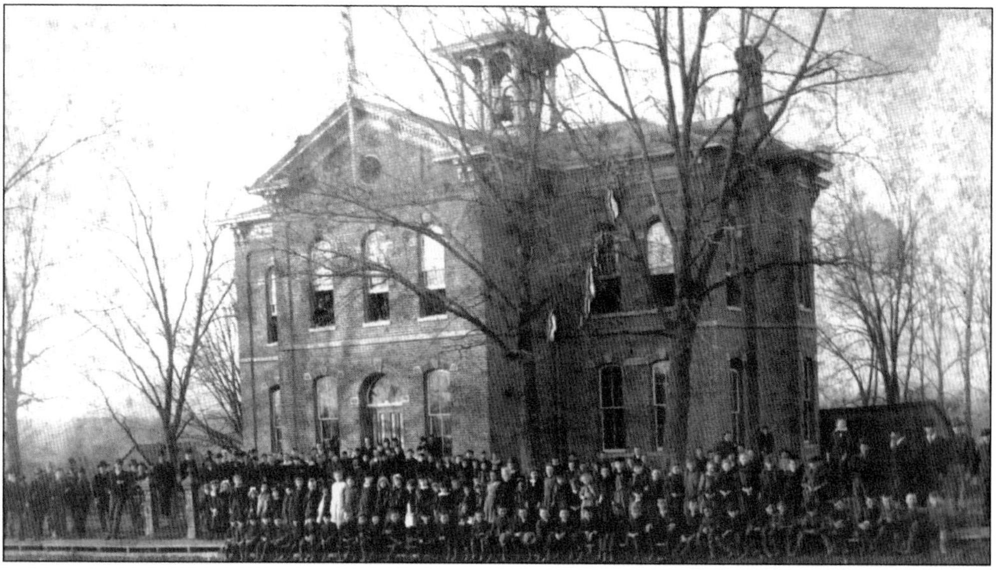

The first public school in Westfield was a log building built in 1835, which served until a two-story frame building was constructed in 1852. That building burned in 1881, and a four-room brick structure replaced it in 1882. Later two more rooms were added. This structure served as both elementary and high school until the high school district was organized in 1916, and the high school students were moved to the old college building, which burned in 1917.

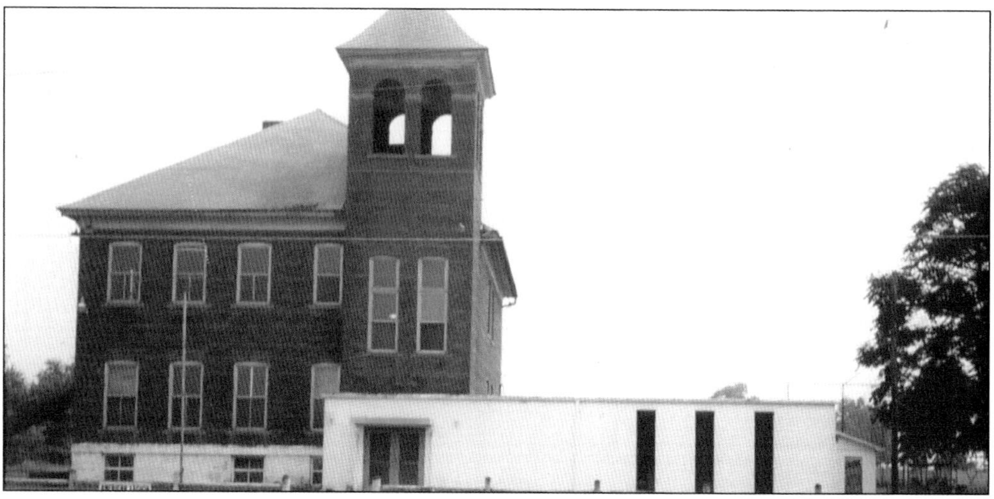

This West Union School, built in 1910, served both elementary and high school students until closing in 1970. The original building was demolished in 2007. The lower addition has been kept and is used as a community center.

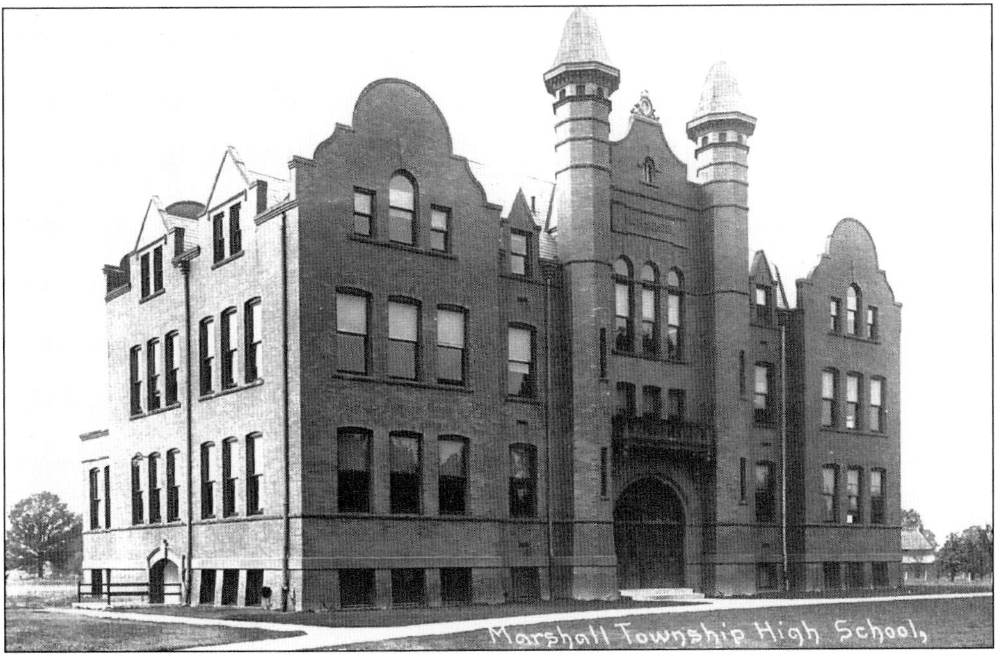

Marshall's first high school was built in 1904. Prior to that, high school students were taught in the old North Side School, which had been built in 1875. The 1904 high school was damaged by a tornado in 1947, and a new high school was built three years later, utilizing the old gym and another small area.

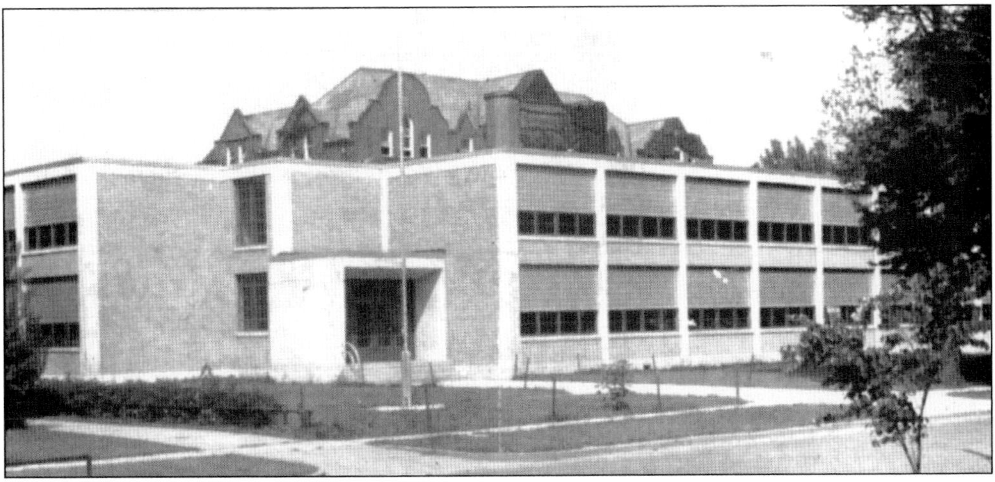

The old Marshall High School looms in the background as the new high school is completed in 1950. A 1956 addition included a large gym, classrooms, and vocational shops. Significant renovations were completed in 2003.

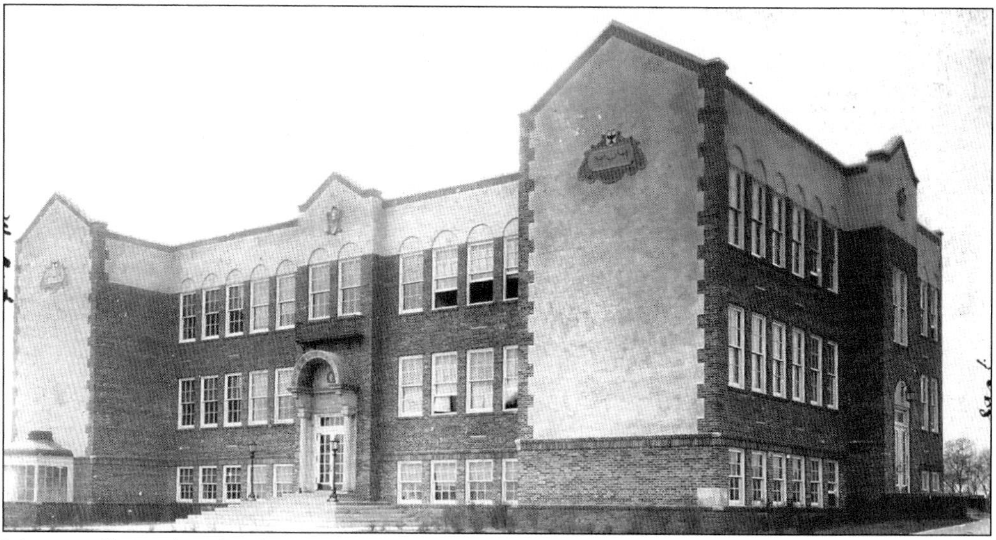

Martinsville High School was constructed in 1921. High school classes were taught in the old South Side School as early as 1885, but only two students were graduated from that first class. A gym and classroom area was added to the east side of this building, but efforts to fund a new school have stalled. In 2008, heavy rain and disastrous flooding forced students into portable classrooms.

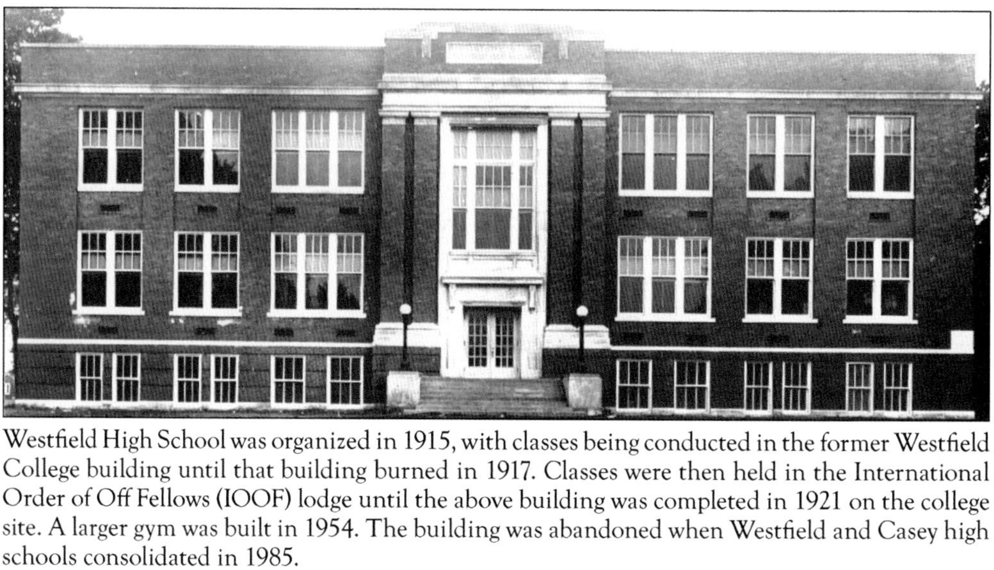

Westfield High School was organized in 1915, with classes being conducted in the former Westfield College building until that building burned in 1917. Classes were then held in the International Order of Off Fellows (IOOF) lodge until the above building was completed in 1921 on the college site. A larger gym was built in 1954. The building was abandoned when Westfield and Casey high schools consolidated in 1985.

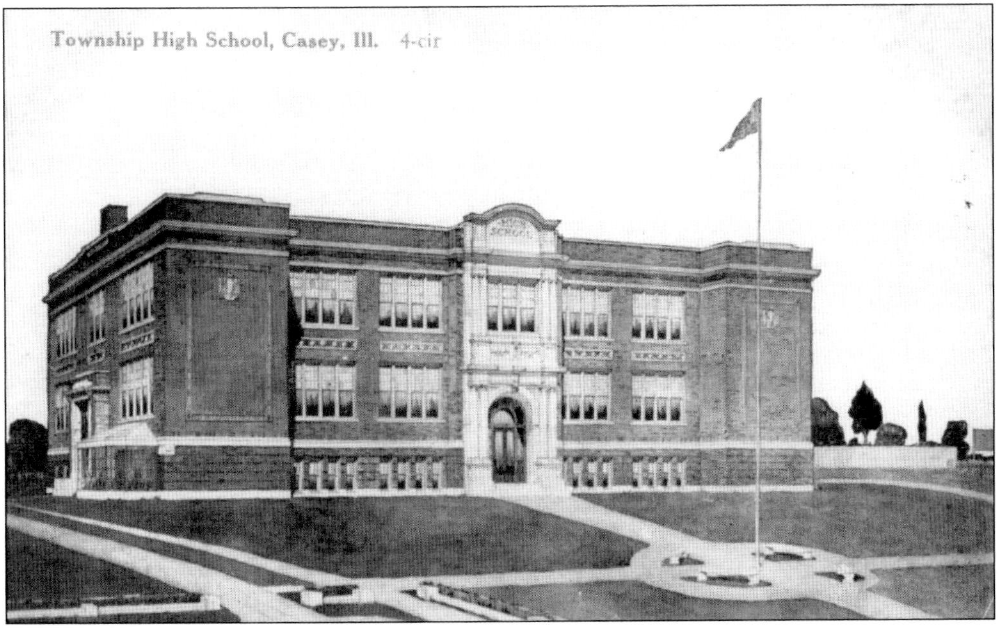

Informal high school classes were set up in Casey in 1892, and made official in 1895. Students met in various locations until the above building was built in 1918. In 1930, a gym was added west of this building. In 1956, the main building and gym were connected, adding classrooms, offices, and a cafeteria. A vocational wing was built on the west side of the gym that same year.

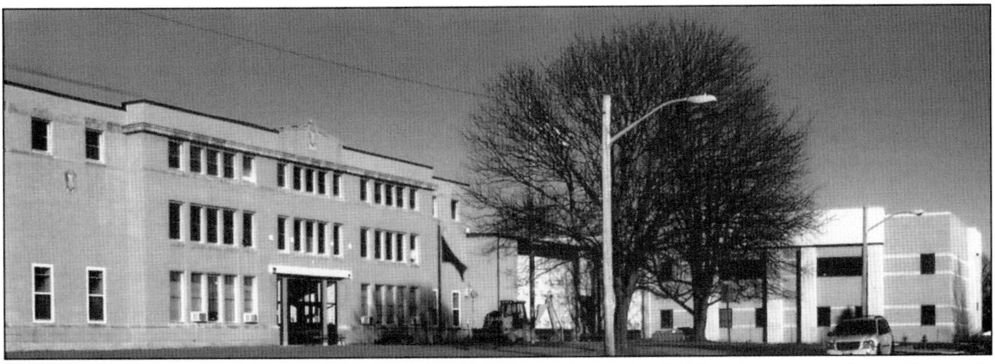

Casey High School's original main building was torn down in 2008 after it was deemed unsafe and too expensive to repair. A new structure that extends almost to the street replaces it. In the above photograph, looking northeast, the new structure is on the extreme right, and the gym is on the left.

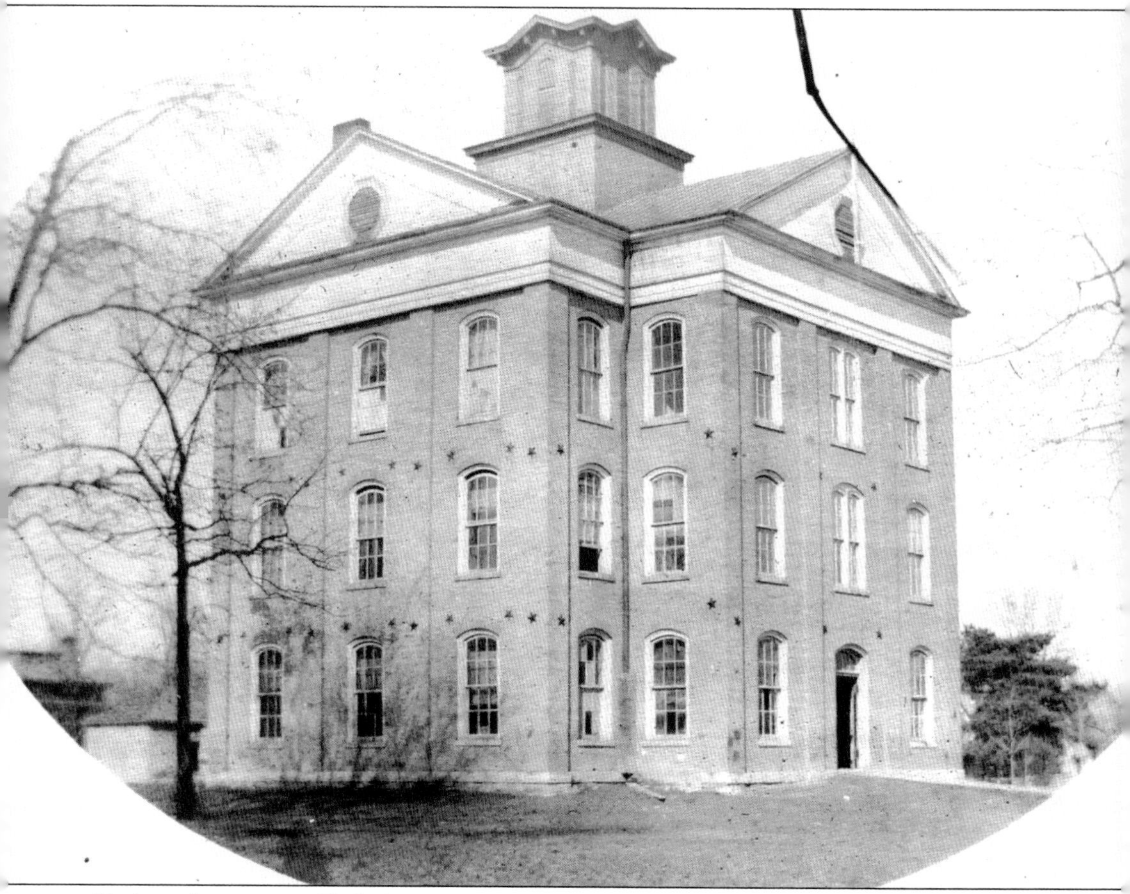

Higher education in Clark County got its start in Marshall in 1852 when Rev. Dean Andrews erected a brick building and organized Marshall College with the help of local supporters. The school seemed to prosper until the Civil War broke out. Around 1861, the college was sold to the Methodist organization, who operated the school for awhile, but ran into financial difficulties and finally closed in 1867 or 1868. The Methodists transferred the college operations to Illinois Wesleyan in Bloomington. The Marshall property was sold to the local public schools in 1871, and the building was extensively remodeled to serve as a grade school.

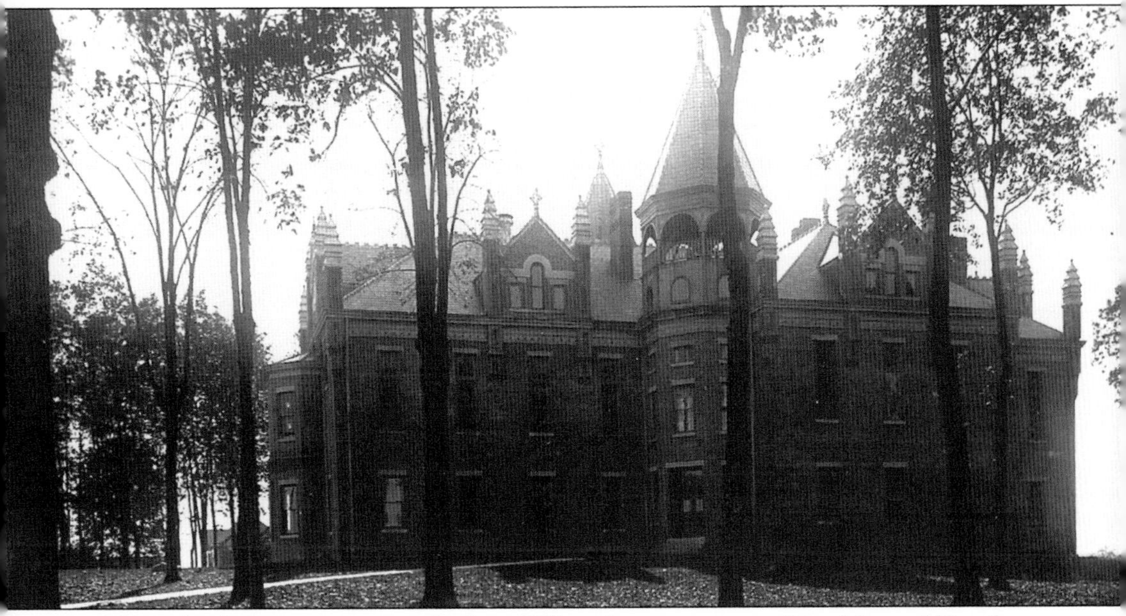

Westfield College's first structure was built in 1852 at the intersection of Franklin and Hamilton streets as a United Brethren church, then in 1861 used as a seminary. In 1863, a two-story building was completed on three wooded acres on the most elevated part of town. In 1865, Westfield College was chartered by the Illinois General Assembly, and in 1870 was offering both bachelors and masters degrees. The curriculum included Latin, Greek, algebra, geography of the heavens, philosophy, and psychiatry, as well as music programs. In 1867, the building was expanded with a new addition. Ground east of the college was purchased in 1871 when the enrollment peaked at 225 students, and a women's dormitory was built. Male students continued to rent rooms in local residences. The opening of state-supported Eastern Illinois Normal School at Charleston in 1895 proved to be competition that Westfield College could not handle. Enrollment dropped to 124 students by 1905, and the college closed in 1914. The building was then used as Westfield High School until it burned in 1917.

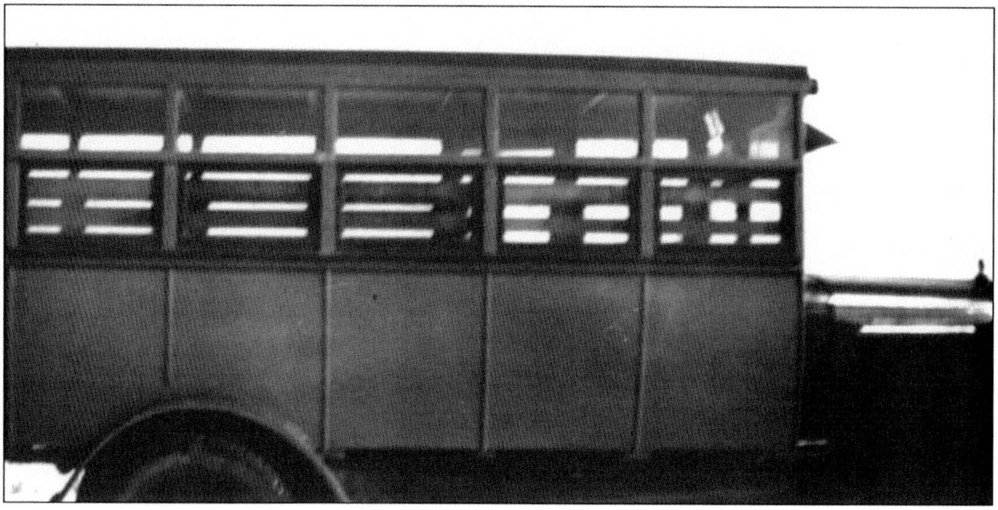

This early school bus served Marshall students in the 1920s.

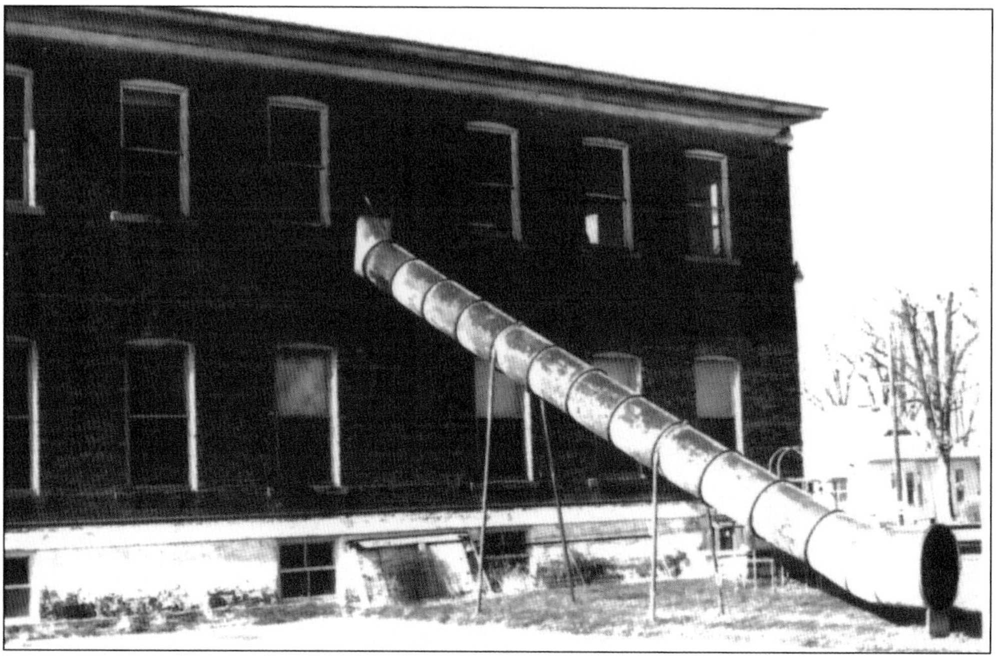

A common "fire escape" for schools at one time was a chute like this one at West Union. Did the airlines adopt the idea?

Four

THE CITIES

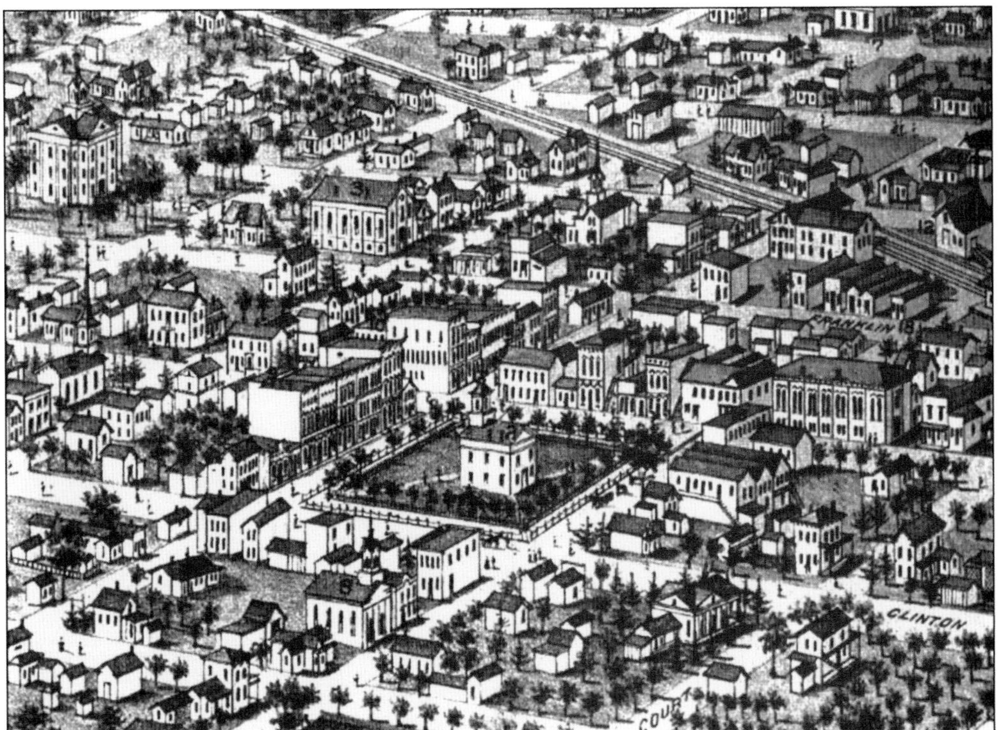

This bird's-eye view of Marshall in 1880 shows how Marshall grew from its founding in 1835. Pictured are such landmarks as the courthouse, the railroad down Michigan Avenue, the Marshall (Sherman) House, the Archer (Madison) House, and churches. It was drawn by H. Wellge, lithographed, and sold.

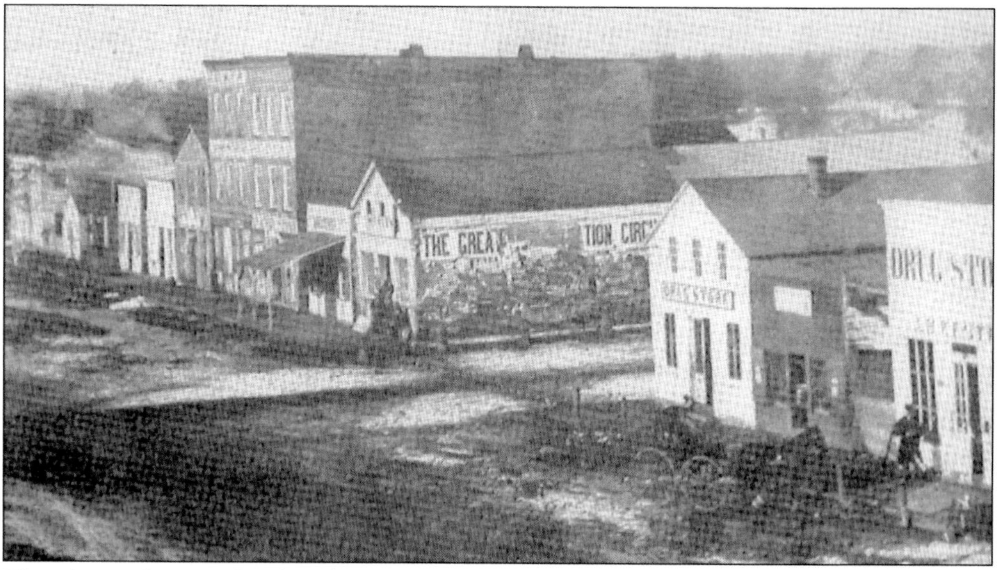

The above photograph, though not in good condition, may be the oldest (1860s–1870s) available of downtown Marshall. It shows the intersection of Charleston Road (Sixth Street) and Cumberland Street (Archer Avenue), looking northwest. The building on the northwest corner sits on the first lot sold in Marshall ($12.50). Woodford and Dulaney built a one-and-a-half story frame building on the lot. Rachel Grabenheimer bought that building and erected another one in 1872. That building was demolished, and the present three-story building was erected in 1889 by Meyer Grabenheimer. The double wide, three-story block building west of the corner in this photograph, built in 1852–1854, is still standing, and is the location of Travel Time and Courthouse Realty. The lower photograph, though of poor quality, shows the house that once stood at the northeast corner of Archer Avenue and Fifth Street.

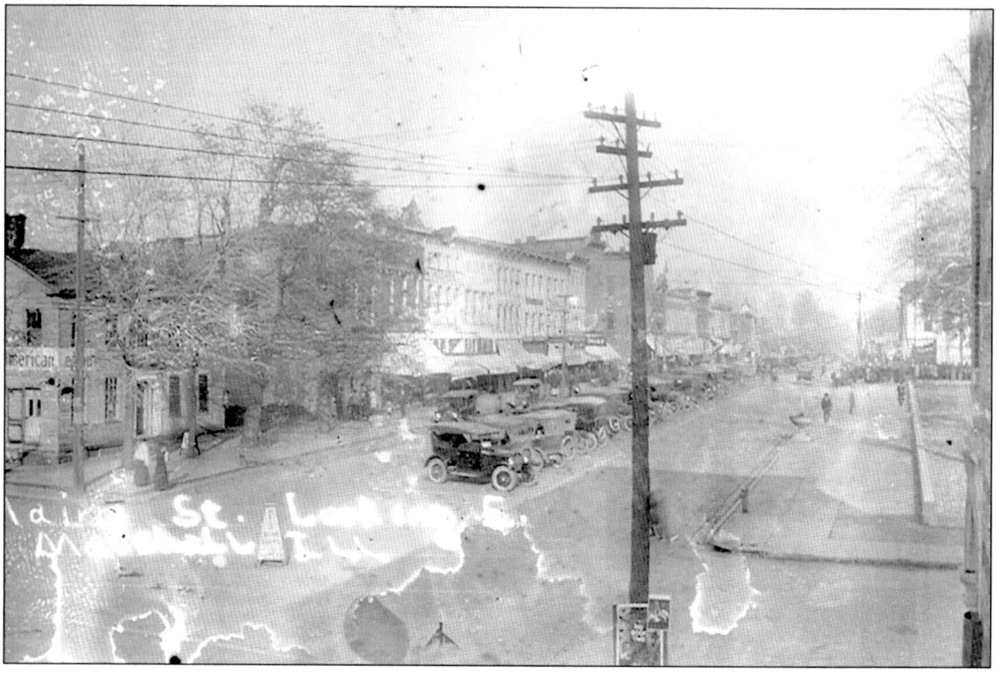

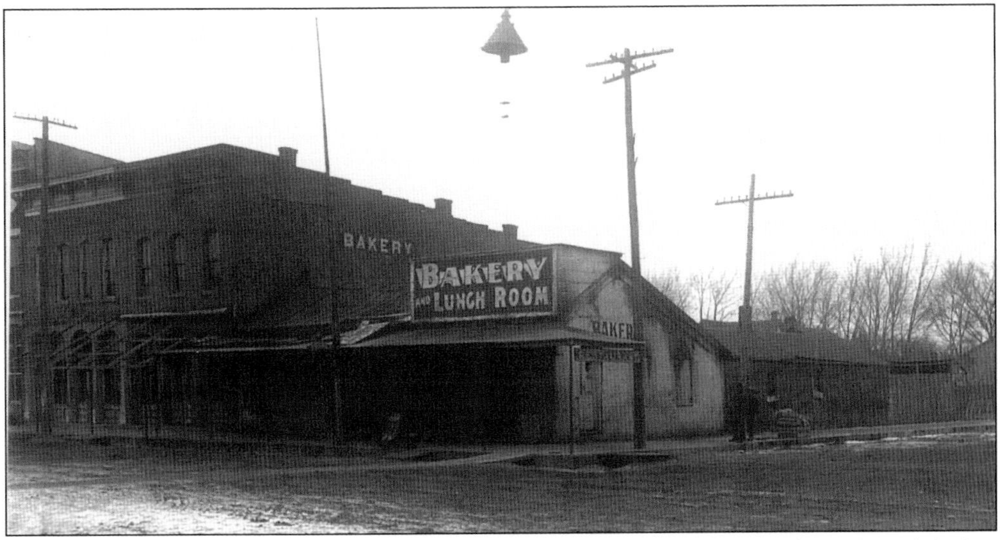

Jim's Bakery and Lunch Room (above) was at the northwest corner of Seventh Street and Archer Avenue. The building was torn down between 1901 and 1906, and in 1908 a two-story brick building was constructed, as shown in the current photograph below. Moye Grocery was once in the building, and Moye's potato chip factory was on the second floor. The building was later used as a duck pins bowling alley, a variety store, and is currently Happy China restaurant.

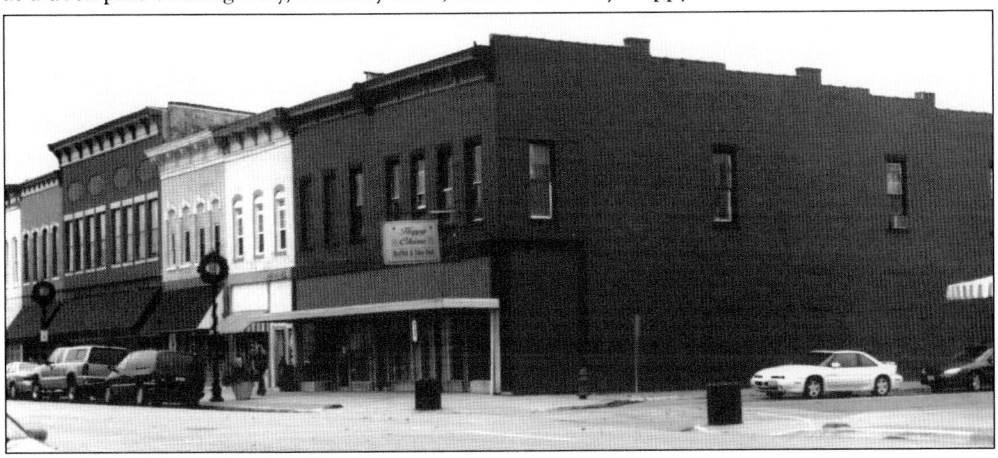

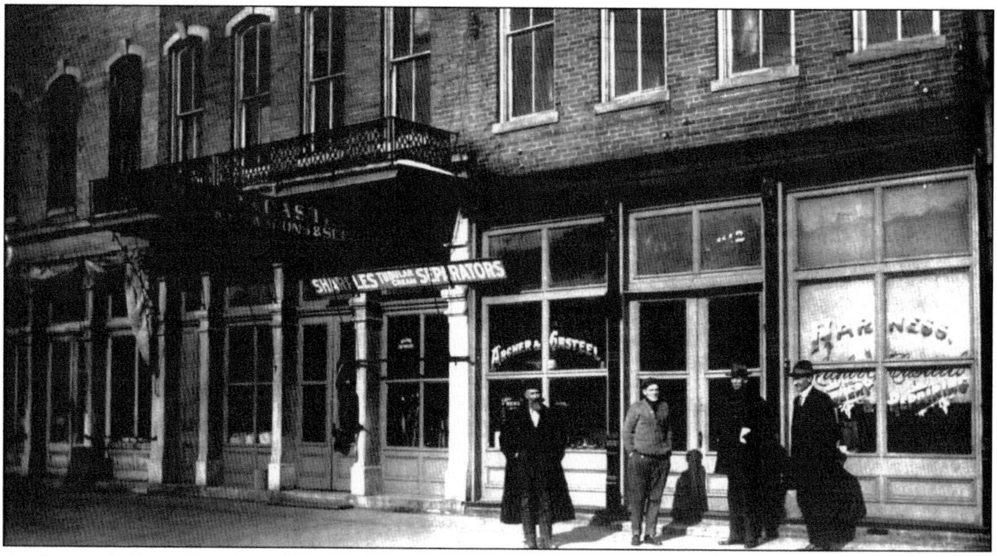

Archer and Casteel at 610–612 Archer Avenue sold implements, harness, wagons, and seeds. The site was later used by Paul Martin Drugs (610), the Advocate (610), the Marshall public library (612), then as the Dale McConchie library meeting room (612) when library expanded to the east. From left to right are unidentified, Dandy Archer, *Marshall Herald* editor Scott, and Harry Casteel.

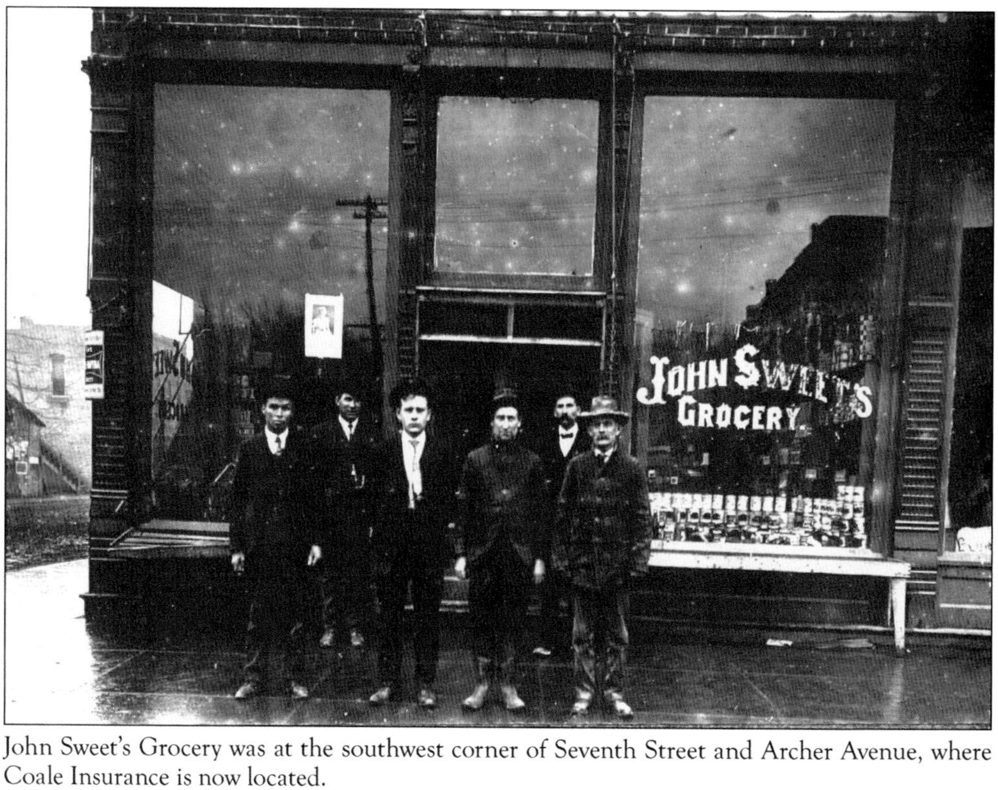

John Sweet's Grocery was at the southwest corner of Seventh Street and Archer Avenue, where Coale Insurance is now located.

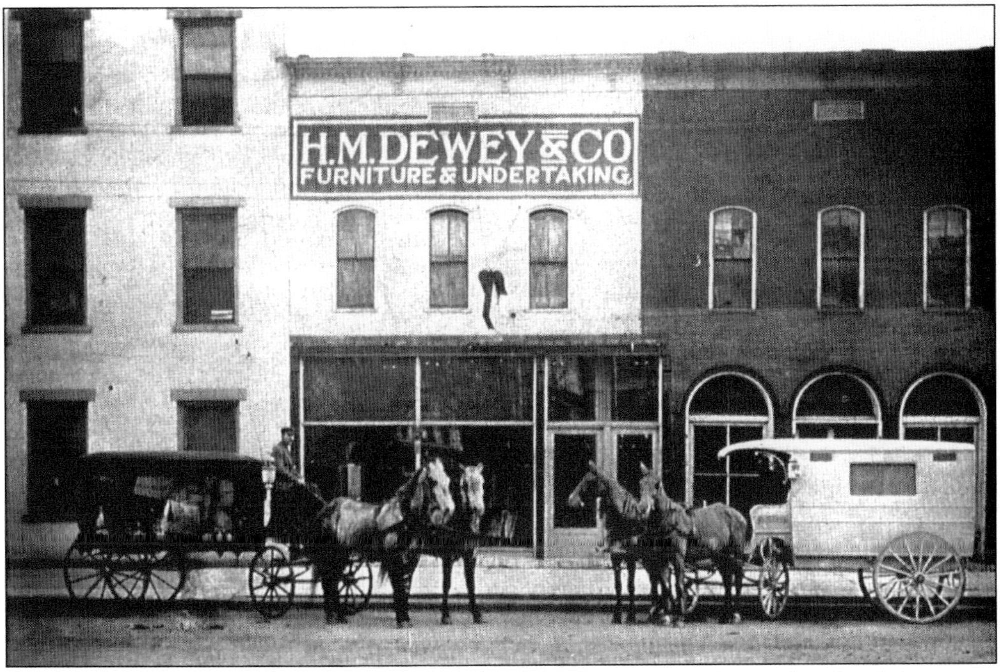

Horace M. Dewey ran this furniture and undertaking business on the south side of the square until 1929. I. F. Pritchard had operated a similar business there from the 1870s to the early 1900s. It was later Marrs Furniture and is now the genealogical library. The building at the extreme left is the ill-fated Marshall House, which burned in 1983.

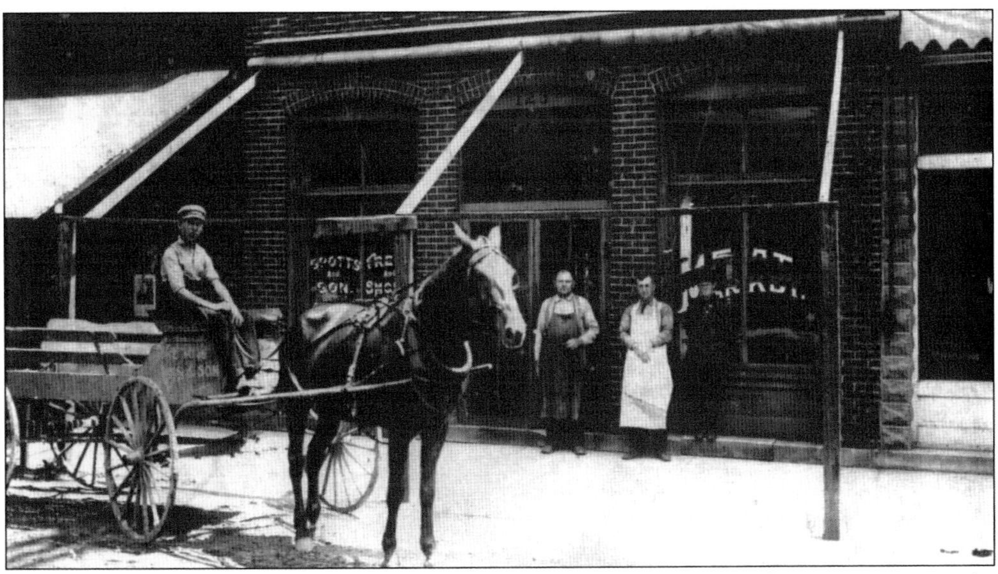

Spotts Meat Market was at 123 North Sixth Street. Charlie "Coal Bucket" Pennington is in the wagon, and Eugene Spotts and Walker Spotts are standing outside their store.

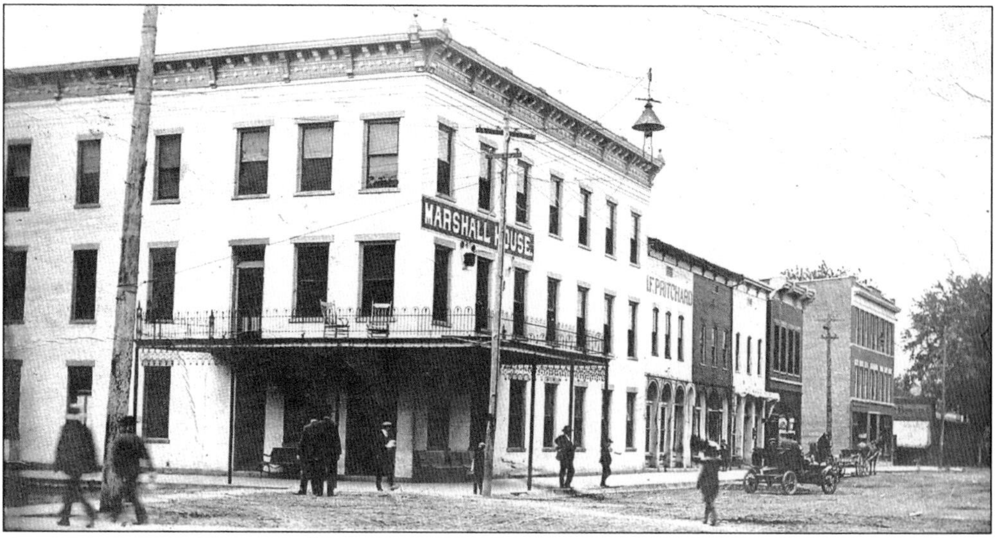

Construction on the Marshall House was started in 1855 by a Mr. Sherman and finished by James Wright. It was known as the Wright House, the Sherman House, and the Bennett House before being called the Marshall House. In 1971, Johnie Snedeker converted it to the Marshall House Apartments, which burned in 1983. The Pythian Temple (Strand Theatre) is at the far right.

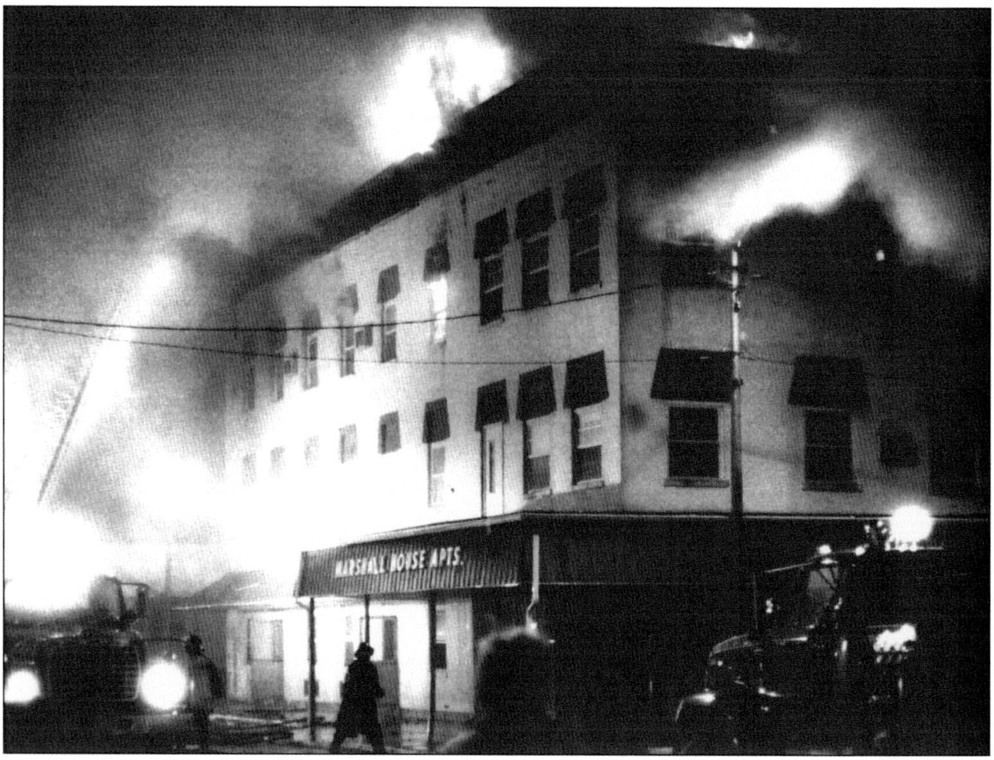

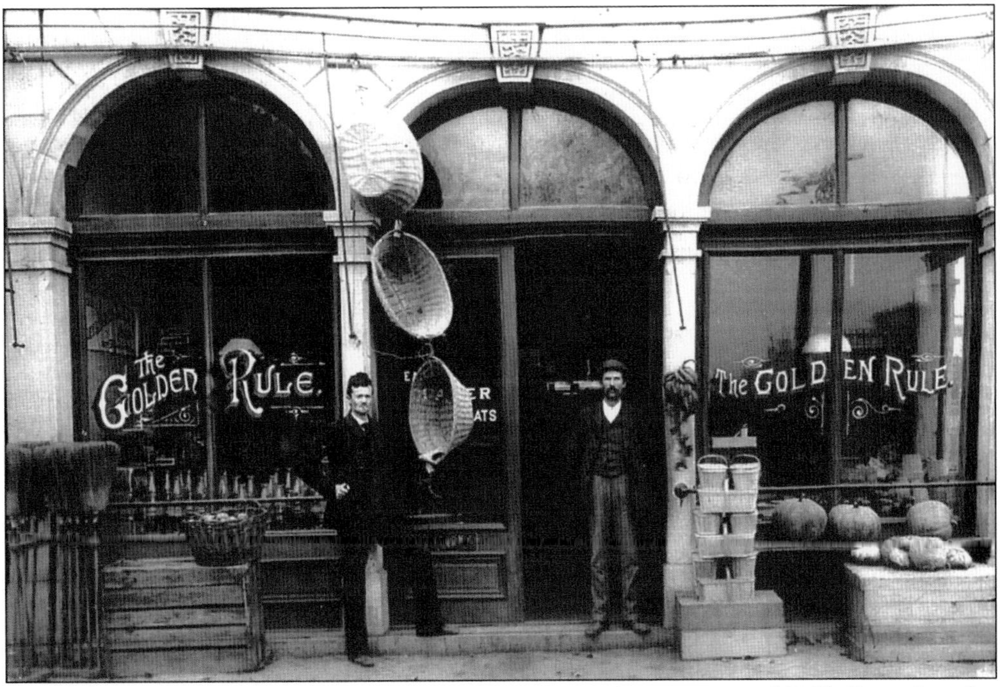

The Golden Rule Grocery on the southwest corner of Archer Avenue and Fifth Street has also been the home of I. C. Claypool's grocery, James Myers Produce, A. G. Dow Produce, Otwin and Bishop's Grocery, McDaniel's Grocery, Sowers Grocery, and the Marshall Hatchery. It was razed to make room for the Dulaney Bank in 1976.

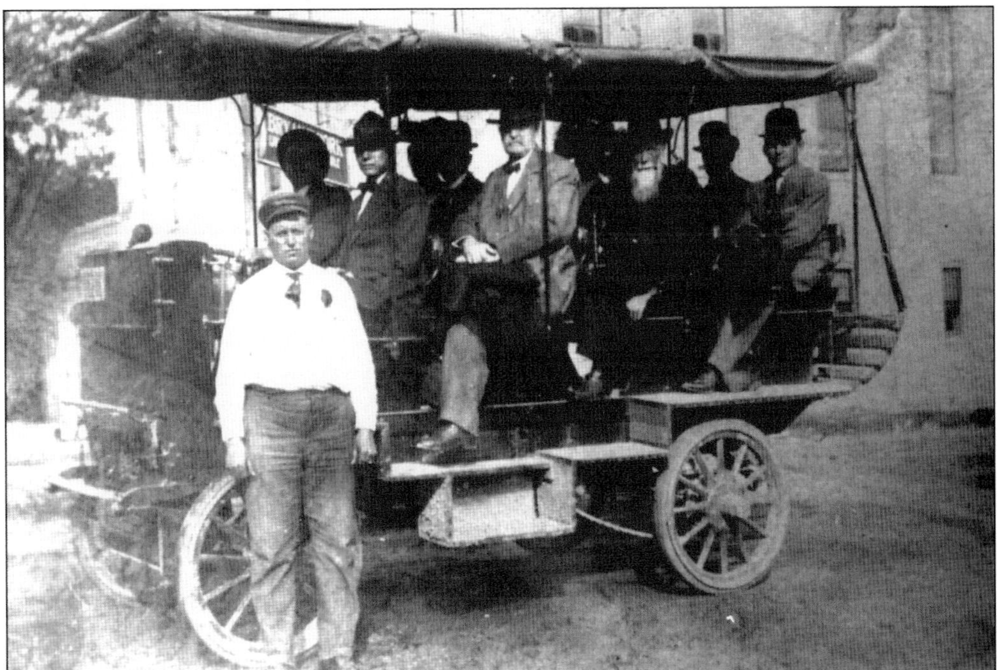

The jitney service ("the bob"), operated by John and William Rector, picked up train passengers at the two railway depots and transported them downtown.

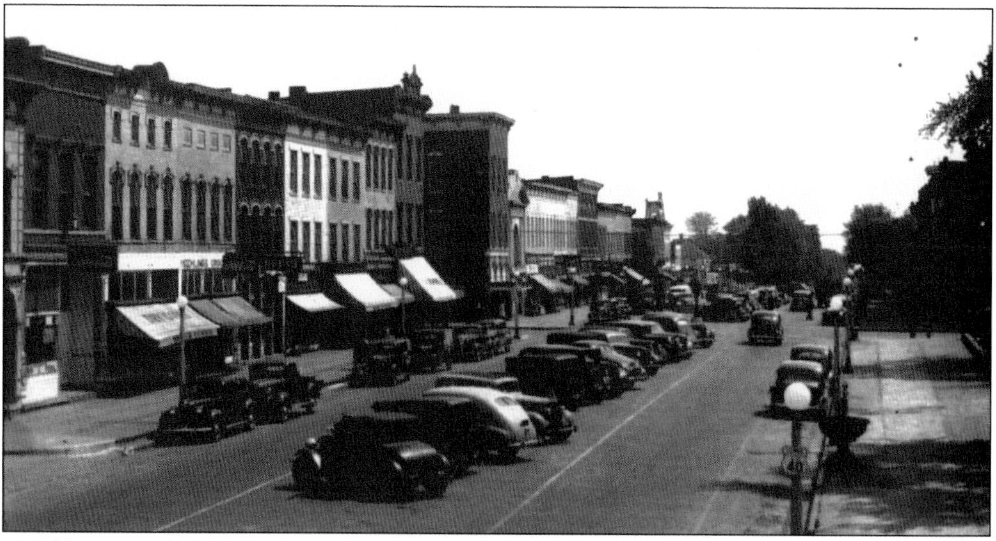

In addition to changes in parking, Archer Avenue looking toward Sixth Street has seen other changes. The tall building at the northeast corner of Sixth Street and Archer Avenue is no longer there, having been replaced by the Dulaney Bank, which tore down that building and constructed a shorter building (current photograph below). In 1976, Dulaney Bank left this building, which now houses Shore-Murphy Insurance, and built at the southwest corner of Fifth Street and Archer Avenue.

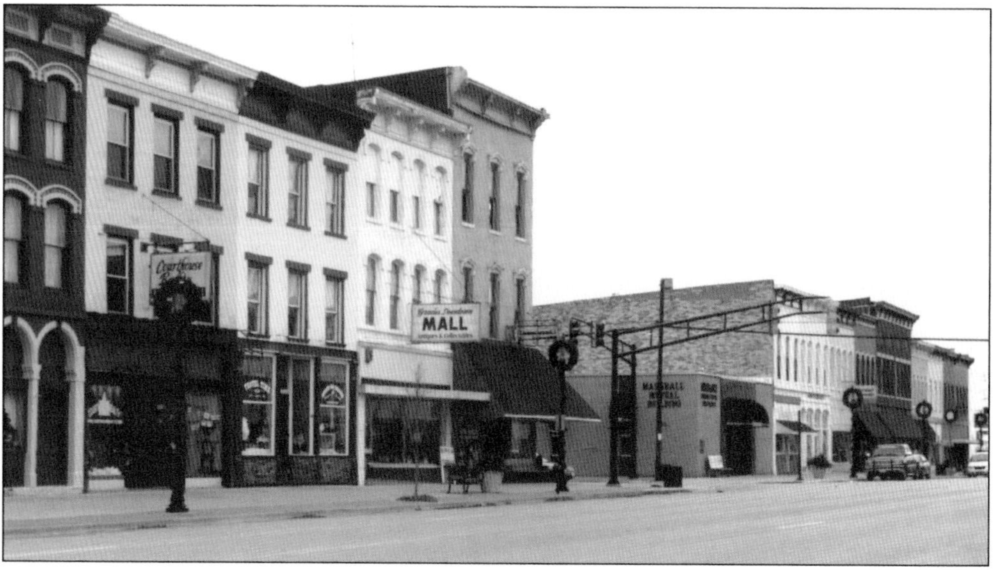

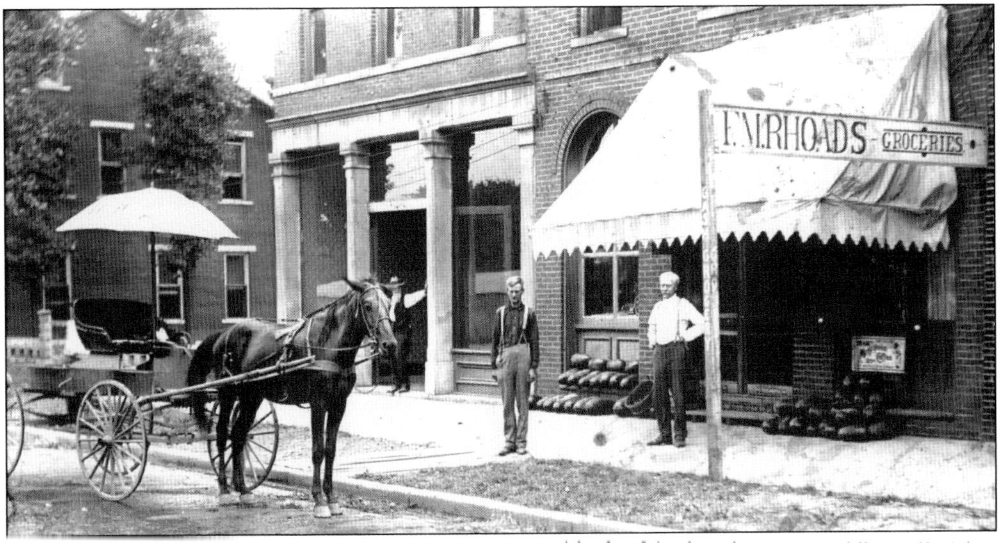

Standing outside the F. M. Rhoads Grocery in the 700 block of Archer Avenue are Cletus Perisho, left, and Frank Rhoads. The building to the far left is the Archer House, showing an exposed west side.

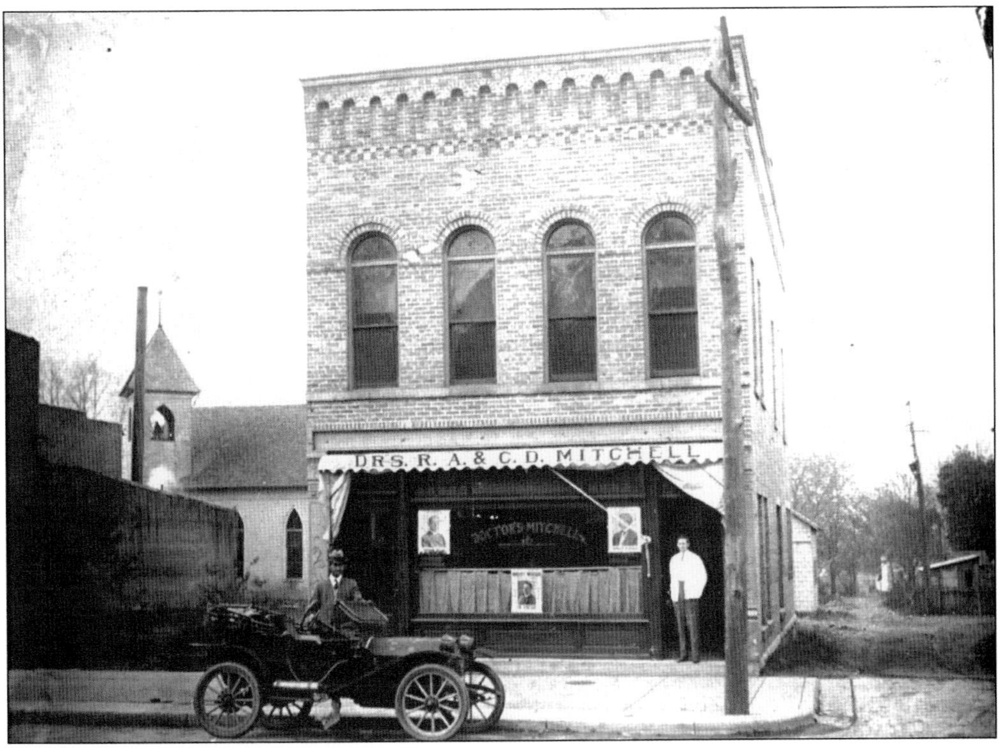

Dr. Roscoe Mitchell, father of Dr. George Mitchell, had this building constructed in 1910 at 116 South Fifth Street, opposite the courthouse. His brother, Clarence, a dentist, joined him. Beyond is the Christian church, on Locust Street, built in 1860.

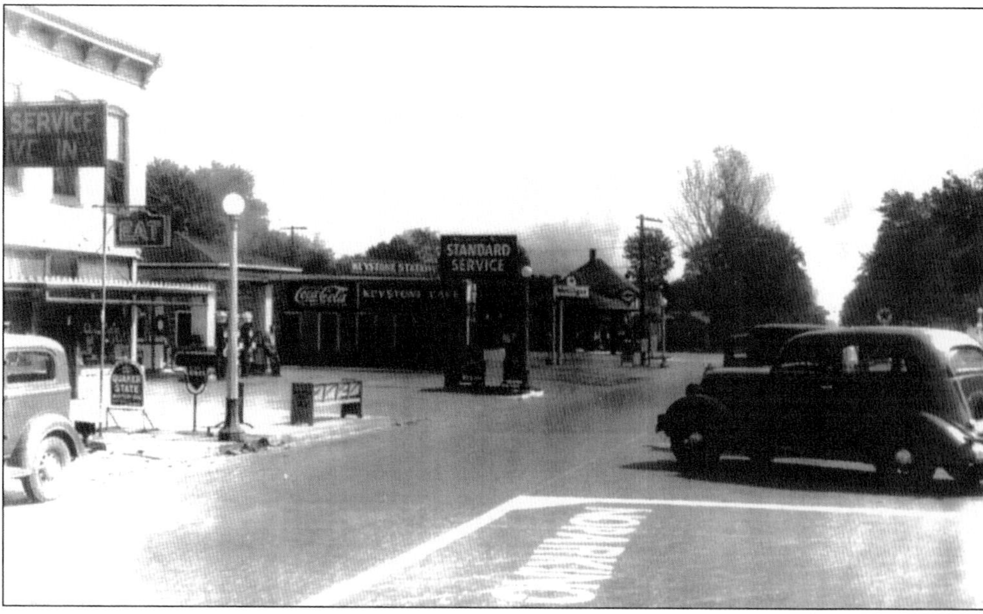

This view, looking east at the intersections of Michigan Avenue, Eighth Street, and Archer Avenue in Marshall, shows the Owl Cafe, owned by Mr. and Mrs. Tom Crump, at the extreme left, where Bishop's Cafe is now located. Next is a Standard service station, then the Keystone Cafe, so called because of its shape, which was built at the site of a Big Four railroad wagon yard. Tom Koutsoumpas was a cook at the Keystone Cafe prior to opening his restaurant across the street. A Mobil gas service station was just east of the Keystone Cafe. The photograph below, looking northwest, shows the demolition of the Keystone Cafe and Marathon station in 1974 to make room for the Marshall fire station. Note the laundromat, which had replaced the Standard service station and which was later razed.

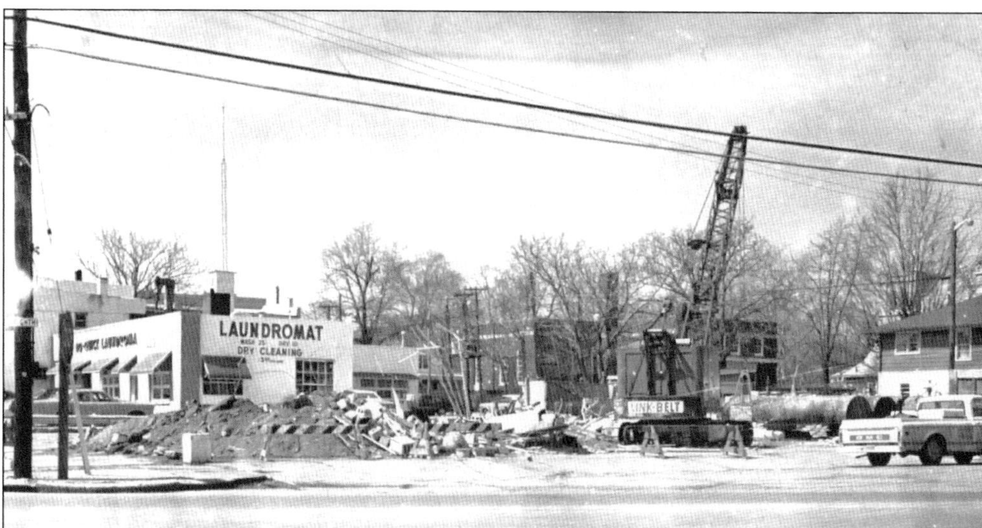

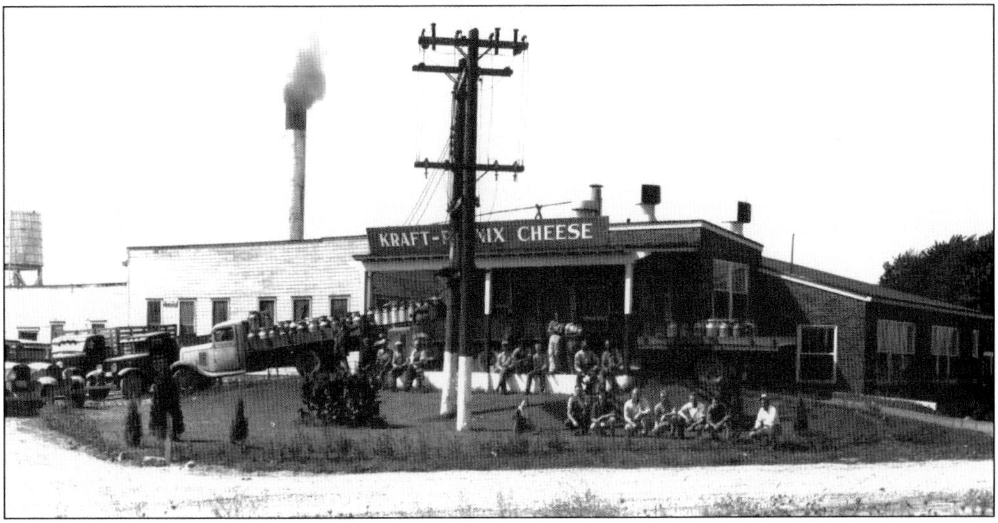

Marshall's manufacturing and processing operations have often included major brands, such as this Kraft Phoenix Cheese plant located on the Clarksville Road a half-century ago.

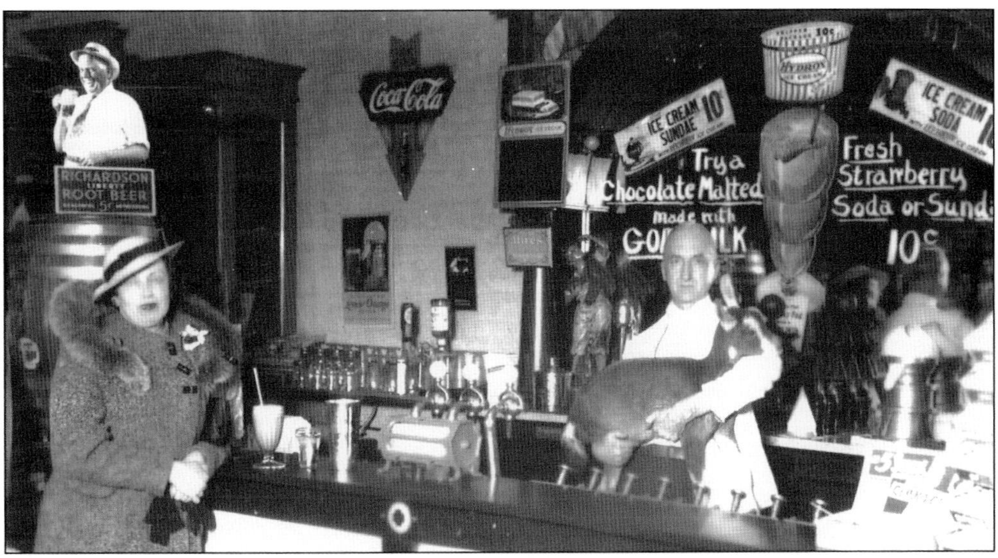

The Keifer Drug Store at 522 Archer Avenue was unique in featuring goat milk products, as Fred Keifer, the owner, was a noted goat herdsman. This photograph was taken about 1916. Gracie's Downtown Mall is currently at this location.

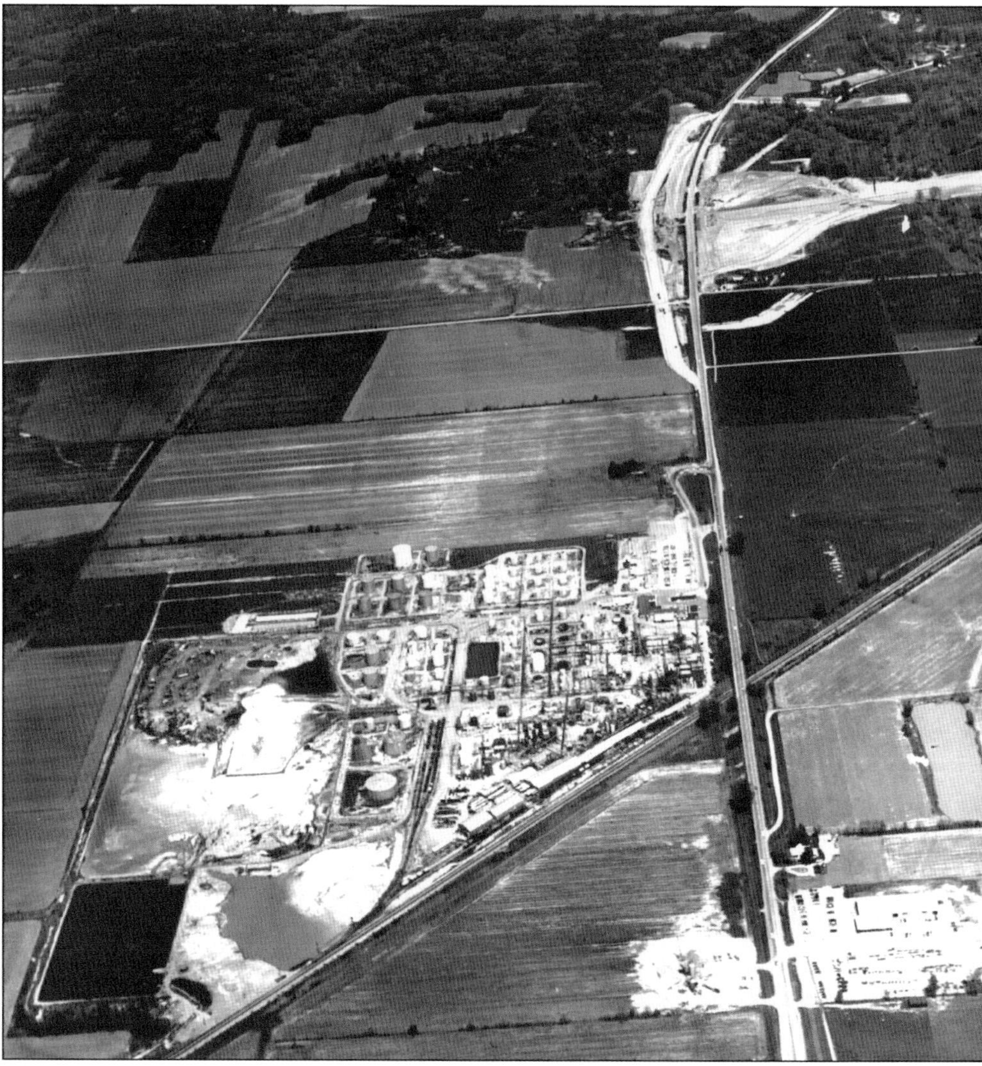

The Velsicol Chemical Corporation on north Route 1 in Marshall provided good employment for hundreds of workers from its construction in 1936 to its closing and dismantling in 1988. An EPA cleanup was ordered for the site, which has been stabilized, and will be monitored for 30 years. The upper part of this photograph shows the I-70 interchange under construction.

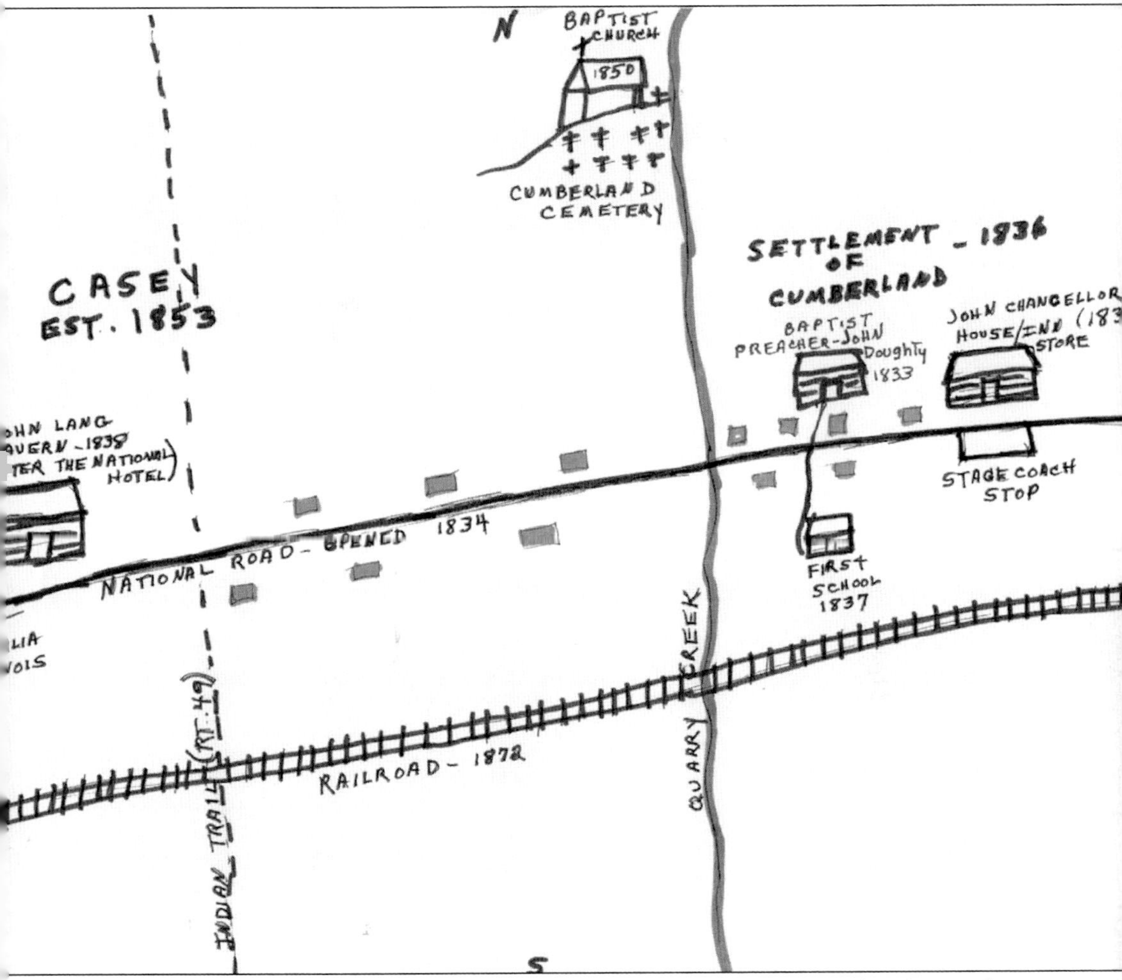

The first permanent settler in the Casey area was John Doughty, a Baptist preacher from Indiana who came to the area in 1833. In 1836, Ewing Chancellor laid out the town of Cumberland, which already had a post office. Cumberland soon had shops, a Baptist church, a Baptist cemetery, and a log school. A north-south road (now Route 49) crossed the National Road a mile west of Cumberland, forming the intersection of what would become Cumberland (Main) and Jasper (Central) Streets. John Lang had settled in the Casey area in 1838 and soon built a hotel called the National House, just west of this intersection on the north side of the street. The town of Casey was platted in 1851, the name coming from the fact that people in the area had gotten their mail at the Cumberland post office, which had been named for Zadoc Casey, a prominent political leader. Casey grew slowly, but in 1869, Rufas Neal built a three-story steam mill on the west side of town, and the railroad came through in 1870. In 1878, the Hammond mill was moved to Casey. Shortly after 1900, the oil boom north of town poured business and money into Casey, creating a solid base.

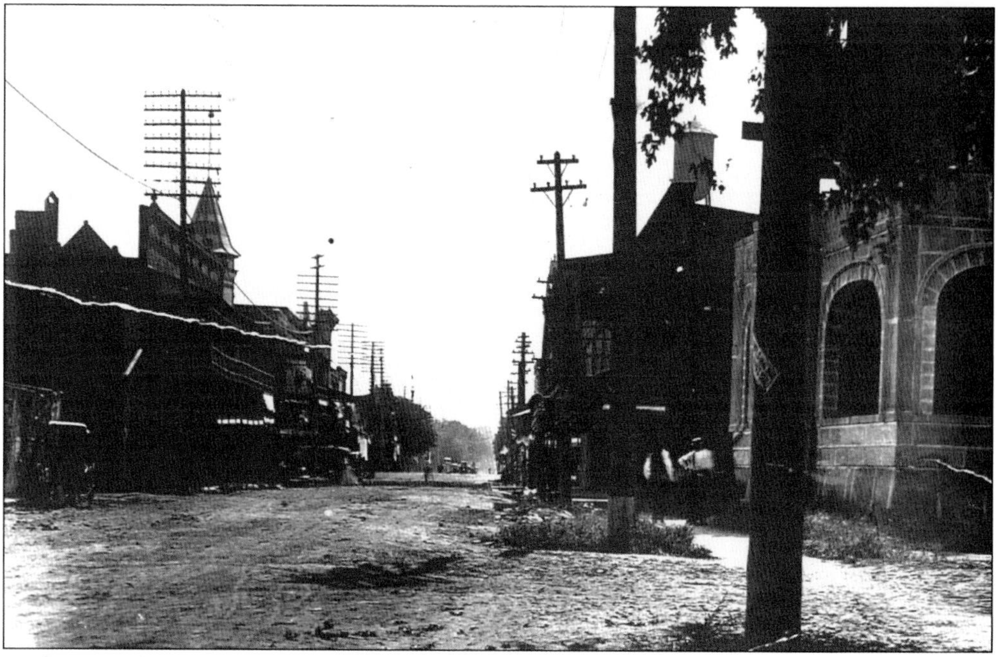

Looking south on Jasper (Central) Street, just north of the intersection with Cumberland (Main) Street, the old city hall is at the extreme right.

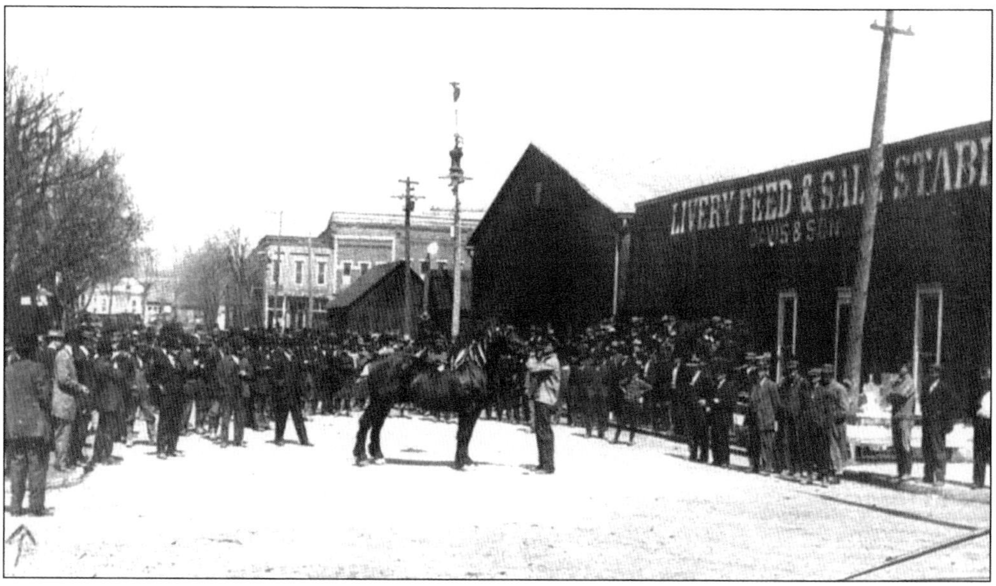

James Davis and son operated the Livery Feed and Stable on First Street, facing the railroad.

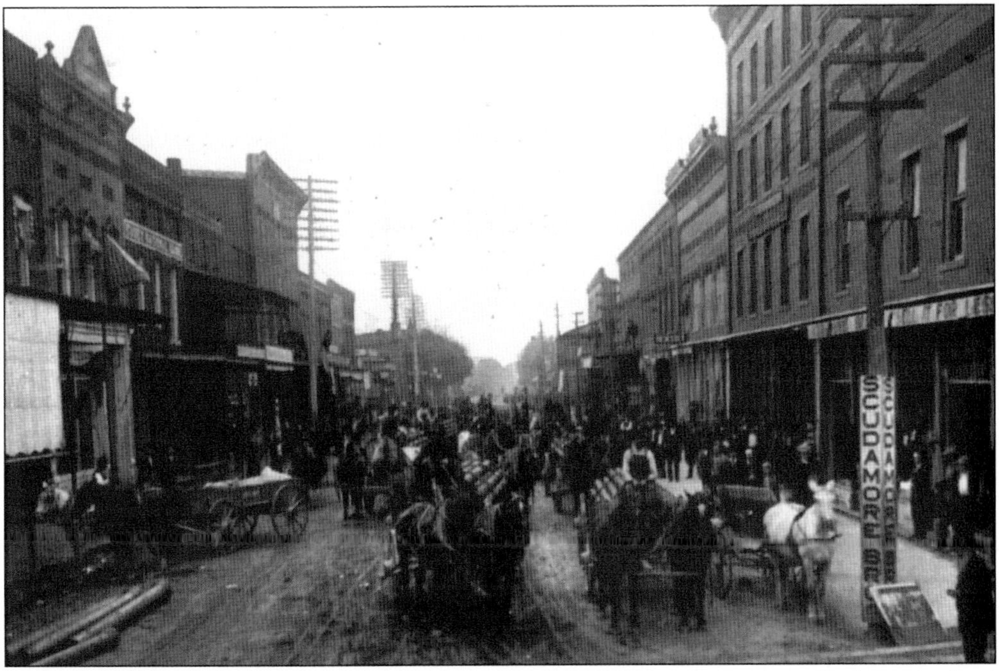

Here is the same street from two different time periods. The main intersection of Cumberland (Main) and Jasper (Central) Streets, looking south in this photograph, has always been a center of activity in Casey. During the oil boom shortly after 1906, it was often a chaotic scene. Note the two nitro wagons in front. By the 1920s and 1930s, things had settled down.

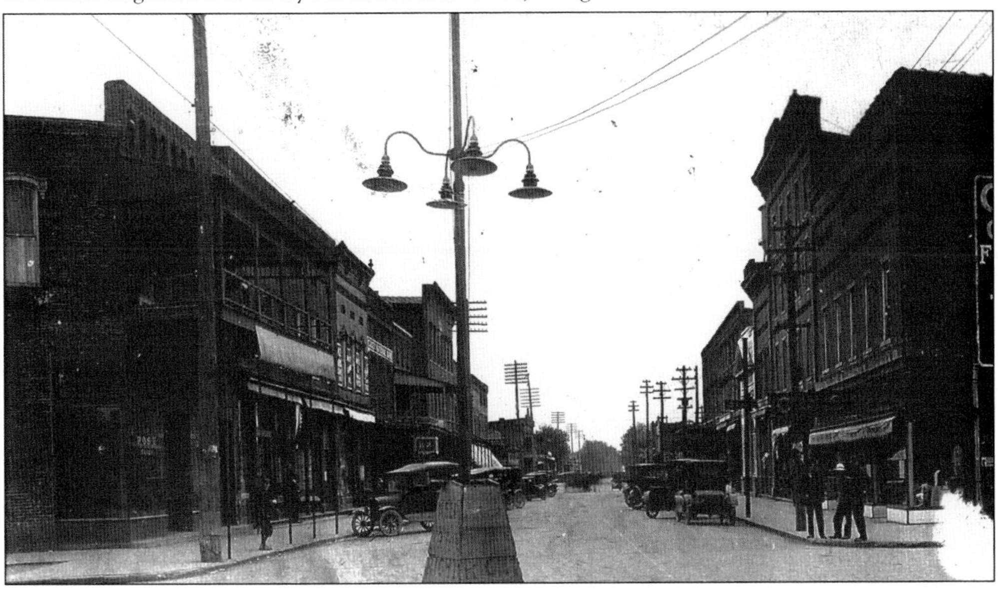

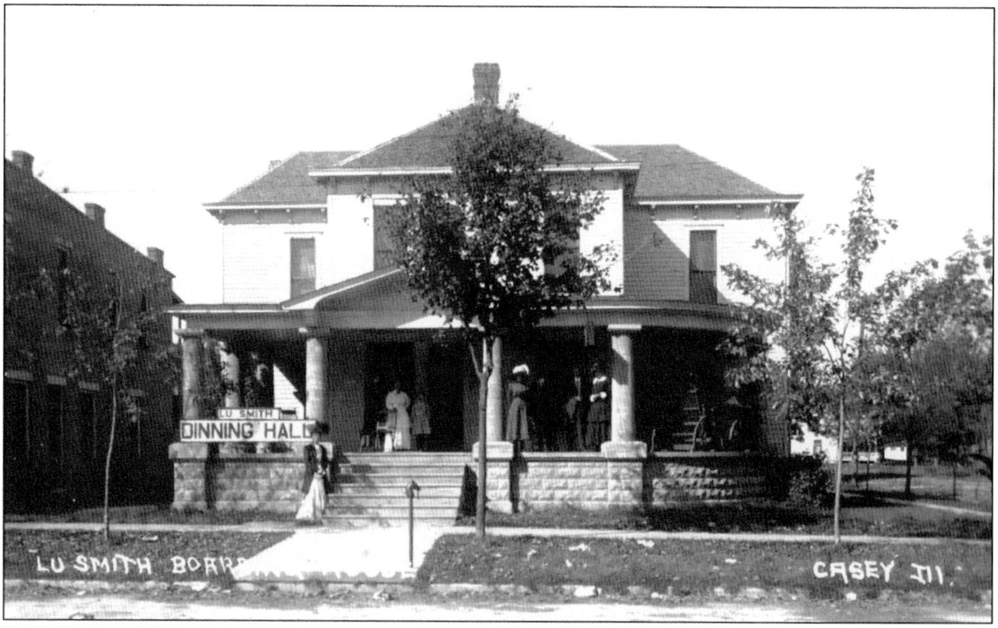

Aunt Lu Smith's Dining Hall and Boarding House at 110 East Main Street in Casey was purchased in 1924 by A. V. Meeker, who converted it to the Meeker Hotel. The Meekers apparently added the brick facing which it has today. Its most recent use has been as the Arbogast Law Office.

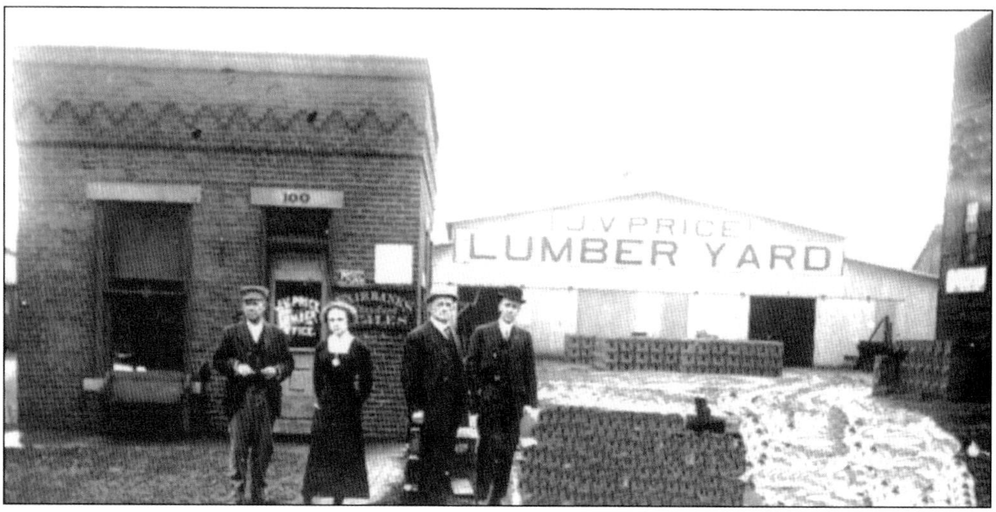

The Sanford and Price Lumber Yard, located on West Cumberland (Main) Street across from the current Kirchner Lumber Yard, became the Price Lumber Yard in 1894 when J. V. Price became the sole owner. On the right in this photograph are the remains of the prefab Hammond Mill, where concrete blocks were later made.

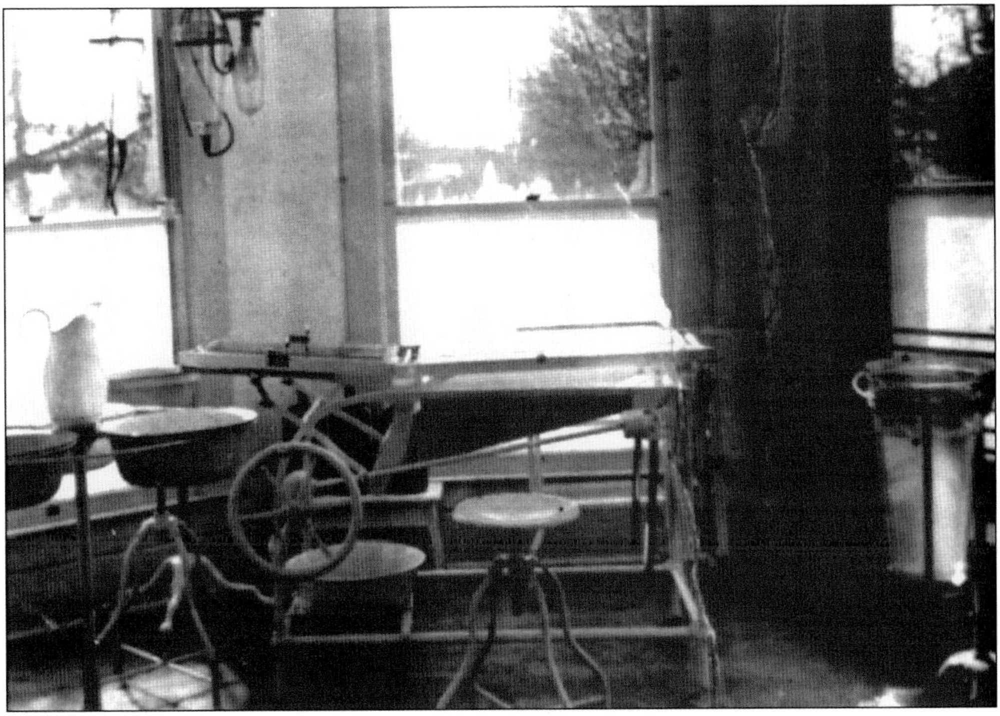

Casey Union Hospital was set up in 1907 by Dr. T. W. Williams in the W. S. Peters house, which was purchased for that purpose by a stock company. The venture was not successful, however, partially due to a malpractice suit, and the house was taken over by Dr. L. H. Johnson in 1909 as a residence. He lived here until about 1950. The house was torn down in 1961, and the site occupied by the Red and White Grocery, then by Dollar General. The above photograph shows the operating room. In the photograph at right, Dr. Johnson is leaning on the porch post.

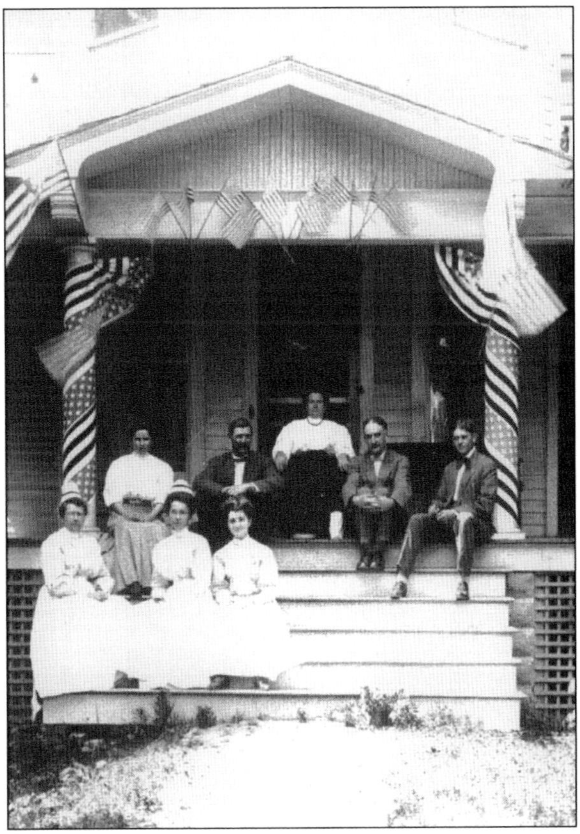

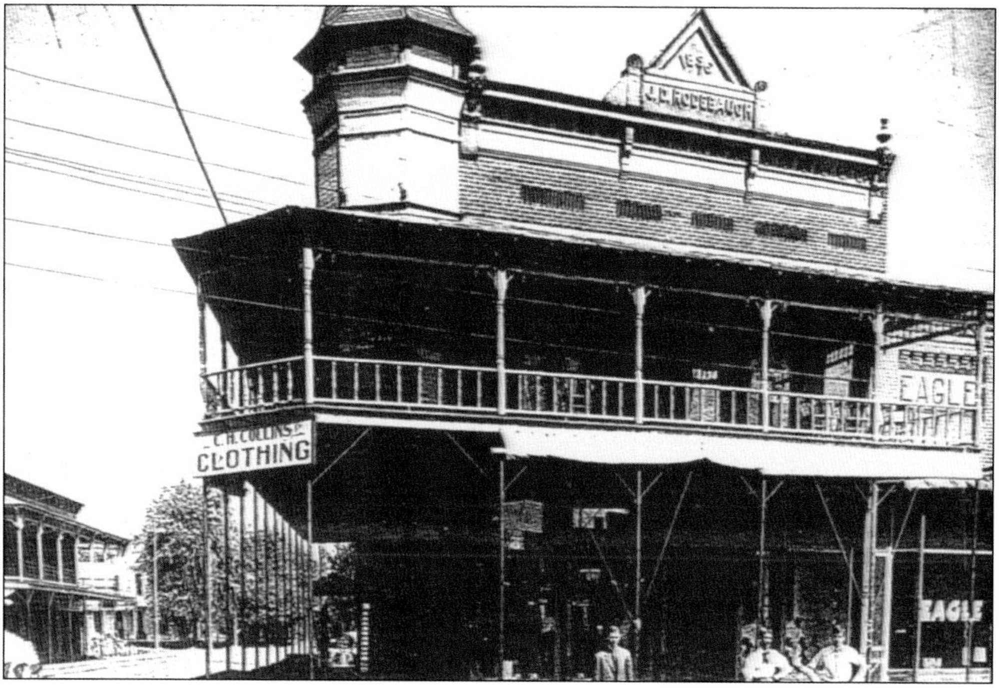

Built by druggist J. D. Rodebaugh in 1896, this building was serving as the C. H. Collins Clothing Store when the photograph was taken around 1906. Collins is on the left. In 1928, the Main Street Pharmacy (below) was opened at this location, and later it was Walgreens. Dave Millikan bought it in 1969.

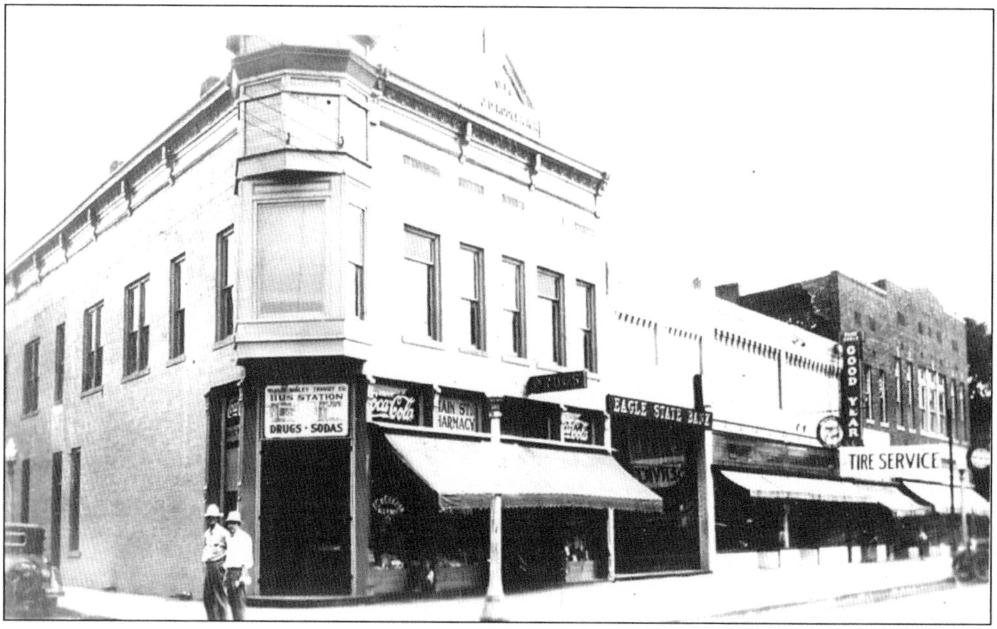

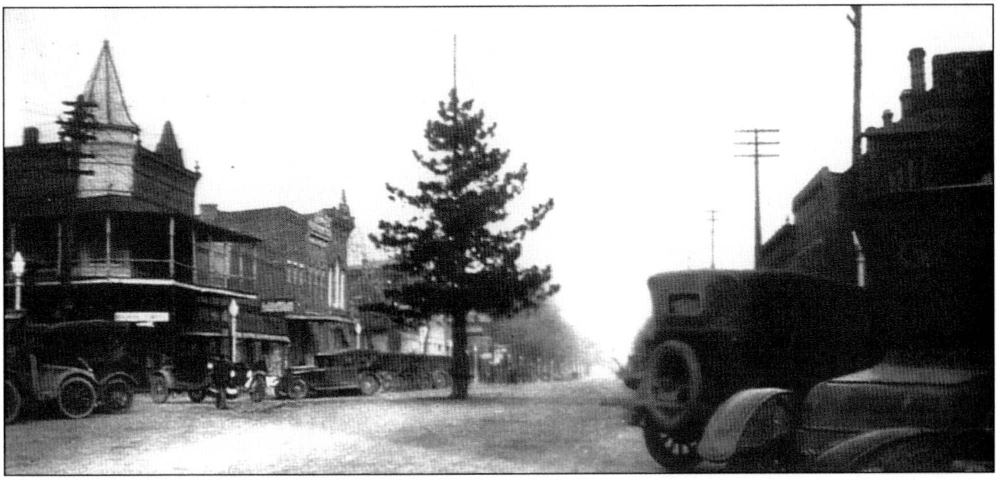

The intersection of Main Street and Central Avenue was a gathering point for Casey residents and visitors, featuring such attractions as Wednesday night band concerts and speeches from a temporary platform. This 1917 photograph shows the large Christmas tree that was placed at the intersection and decorated.

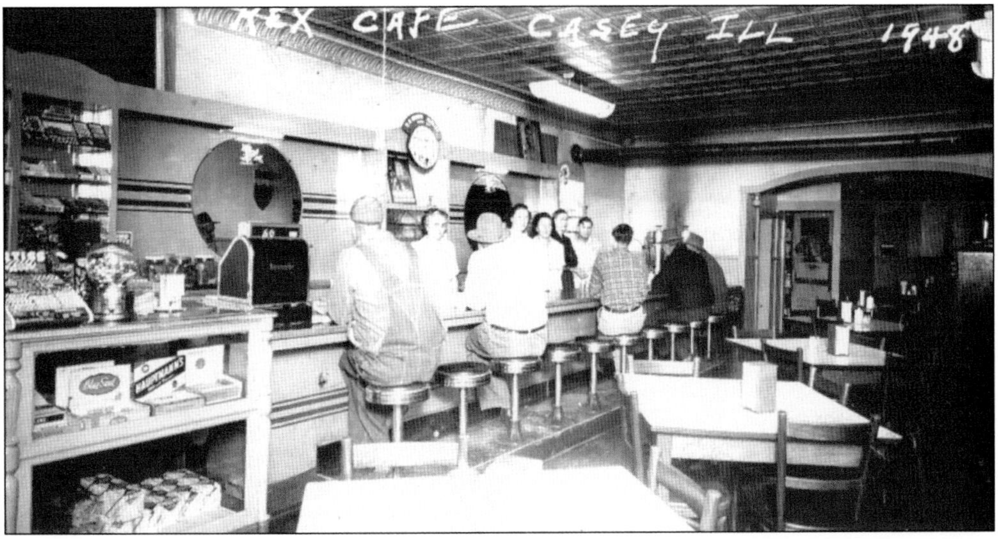

The Rex Restaurant on North Central Avenue was opened prior to 1910 and had numerous owners over the years. Russell Vernon operated the restaurant from 1940 to 1951, when the above photograph was taken. Ben Bertram bought it from the Vernon estate. In 1961, Mr. and Mrs. Art Hayden bought the restaurant, then Frankie Blakeman, and finally Danny "Dano" Doniphan. Charlene Williams operated a children's shop at the site, then the building was demolished in 2000.

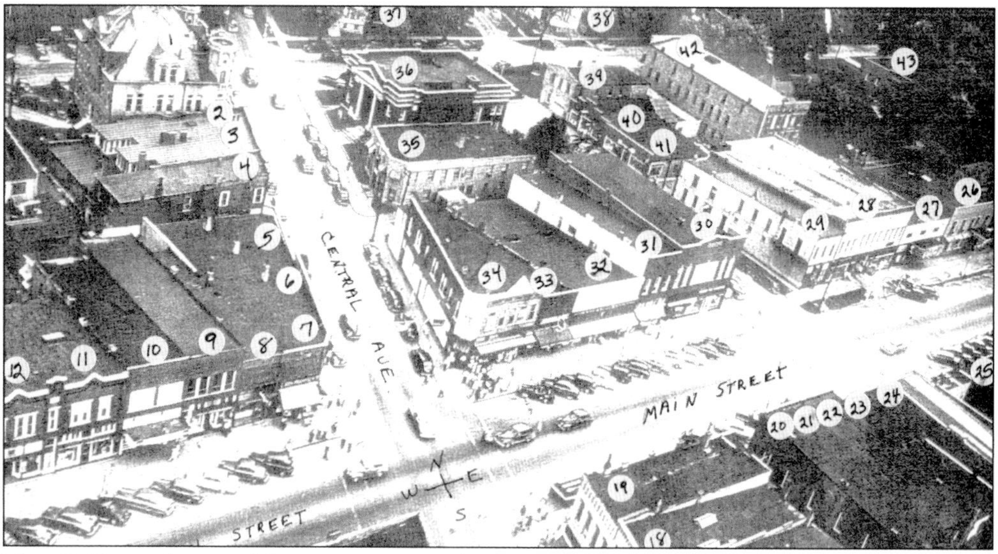

This 1948 aerial view of downtown Casey shows many changes during the past 60 years. Seen here are the city hall (1); Ohio Oil office (37); Bertrams (10); Hotel DeLite (26); Lyric Theater (27); post office (19); Kroger grocery (13); Dr. I. W. Lee, M.D. (3); Ettelbrick Shoe Company (25); Banner Times newspaper (29); Dulgar Grocery (20); and Baptist church (38).

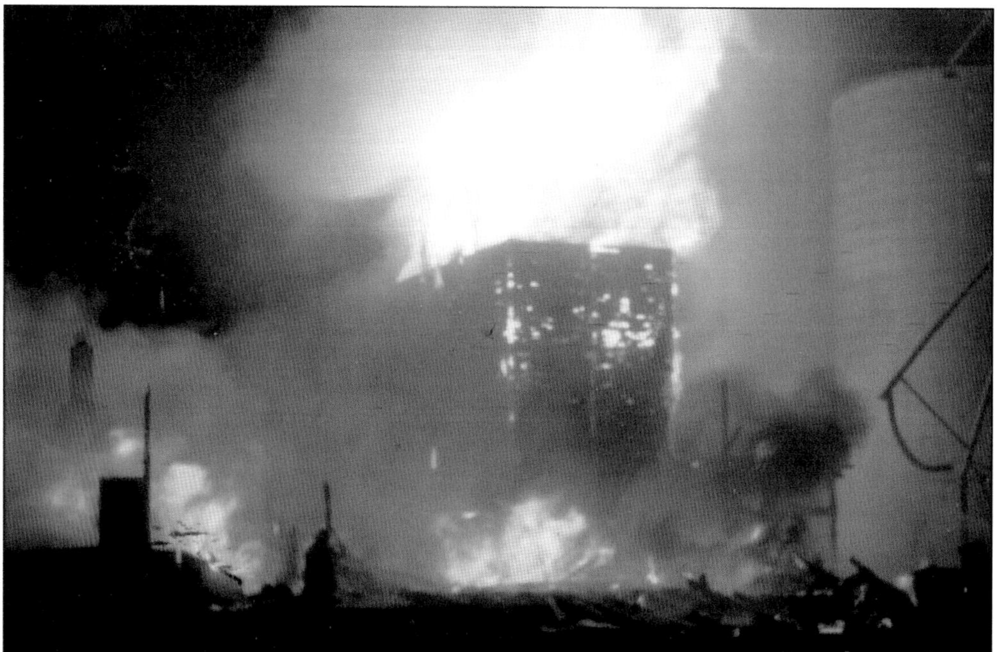

The worst fire in 70 years burned three-fourths of a block in Casey on December 17, 1975, destroying Sav-Mor, Brown's Jewelry, Tylman Studio, Grafton Café, and Vogue Villa, where the fire started. Damaged were the telephone office, Shawver's Clothing, the Cutright Store, and the KZ Newsstand. The arrival of Olney's snorkel truck was the turning point in the battle by the Casey Volunteer Fire Department and firemen from nine other cities.

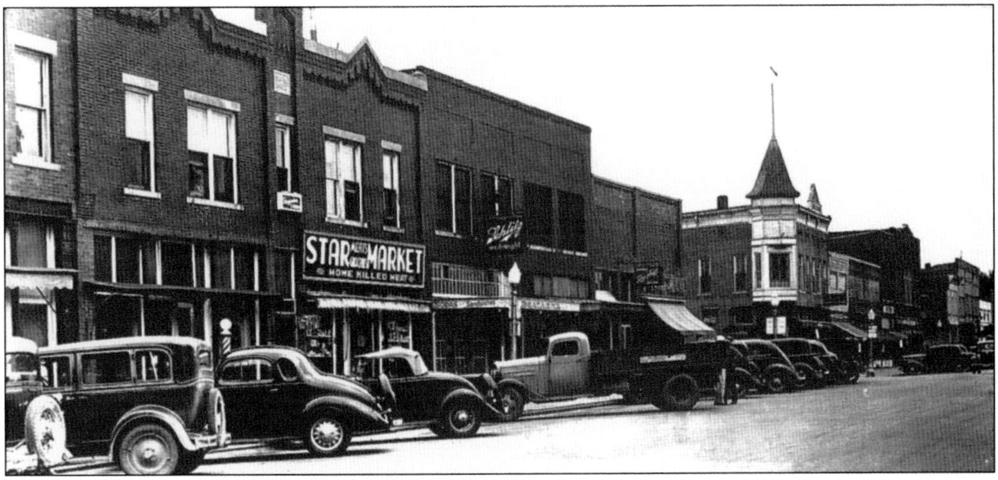

The north side of Main Street featured the Dunn and James Barber Shop, the Star Market, Bertram's soda fountain and news stand, Fitzpatrick Dry Goods, the Main Street Tavern, and Ben Franklin Variety Store. Across the street to the east was the Walgreen Pharmacy, Lehman Clothing (once the site of Eagle Bank), Arndt's Dime Store, Morgan Market, and Ferren Furniture.

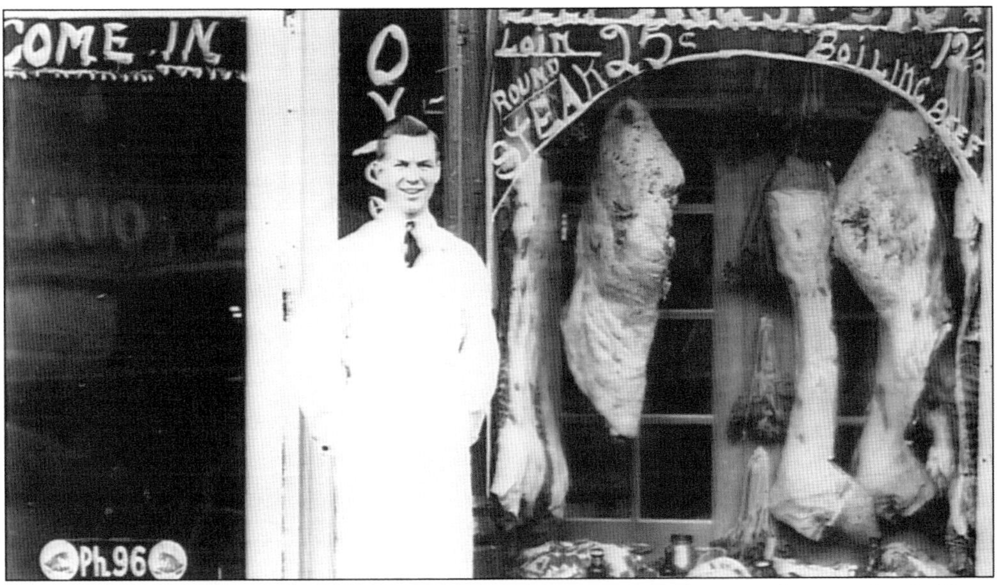

The Star Meat Market at 10 West Main Street was operated by Bill Davis, above, and wife Clara, who did their own butchering. The business was sold to Mr. and Mrs. Cook; then in 1945 Tom Baker became the new owner. He built a larger Star Market at 106 West Alabama Street, the first self-service grocery in Casey.

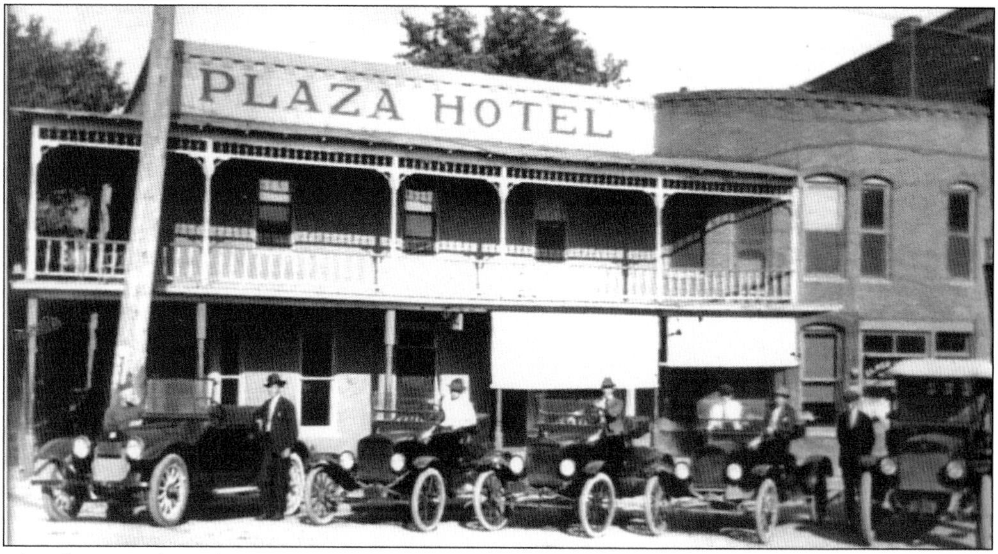

The Plaza Hotel, on the east side of South Central Street just south of the Vandalia/Pennsylvania railroad track, catered to railway passengers at first but was attracting automobiles by 1912. The site is now the Casey Business Center.

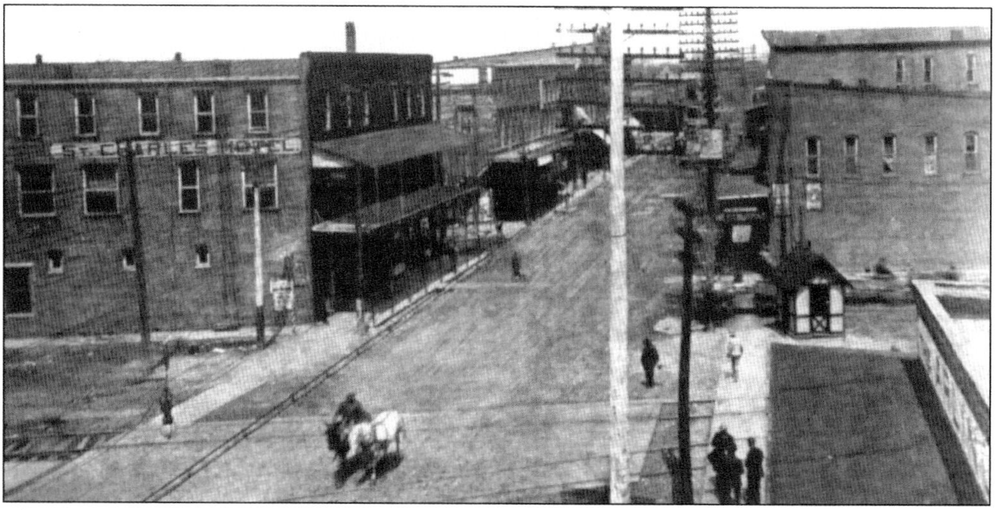

The St. Charles Hotel, north of the tracks on the west side of Jasper (Central) Street, was built in 1897 to attract passengers from the Vandalia Railroad. It contained 30 to 40 rooms and apartments. The hotel, including a bakery and the Davis Brothers Restaurant, burned in 1917. Farther north on Jasper Street was the opera house in what is known as the Sanford Block, which was threatened by the fire, but was saved.

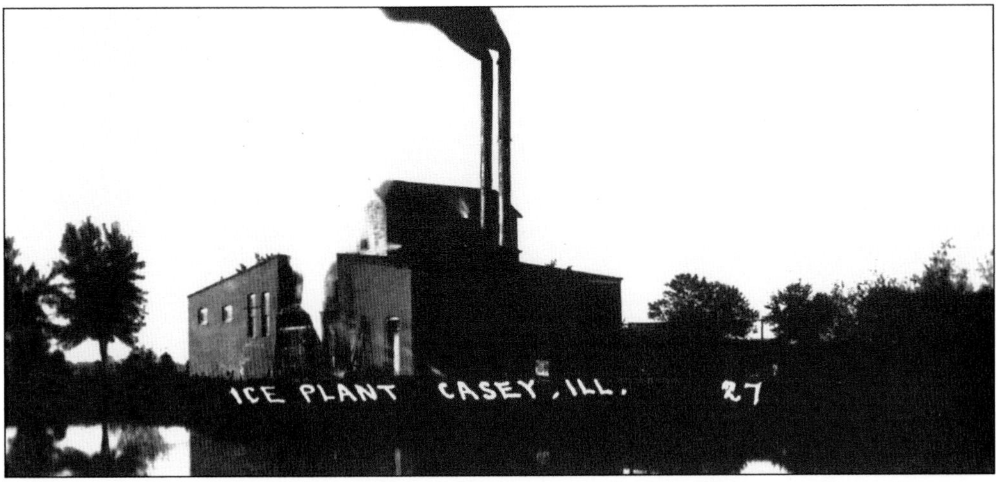

The Weaver ice plant was located on Weaver Pond, just north of the Washington Street Cemetery. The pond has since been drained. Joel Weaver and his son initially depended on nothing more than nature to produce the ice, which they cut and stored in sawdust, supplying Casey and neighboring cities. In about 1903, the Weavers built a modern plant that produced artificial ice. That plant was destroyed by fire in 1911. Before the ice business was created, the Weavers had a brickyard, which furnished many of the bricks in Casey buildings.

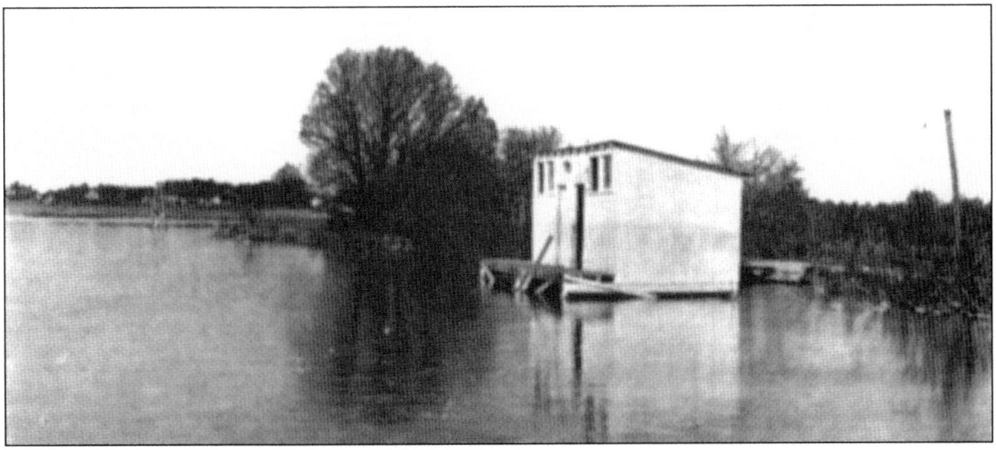

In 1910, a group of about 40 young men leased Weaver Pond for bathing and fishing. Above is the rather primitive bathhouse that they erected. The pond was about four blocks in length and about one block in width. As noted above, it has been drained and is now a residential area.

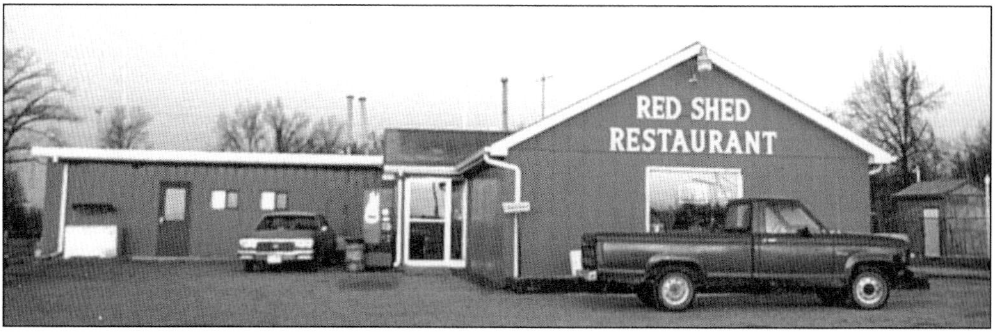

The Red Shed Restaurant operated from 1972 to 1988 on the west side of Route 49, north of Casey. It was owned by Joe Hardway and Virgil Streater. They also operated the Safari Campgrounds north of the Red Shed, which included a Texaco service station. The restaurant originally featured a smorgasbord and a large banquet room, which catered to meetings. Later when Vera Redman took over, the menu changed to family meals and short order food. Pete and Nancy Davidson took over next and offered entertainment by local musicians. The business was sold to Hardees, and the Red Shed building was bought by Clayton Garrard and moved to Eighth Street for use in his appliance business.

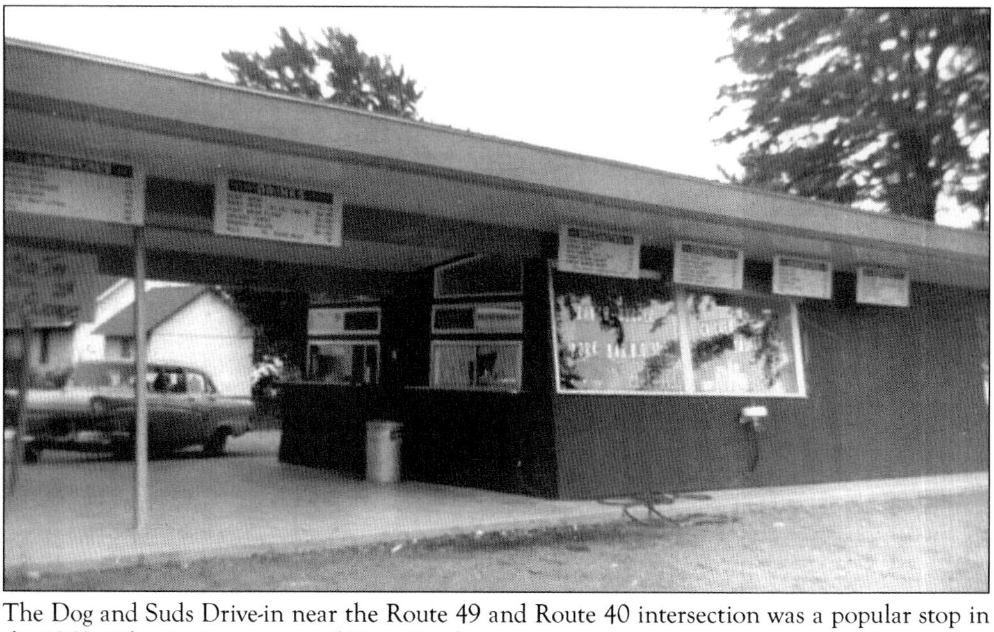

The Dog and Suds Drive-in near the Route 49 and Route 40 intersection was a popular stop in the 1960s. The site is now part of Casey Implement.

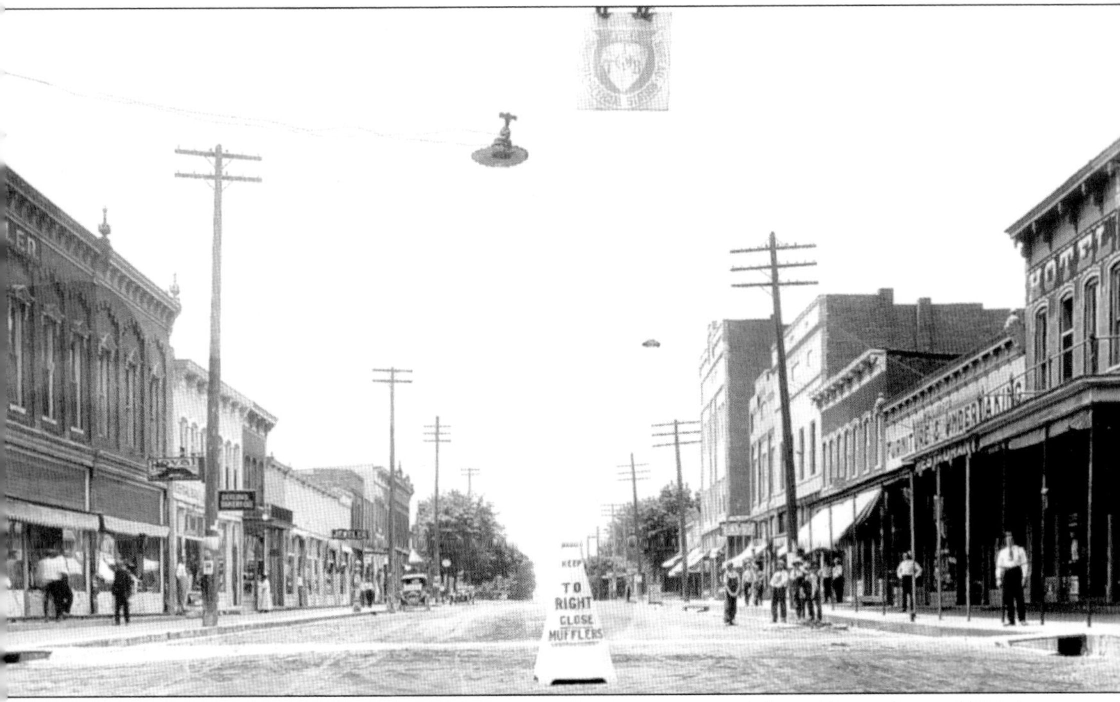

John Chancellor was the first resident of Martinsville, having moved from Kentucky in 1829. In 1830, he constructed a two-story log house as lodging for National Road workers. Amos Potts came from Ohio in 1830 and built a house, then sold the house to Joseph Martin. Martin laid out the town of Martinsville in 48 lots in 1833 along the new National Road. Fitch and Redmon opened a log cabin grocery around 1834, then in 1836 Stockwell and Chenoweth brought goods from Darwin and opened a store. The first regular hotel, made of logs, was built in 1837. The first blacksmith shop was built in 1838 by Cornelius Jenkins. In 1854, a gristmill was built and Samuel Macey opened another gristmill in 1868. The Vandalia Railroad came through in 1870, and Sallee Brothers' sawmill was opened in 1880. The above photograph of downtown Martinsville, looking west, shows Miller's general store on the left. It served the community for 70 years, closing in 1956. At one time 50 clerks were employed, and Miller's issued its own money tokens.

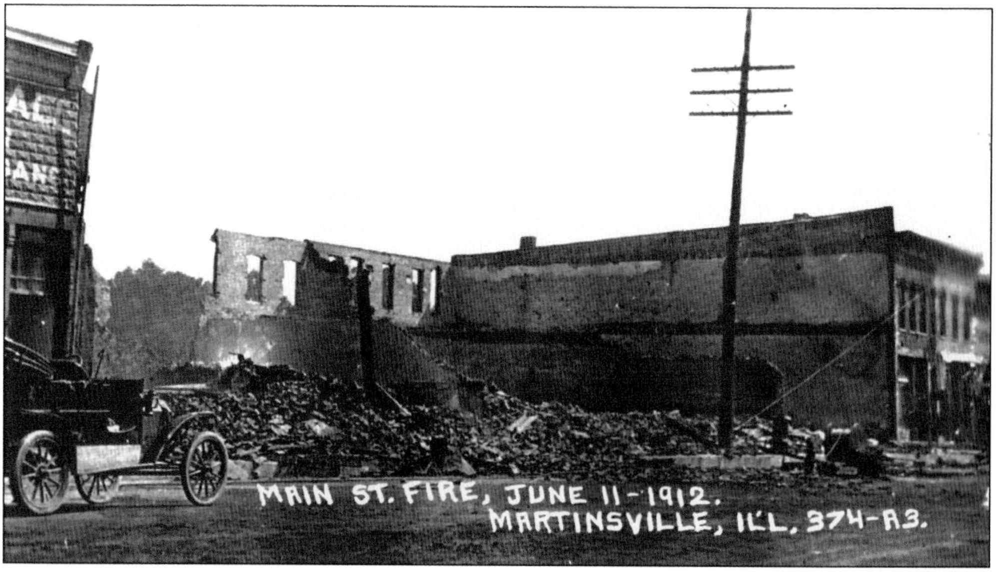

The fire that struck the north side of Main Street in 1912 destroyed the 40-year-old W. G. Delashmutt general store, the IOOF building that housed the Opera House and Alec Millis' restaurant beneath it, and the Winters store to the right. The main means of fighting the fire was the "bucket brigade," as modern fire trucks and adequate water pressure were still in the future.

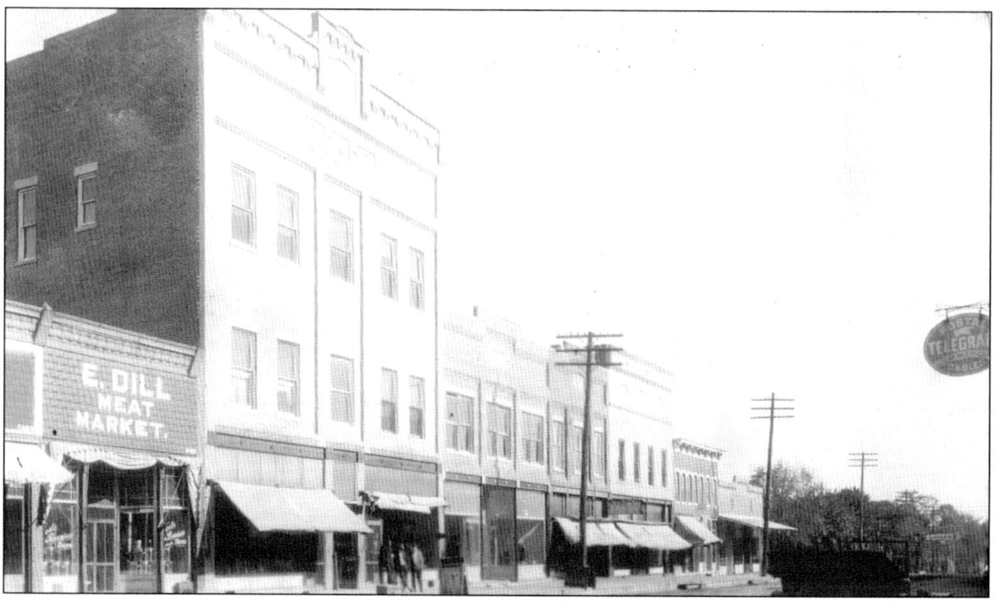

Following the destructive 1912 fire, the three-story IOOF building was rebuilt, including the opera house. Other structures took the place of those burned out, as shown in this 1917 photograph. I. W. Ishler opened a furniture and undertaking business next to the IOOF building in 1918, but another fire in 1923 destroyed this business, as well as that of W. K. McDaniel's dry goods store.

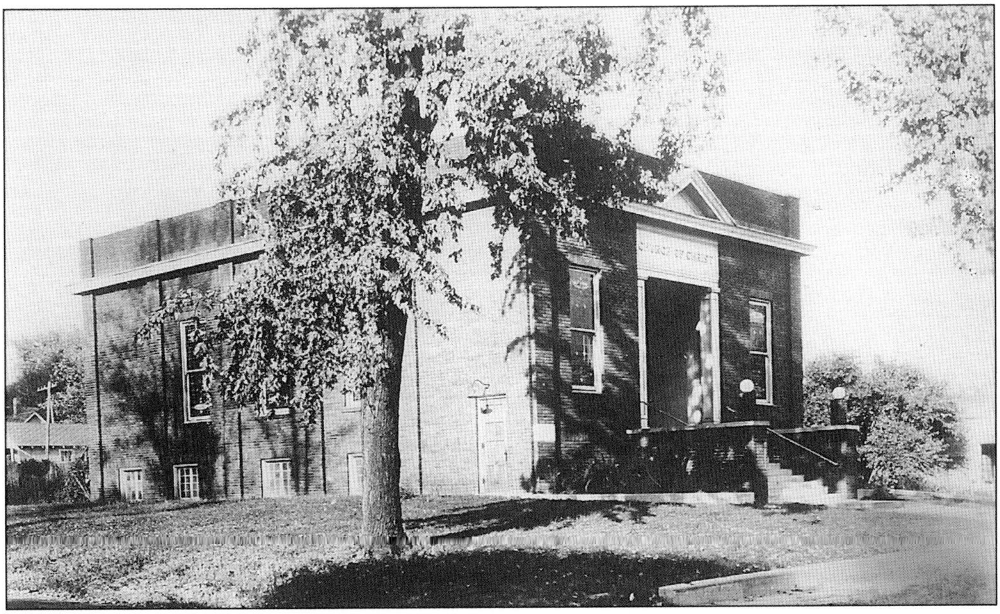

The Christian church on the northeast corner of Cumberland and Union Streets was constructed in 1927, and served the congregation until 1936, when it was sold to the City of Martinsville as a city hall. The city hall was moved, and the church served as a community center until 1948 when the Martinsville library moved in. When the library moved out, the building was razed to make room for an expanded fire station.

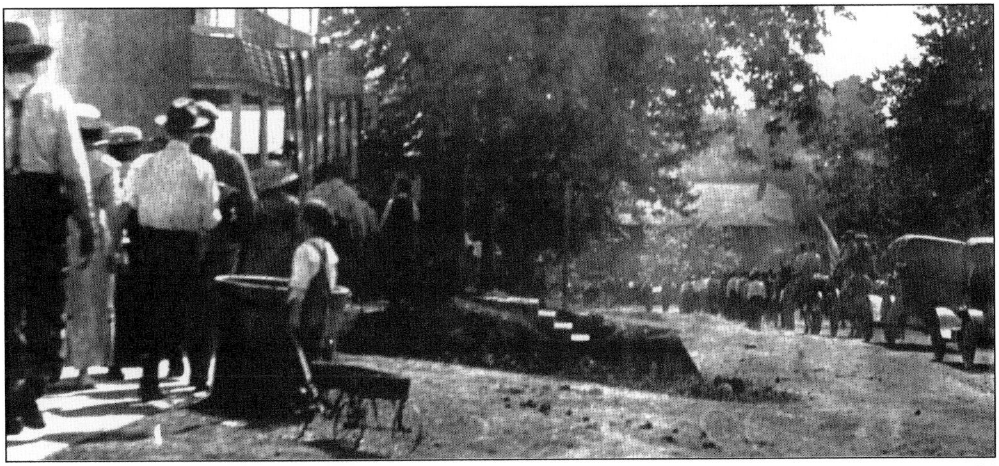

Martinsville residents head down South Washington Street towards the train depot to give World War I soldiers a send-off in 1917.

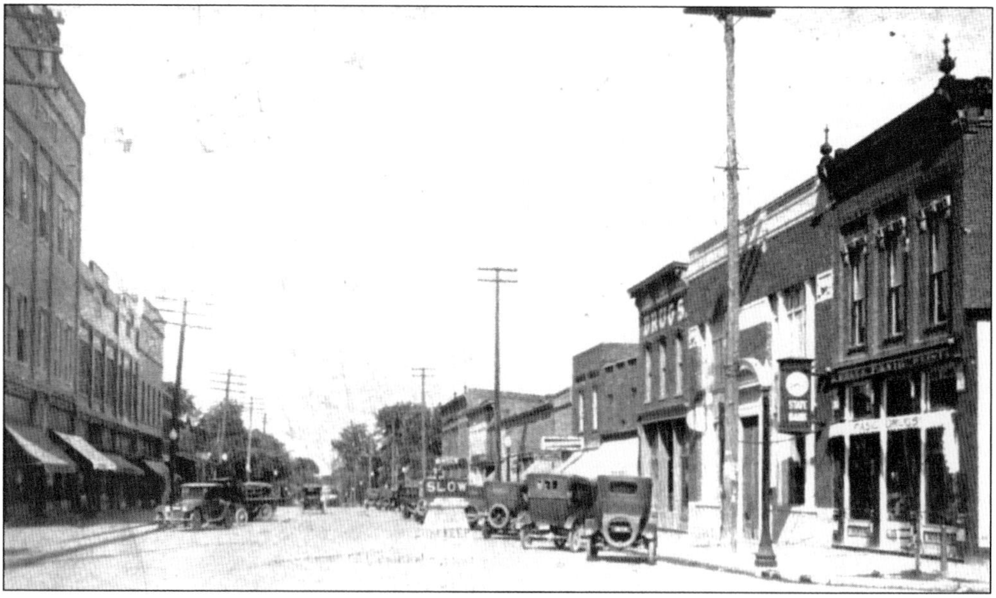

This 1930 card shows the Fasig Drug Store, a popular hangout for young people in the 1950s, on the extreme right (southeast corner of Cumberland and Washington Streets). It was torn down to make way for the Martinsville State Bank's drive-up facility in 1965. The bank is now owned by Regions.

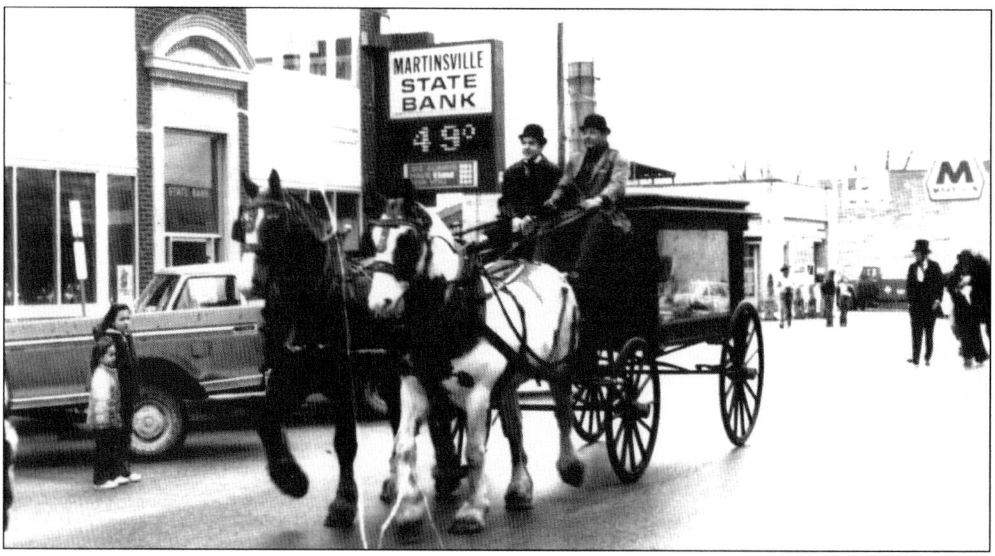

Looking southwest, the Martinsville State Bank is behind the old Greenwell Funeral Home hearse in this Martinsville sesquicentennial parade in 1983. The Marathon service station in the background has been torn down by an expanding Rowe Foundry.

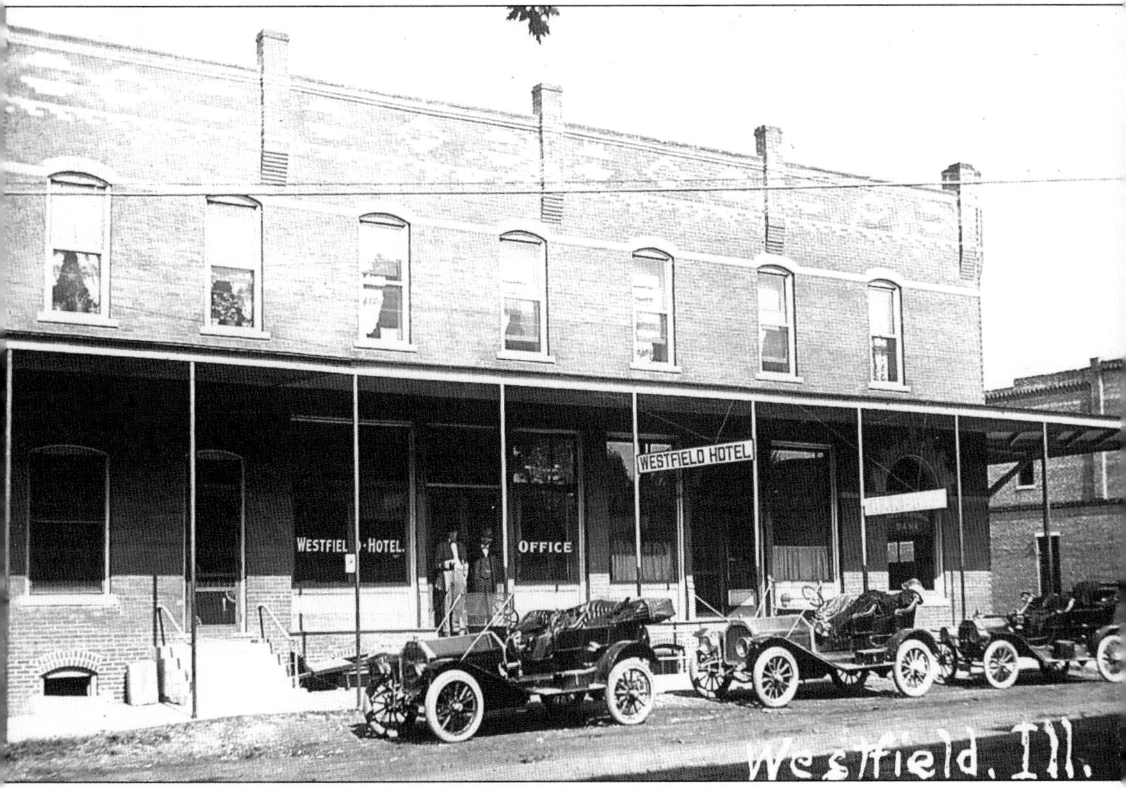

Westfield celebrates 1836 as its founding date, although the town was not platted until 1839 by Col. W. B. Archer, with 46 blocks making up the new village, one designated as a public square. The town was incorporated in 1866. Westfield featured two blacksmith shops, a livery barn, a poultry house, a hardware and implement store, a butcher shop, three brick yards, a tannery, four barber shops, two clothing stores, two wagon shops, a drug store, two saw mills, three grocery stores, two restaurants, a bakery, a lumber yard, a stock yard, a grain elevator, banks, a grade school, a high school, medical doctors, two funeral directors, a grain elevator, an ice wagon, a hardware store, and a newspaper. The Grant House, named after the famous Union general at the time, was built in 1864 as a public boardinghouse. A "pest house" was used to house young people who had smallpox or other communicable diseases, boys upstairs and girls downstairs. The Cincinnati, Hamilton and Dayton Railroad (CH&D) came to town in 1876, serving Westfield until 1930, and Westfield College provided higher education from 1865 to 1914. An oil boom shortly after 1900 gave the town a big boost. One of Westfield's early hotels is shown in the above photograph. It eventually housed many businesses, including a bank, a bakery, a doctor, a laundry, a barber, and the post office.

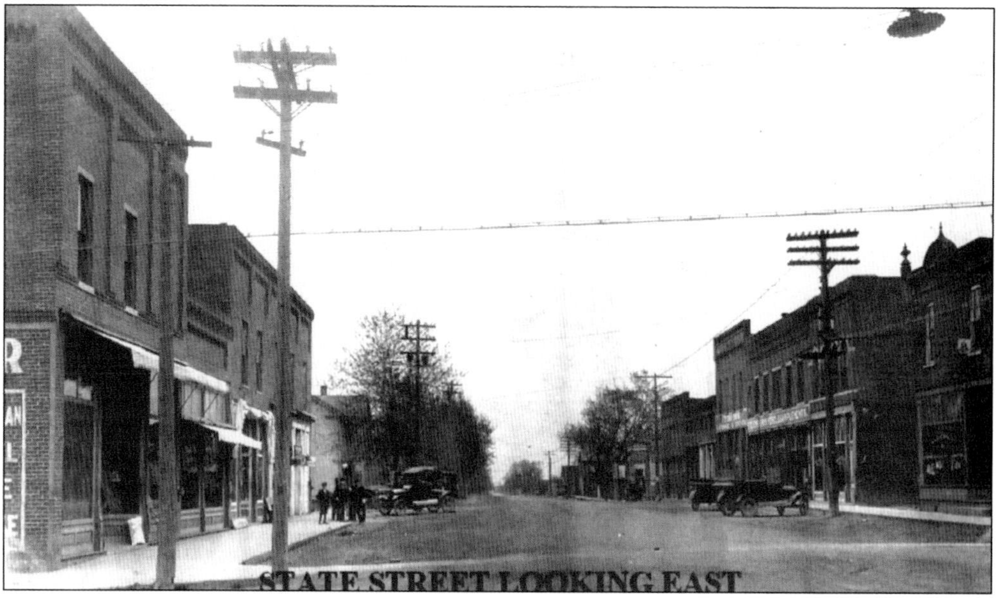

Westfield's State Street was full of businesses in the early 1900s. The Shuey and Rider Store at the extreme left, built in 1900, has been torn down.

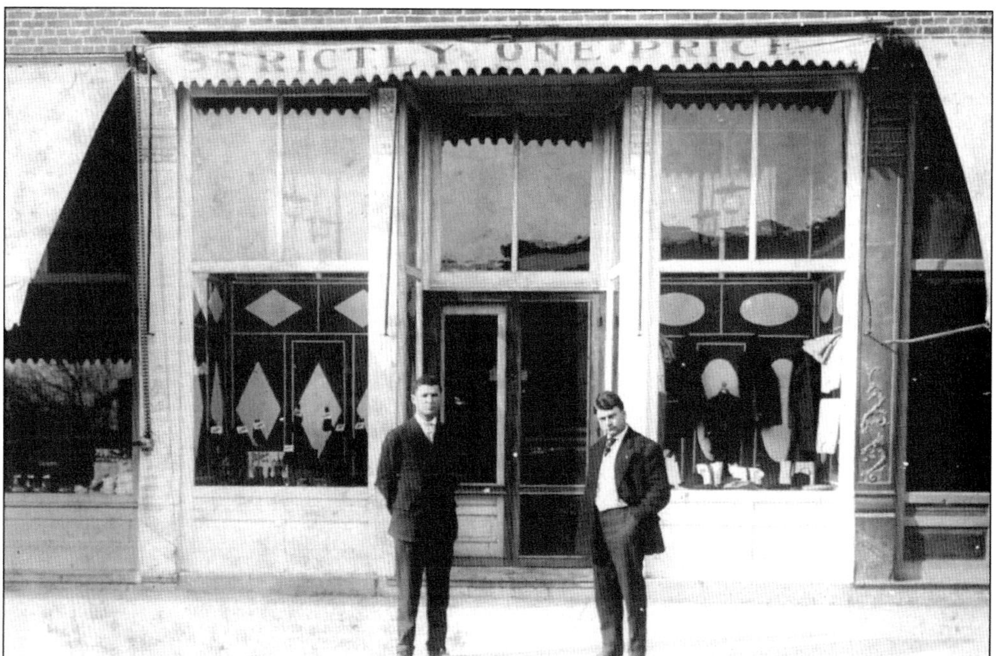

In front of the George P. Kaley store in 1906 are Leonard Parcel, left, and James Kaley.

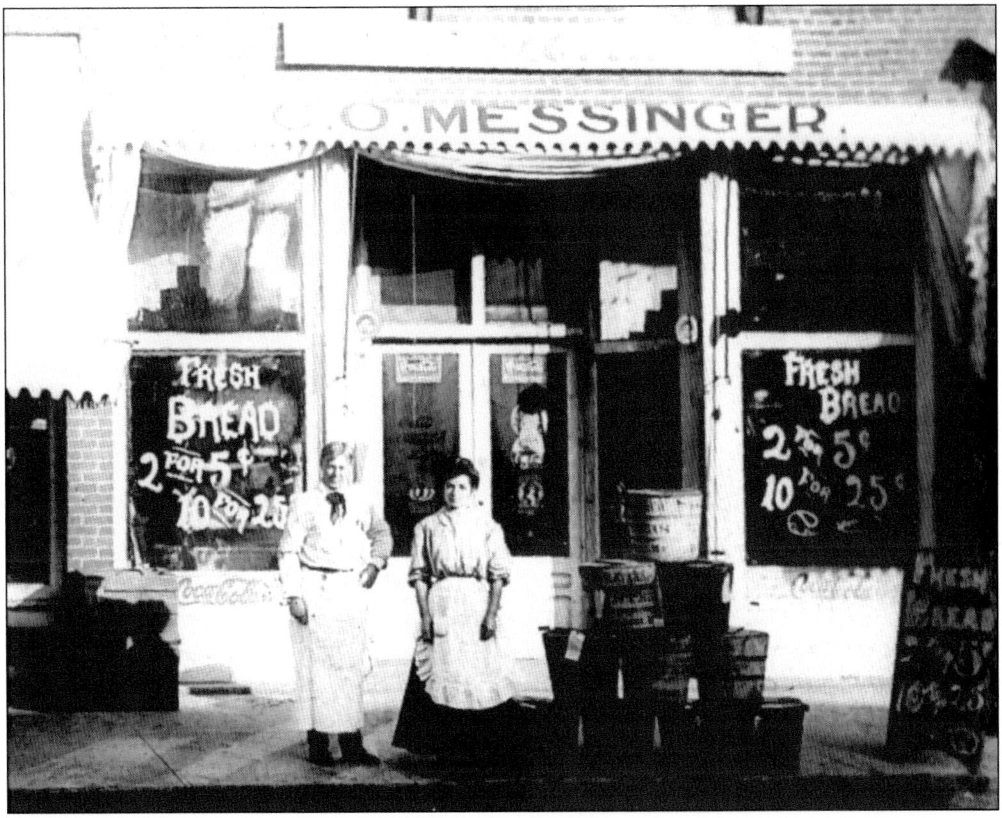

Westfield's C. O. Messinger made his mark on his city with a grocery, the Oyster Bay Restaurant, and an automobile repair garage, and by directing the city band. Outside the grocery, located across the street from the bank, are Carrol and Pearl Messinger in this 1910 photograph. Note the prices.

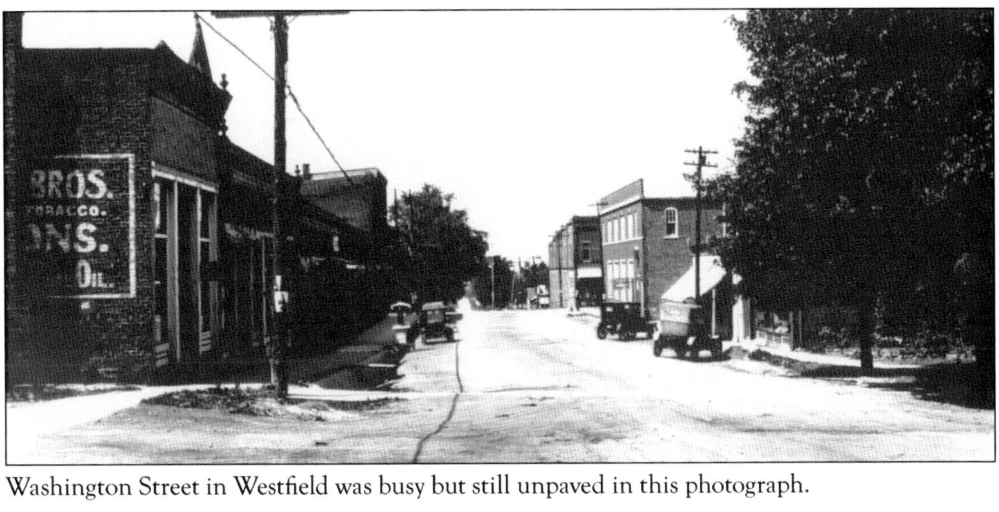

Washington Street in Westfield was busy but still unpaved in this photograph.

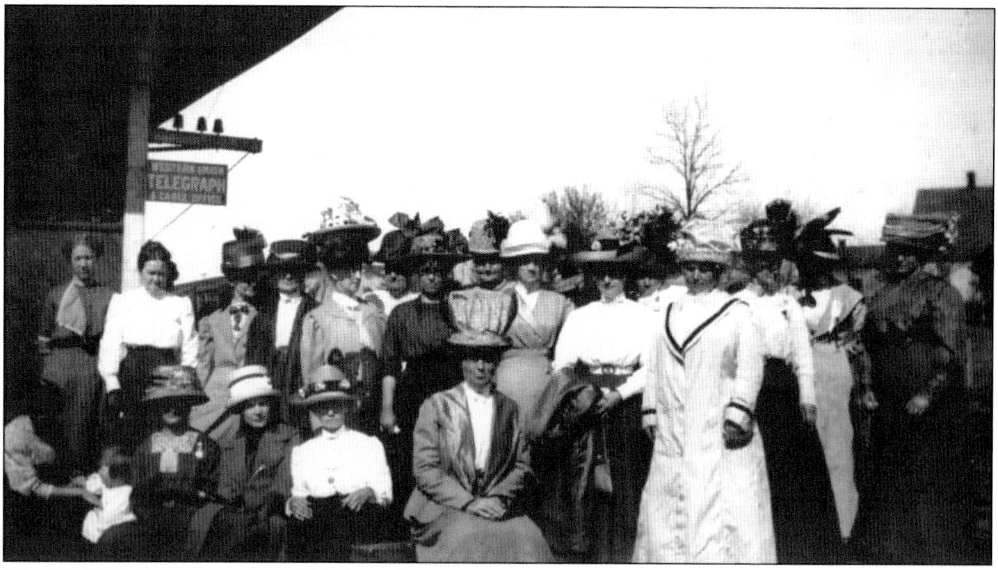

The CH&D depot in Westfield drew large crowds during the oil boom days. This photograph was taken in 1912.

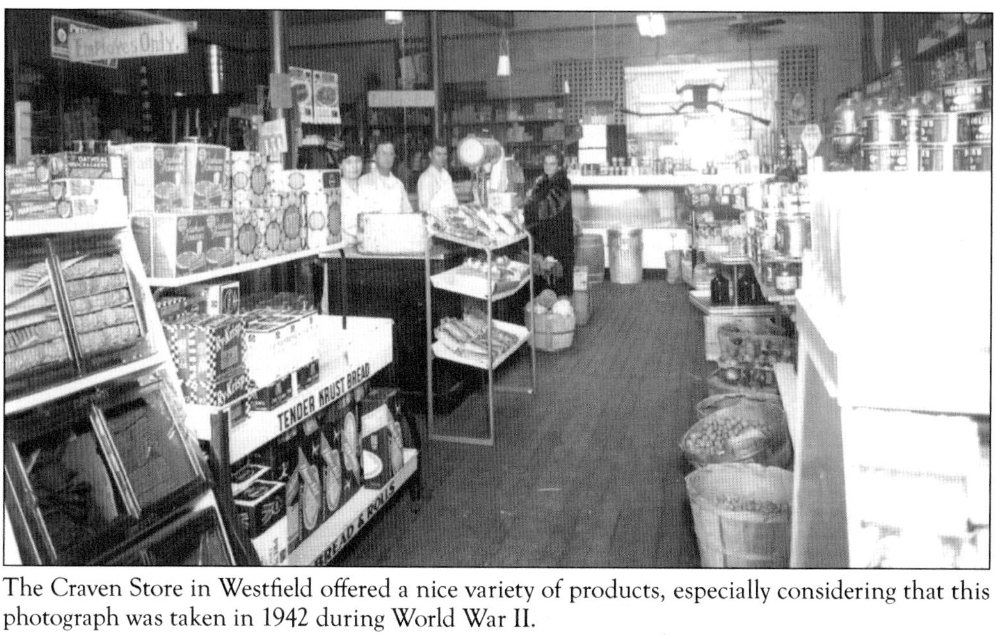

The Craven Store in Westfield offered a nice variety of products, especially considering that this photograph was taken in 1942 during World War II.

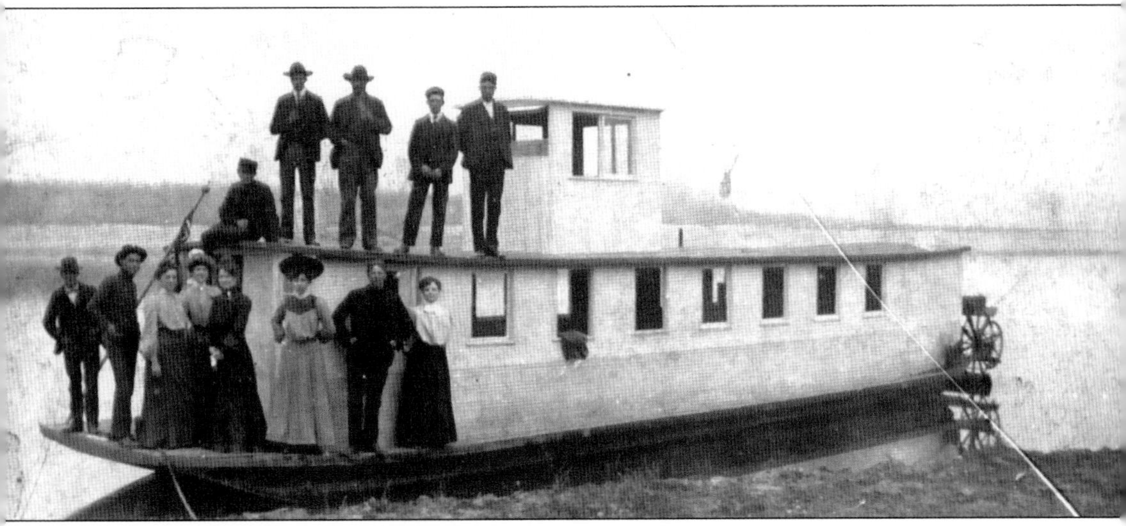

This paddle wheel steamboat at York (Reno Shawler is on the lower right) was smaller and less luxurious than others that made their way up the Wabash between Vincennes and Terre Haute, beginning in 1823. York was an entry point to Clark County and a booming community in the early 1800s when river travel was king. Some steamboats, such as the *Starlight*, were primarily passenger ships. Others, such as the *Zanesville*, would dock for loads of pork, wheat, or corn. During the boom years, York had two large warehouses, general stores, blacksmiths, packing houses, livery stables, a drug store, saloons, and an undertaker. York gets its name from the New Yorkers who settled the area, and even has a street named Broadway. The opening of the Big Four railroad through West Union in 1879 initiated York's decline as train traffic replaced river traffic.

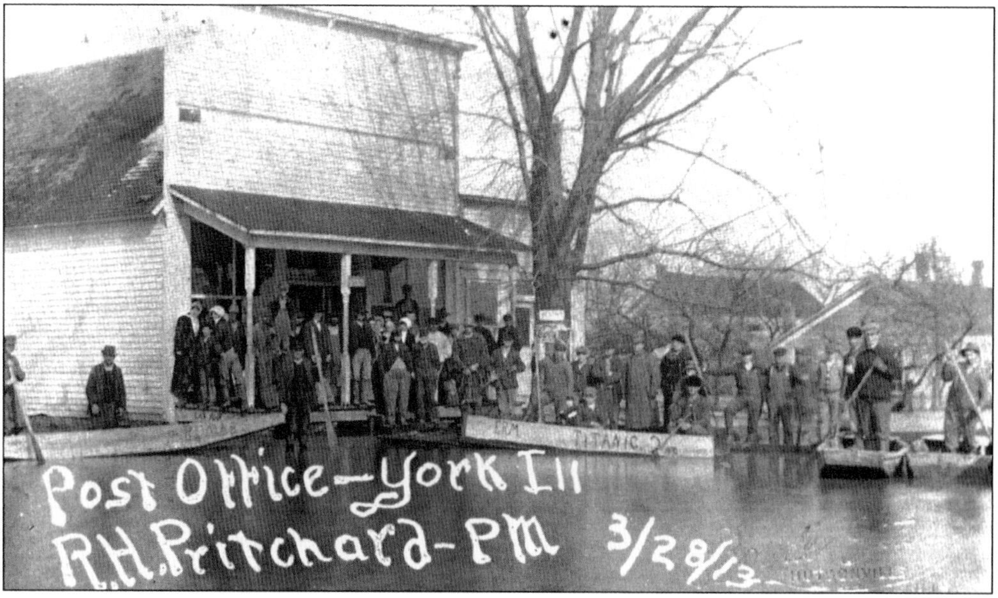

In York, the river has always given and taken away. Much of the city has been subject to periodical flooding over the years. Note the *Titanic* reference.

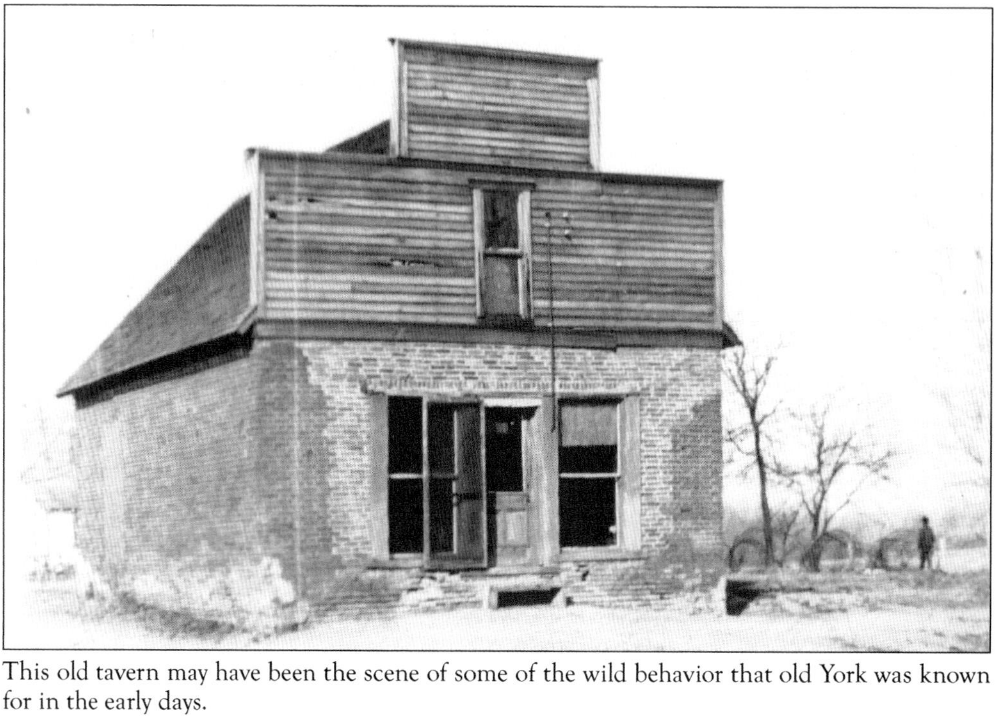

This old tavern may have been the scene of some of the wild behavior that old York was known for in the early days.

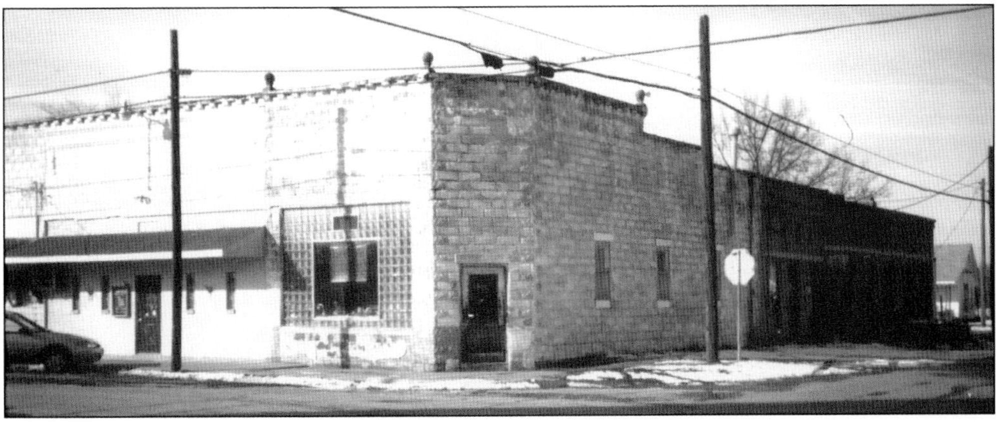

This corner building in West Union was once the Farmers and Merchants Bank, organized in the early 1900s. It became the West Union State Bank, which prospered before becoming a victim of the Great Depression. To the left is the popular Earl's Restaurant, featuring catfish, which attracts visitors from a wide area.

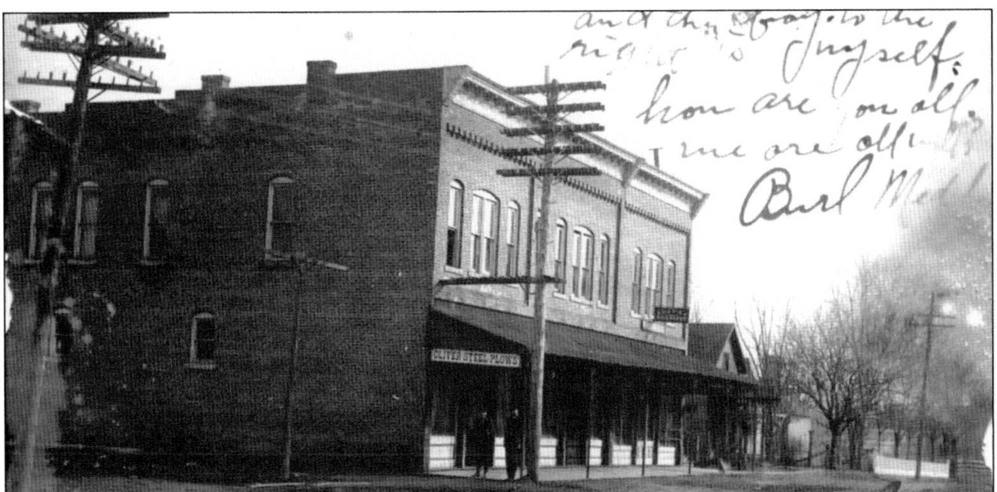

The Charles Prevo Clothing Store building in West Union was built about 1900. The town pump was just west of the building. Dean Clatfelter later had an appliance sales and service business in the building, as has Bill Crumrin.

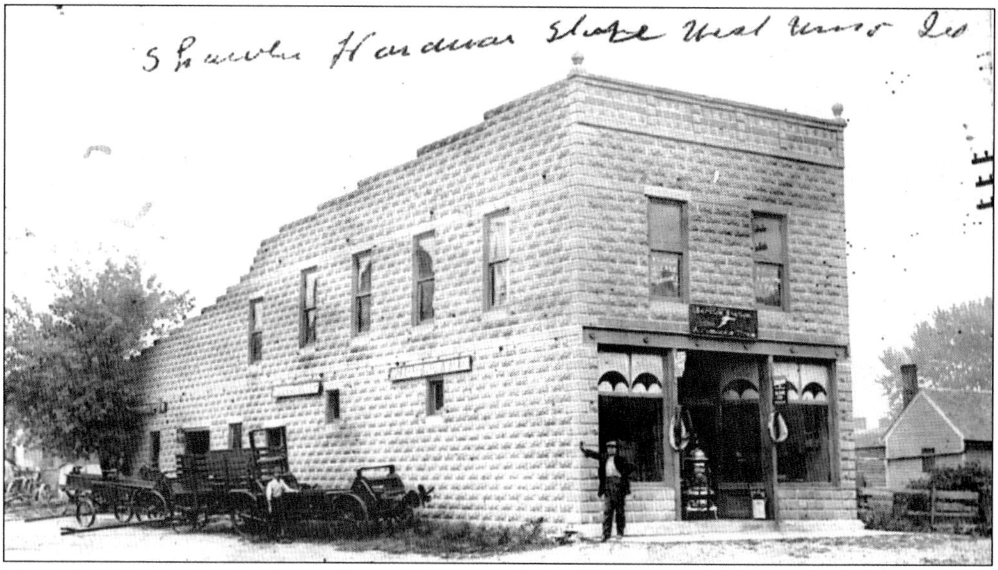

West Union's Shawler Hardware Store, above, was built in 1906. It was owned by LaReno Shawler and Roscoe Richards, with Shawler eventually buying out Richards. The hardware store closed during the Great Depression and was later used by "Doc" Tingley and then Ray Tryon as a blacksmith shop. A house owned by Bill Crumrin was later built on the site.

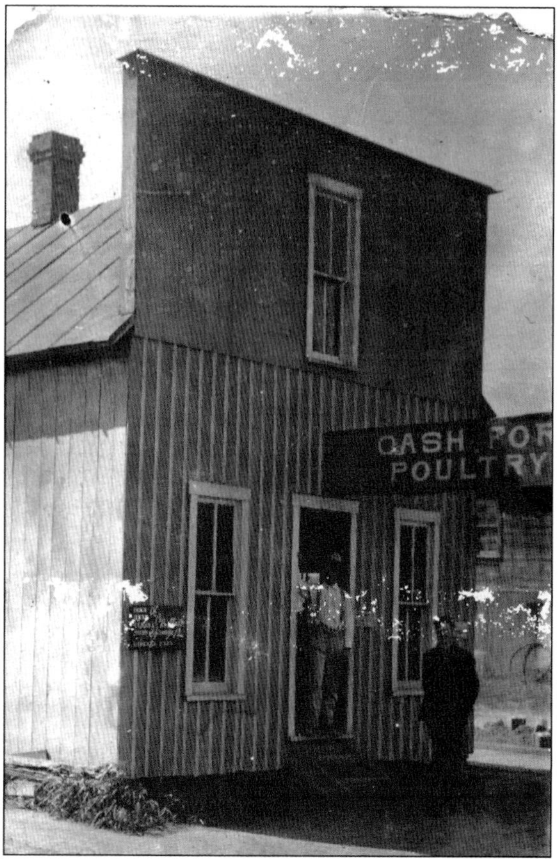

Here's an early poultry and egg business in West Union. In the 1920s and 1930s, West Union businesses included a hotel (Fred Bush), a drug store (Frakes, Tolbert, Keifer), two doctors (Silas Weir and Charles Highsmith), a poultry house (Burl Medsker), a milliner's shop (F. Snyder Reisner), a butcher shop (Oscar Spangler), five groceries, a barber shop, a lumber yard (Simpson), a hatchery, a furniture store, a mill, a bank, and a funeral home (Prust).

Five

Oil in Clark County

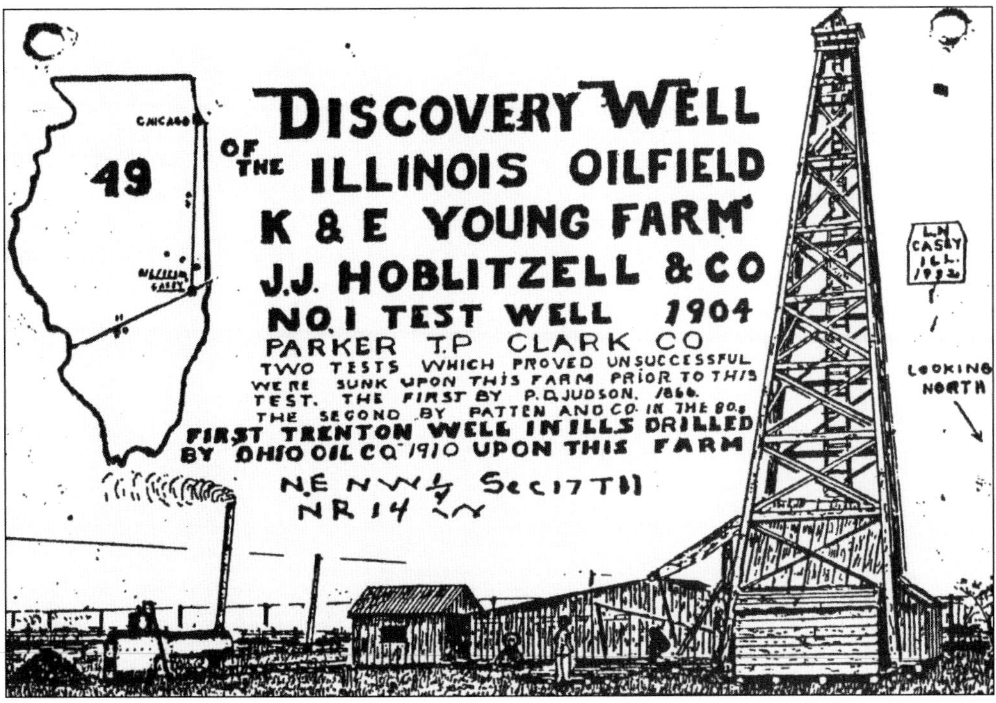

Oil has made a big impact on Clark County during the past 100 years, principally in the western townships. The earliest oil strike occurred in the 1860s south of Westfield, resulting in the building of a hotel, but the primitive method used in drilling proved inadequate, and the excitement quickly died. The real "boom," as outlined in the above sketch by Lee Newlin, occurred in 1904 when the first successful well was produced, making 45 barrels a day.

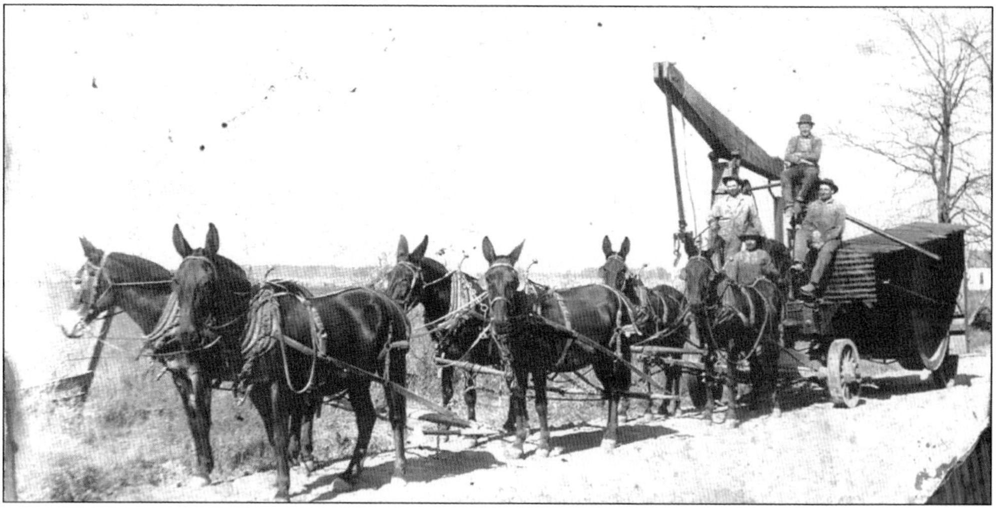

Although steam tractors were usually available, it was mules and horses that did the bulk of the work in moving and setting up oil field equipment, often on ground much too muddy and soft for the heavy steam-powered equipment. By 1905, 150,000 barrels were being shipped out of Casey in railroad tank cars.

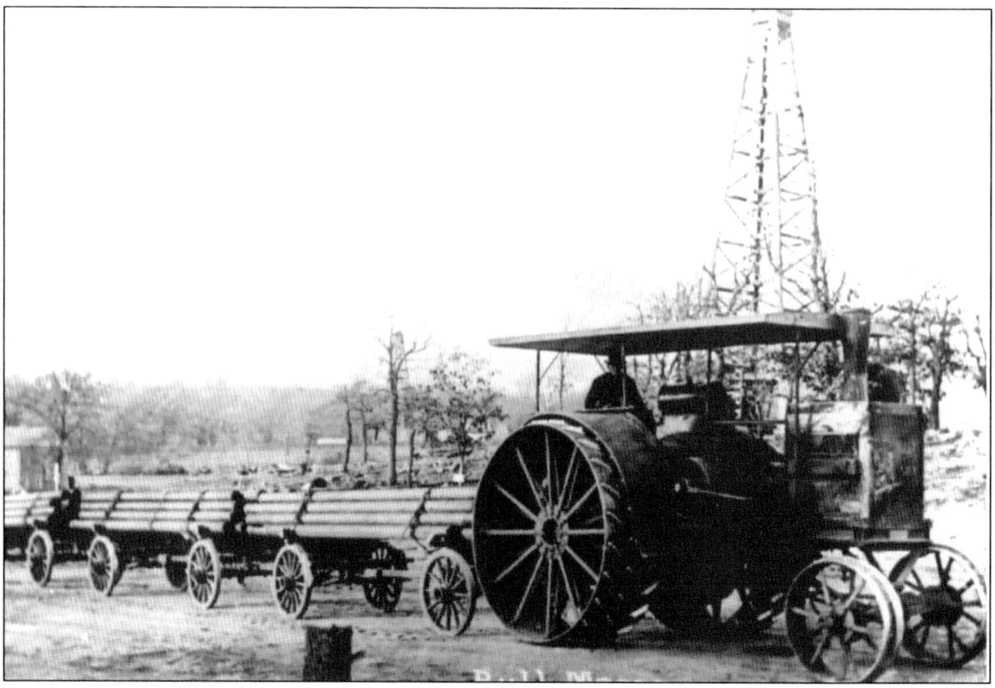

The same steam-powered tractors that were used by farmers were used in the oil fields of Clark County when their expense could be justified and where the terrain was suitable for the heavy weight. By 1907, 2,000 wells had been drilled between Casey and Westfield, and the little village of Oilfield quickly sprang up. Farm operations nearly stopped as workers flocked to the oil fields.

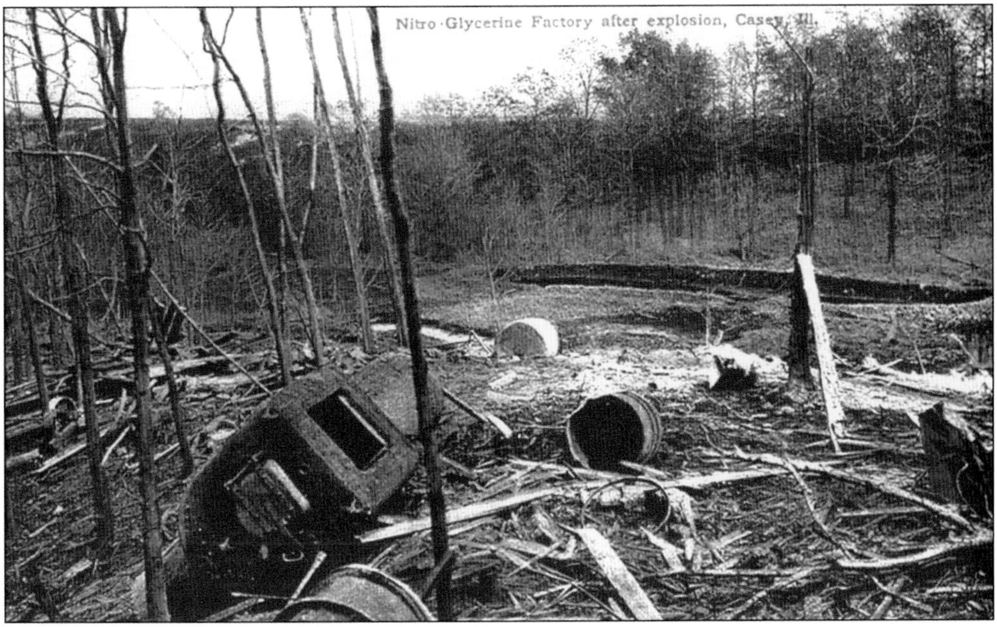

Another local industry created by the discovery of oil was the manufacture of nitroglycerin, an explosive detonated in the drilled hole to loosen the oil sands to create a greater flow of oil and gas. This process is called "shooting" a well. Nitroglycerin was very difficult to deal with, however, and the above photograph shows what happened to one nitroglycerin plant in Casey. No one was injured.

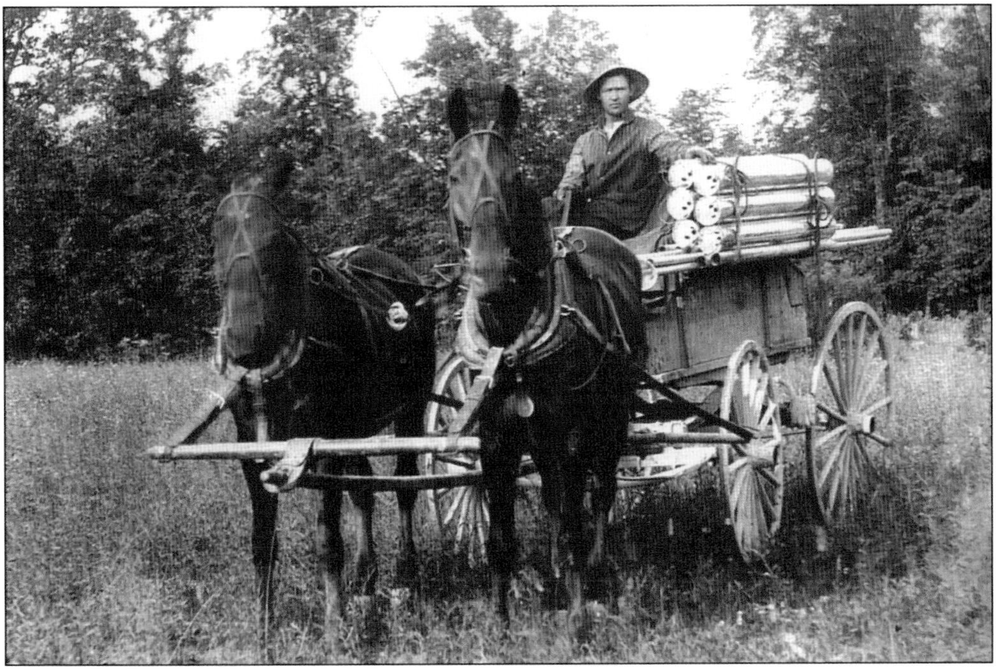

Hauling the nitroglycerin to the well sites was quite dangerous, as it was sensitive to jolts over the rough terrain. Charley Baker is the driver for this load in 1909.

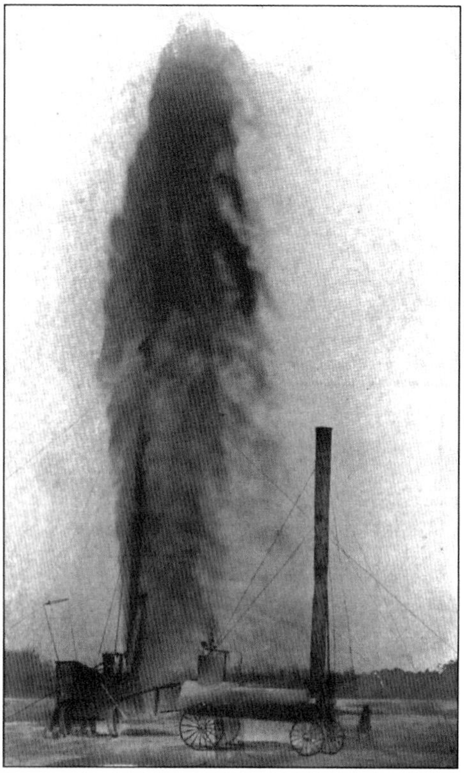

Few things were more spectacular than the shooting of a well with nitroglycerine. As word got out that a well was to be shot, visitors came from miles around, often by train, to view it at a safe distance. The oil was often propelled high over the oil rig by the force of the explosion, the released pressure of gas behind the oil, or both.

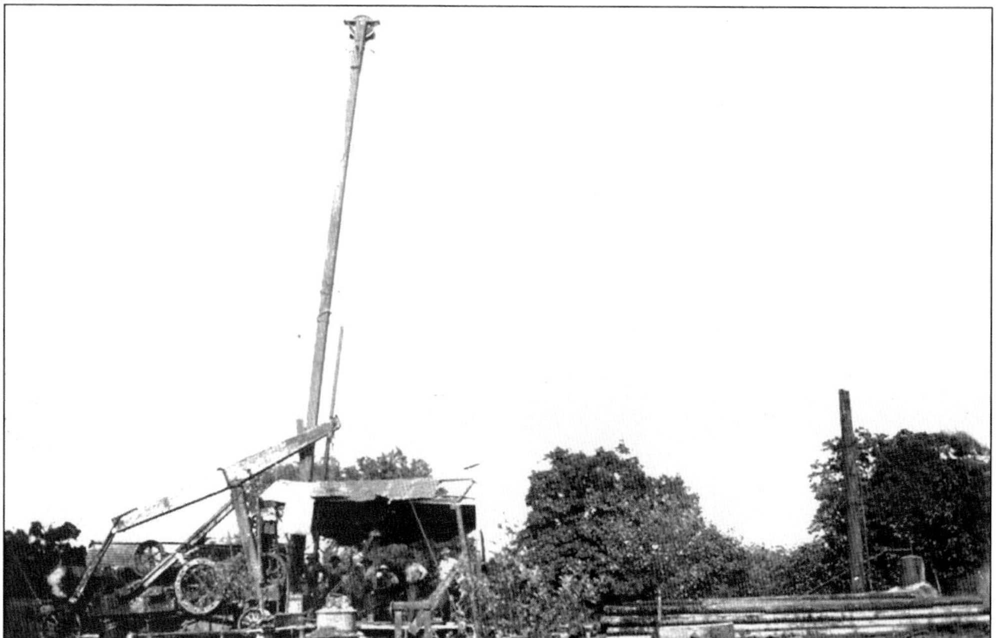

Early oil drilling rigs were quite simple, some with one mast, some with two. The railroads could not handle all the oil, so the Ohio Oil Company laid a pipeline in both directions out of a new pumping station at the Martinsville tank farm. There was so much natural gas that the burning flares could be seen for miles. Casey High School named its yearbook *The Flame*.

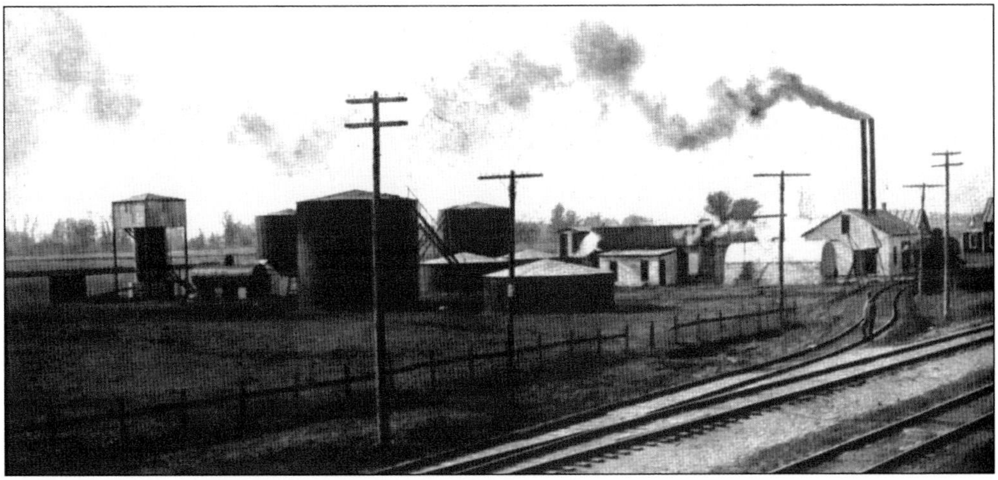

Refineries soon developed in Clark County to meet the demand for turning crude oil into a more saleable product. There were two refineries in Casey, the Leader Refinery above and the Cornplanter Refinery below. The Leader Refinery, built in 1907, covered a 10-acre site a mile west of Casey. It had an initial capacity of 8,000 barrels of crude per month. Gasoline was produced by distilling it from the crude, then condensing it into liquid form before treating it with acids to partially deodorize it and remove foreign matter.The Oil Well Supply Yards and Cornplanter Refinery were located east of Casey on the W. M. Hughes property. Of the three area refineries, only the one in Robinson remains.

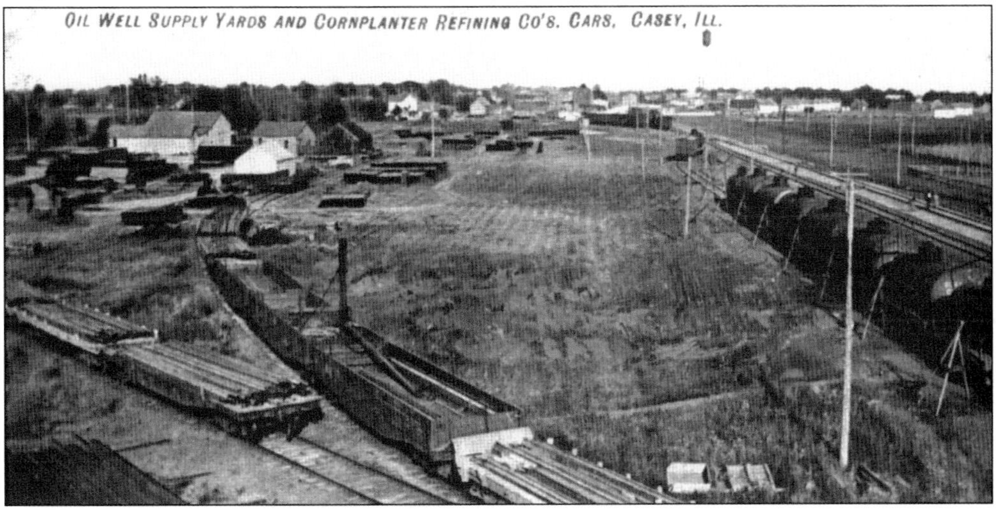

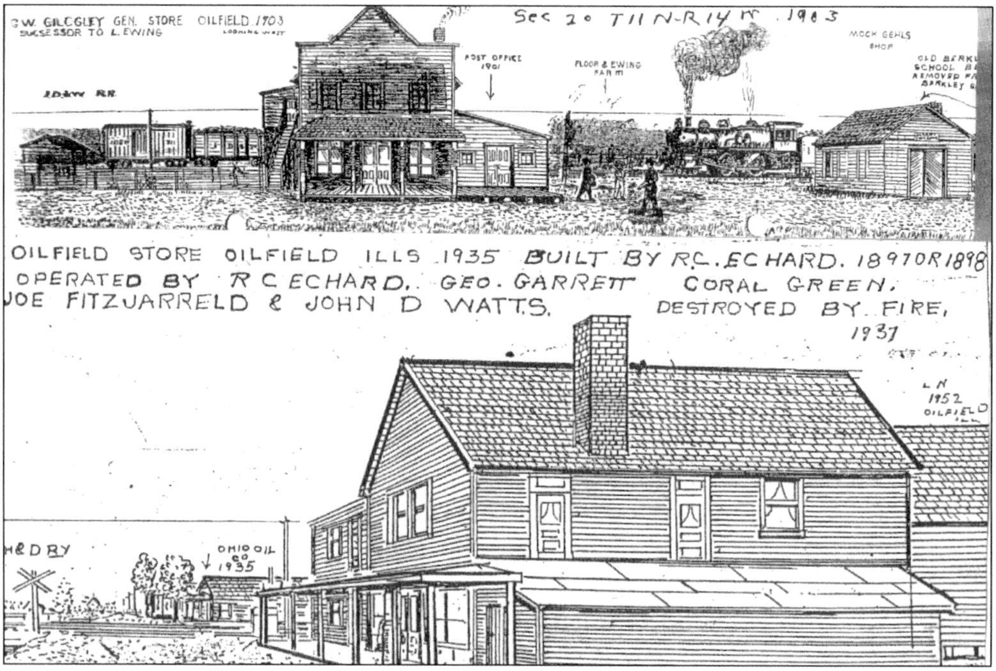

The Oilfield general stores were located along the CH&D tracks that ran west of the current Highway 49, south of Westfield. The Oilfield community grew quickly after 1909 and soon had a remodeled hotel (left from the initial oil discovery just after the Civil War), a grain elevator, schools, service businesses, new homes, and boardinghouses. (Sketches by Lee Newlin.)

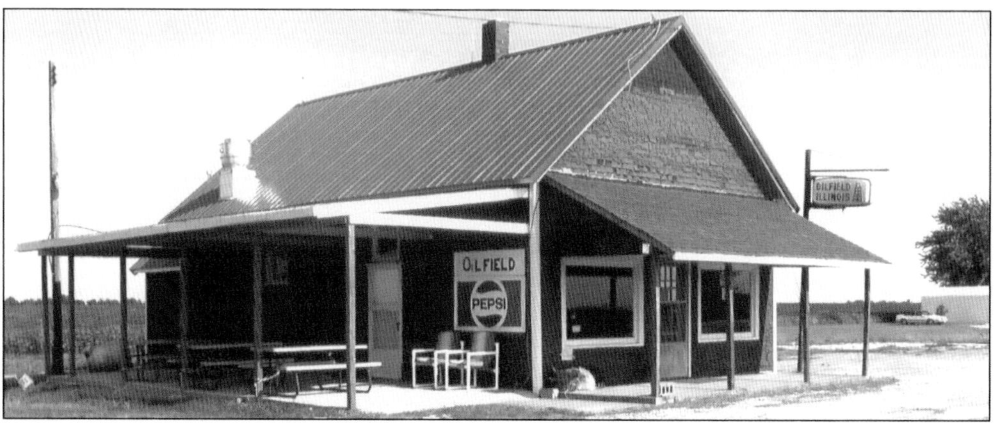

The current Oilfield store may have originally been the Butternut School, built in 1866 and taken apart and moved to the east side of Highway 49 in 1924. Past owners include Hale and Lee Newlin, Arthur Comer and Clarence Warner, Martin "Paddy" Connelly, Bill and Maxine Redman, and Elbert and Mary Ennis. It closed in the 1990s, but reopened as a sandwich shop in 2007 (closed in winter).

When lightning strikes, watch out.

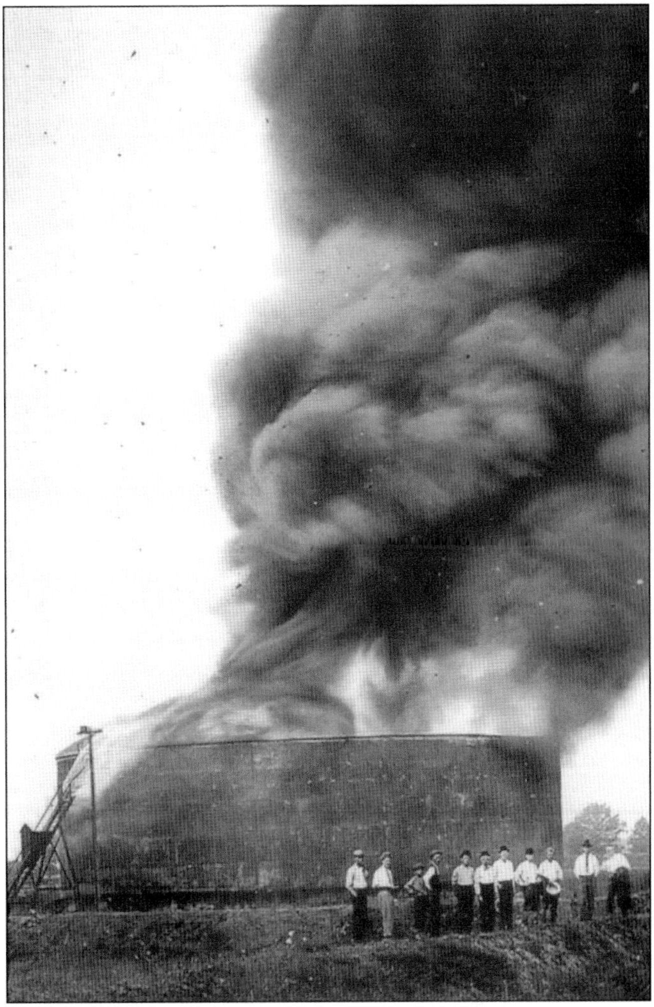

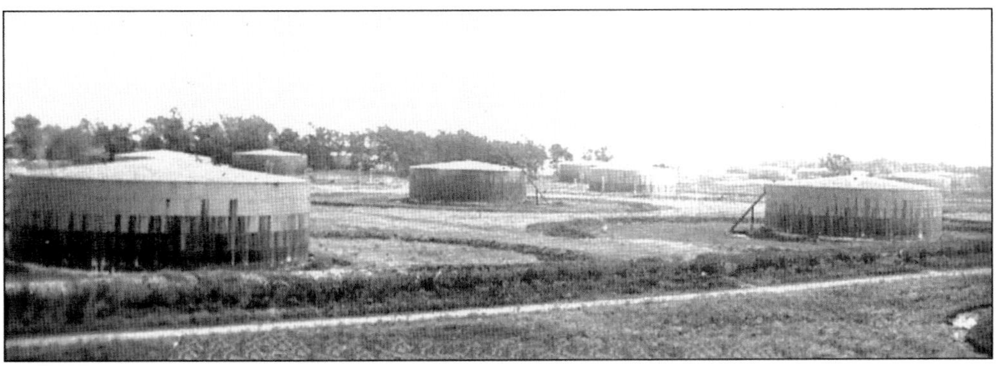

The Ohio Oil Company "tank farm" just west of Martinsville featured 237 tanks, each holding 30,000 barrels of oil.

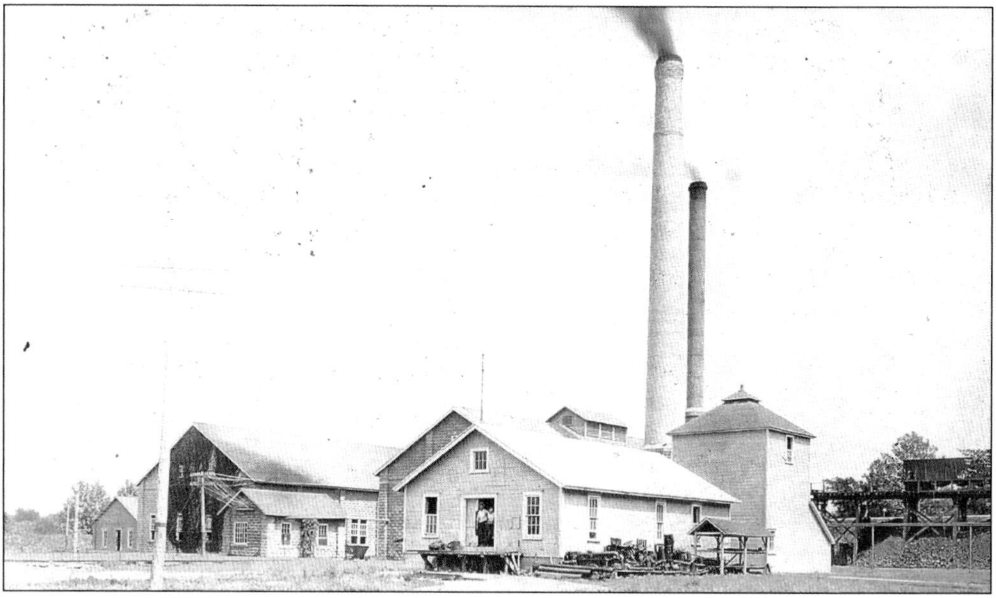

The Ohio Oil Company pumping station at the "tank farm" west of Martinsville pumped through an eight-inch line in 1906, but by 1908, two additional lines were necessary.

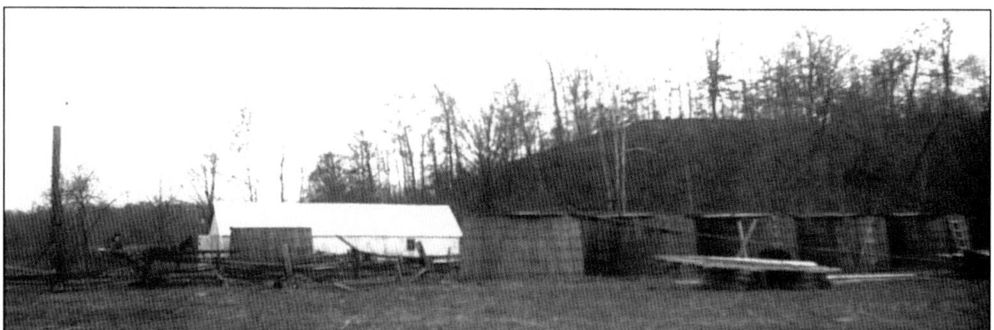

The earlier storage tanks near oil well sites were made of wood, whereas modern tanks are made of steel. When these on-site tanks are full, the oil is transported to refineries for processing, or to larger centralized tanks, such as those west of Martinsville, for storage.

Six

The Handy Writers Colony

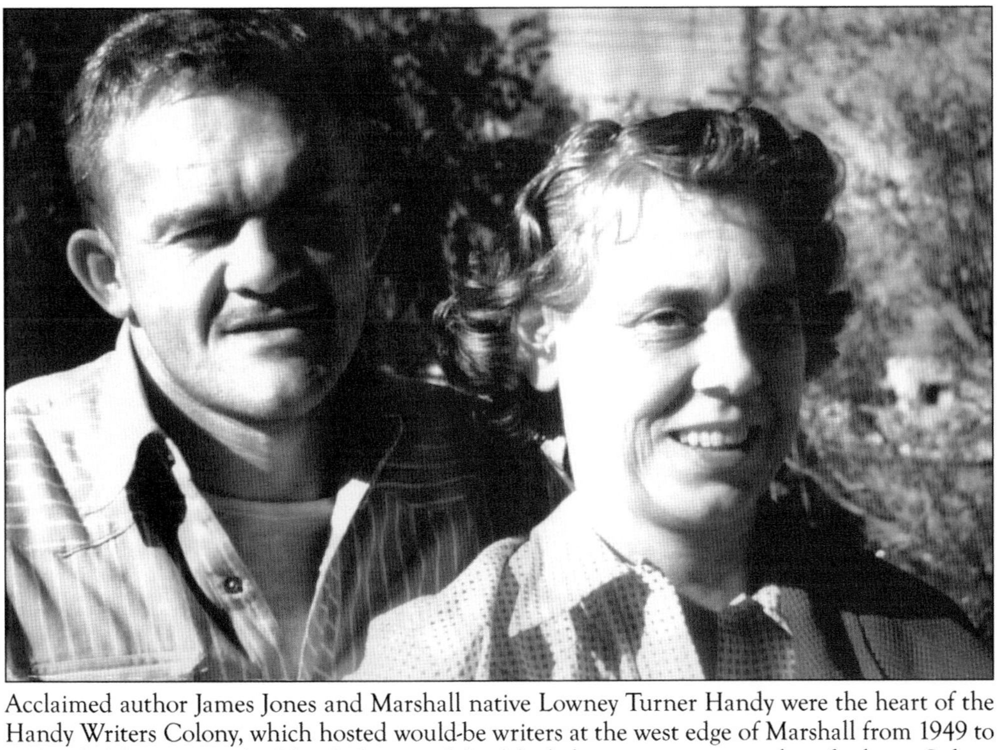

Acclaimed author James Jones and Marshall native Lowney Turner Handy were the heart of the Handy Writers Colony, which hosted would-be writers at the west edge of Marshall from 1949 to 1964. Fledgling writers had free lodging and food for helping to maintain colony facilities. Colony writers published at least 24 books, and five of these were made into Hollywood films. Ironically, respected mentor and taskmaster Handy was not a published author.

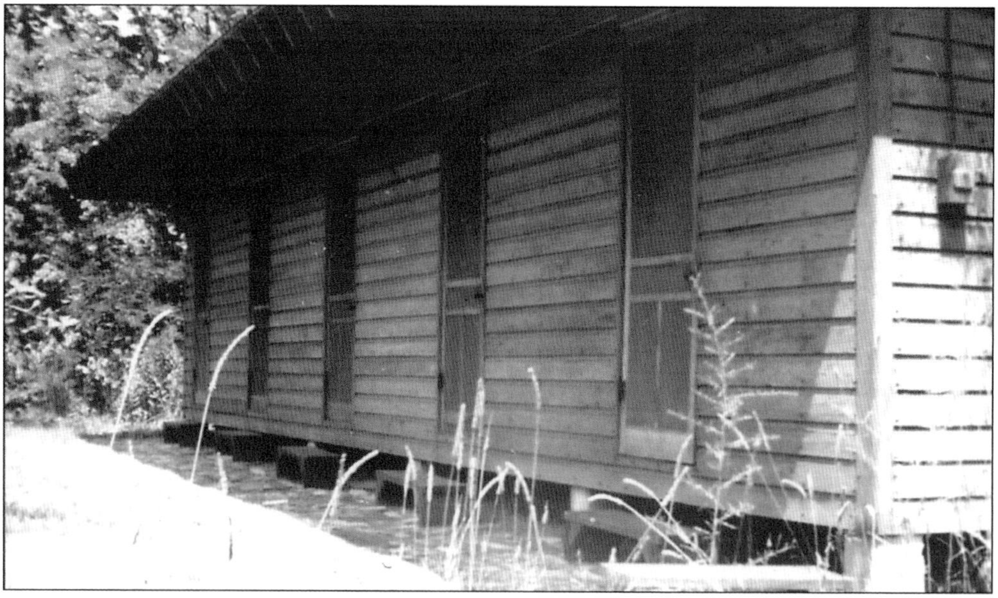

Writers lived and wrote in a single room in the "barracks." They were expected to work alone, copy the works of other writers during the first part of their stay, and discuss what they were writing with nobody except Lowney Turner Handy. They ate simple meals together and in the afternoons helped maintain the colony.

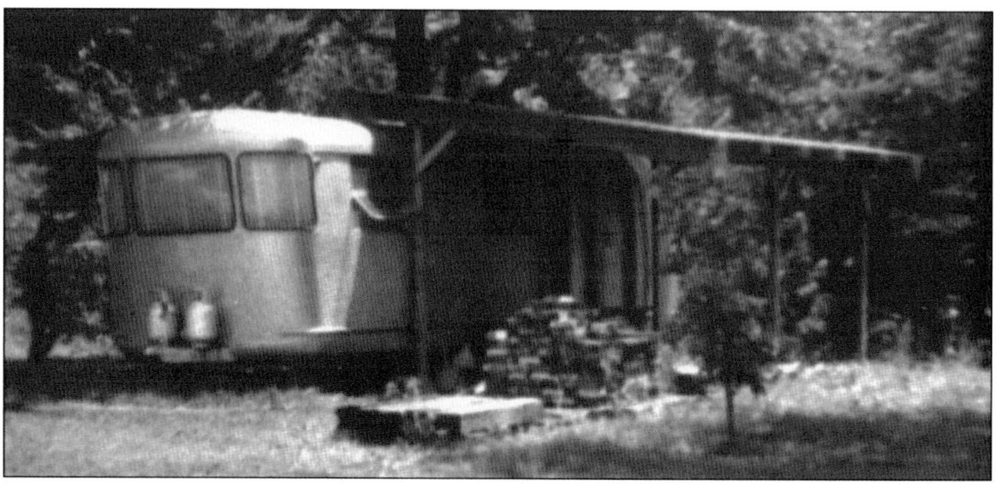

Although the first colony writers lived in tents, James Jones never had to rough it. This is his mobile home on the grounds. After receiving royalties from his blockbuster *From Here to Eternity* in 1951, he had his own house built at the edge of the colony. He also contributed 10 percent of his royalties to the colony. Jones's second novel, *Some Came Running*, was set in the local area.

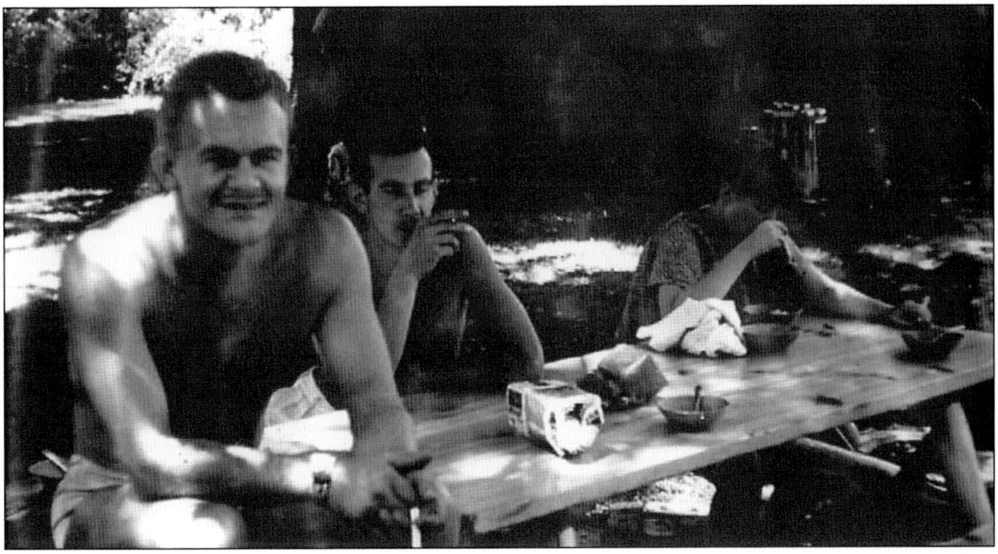

James Jones relaxes with an unidentified colony member and Jones's sister Mary Ann, who died of natural causes at the colony in 1952, the same year James won the National Book Award for *From Here to Eternity*. Lowney Turner Handy had very few women writers at the colony, saying she could not work with them.

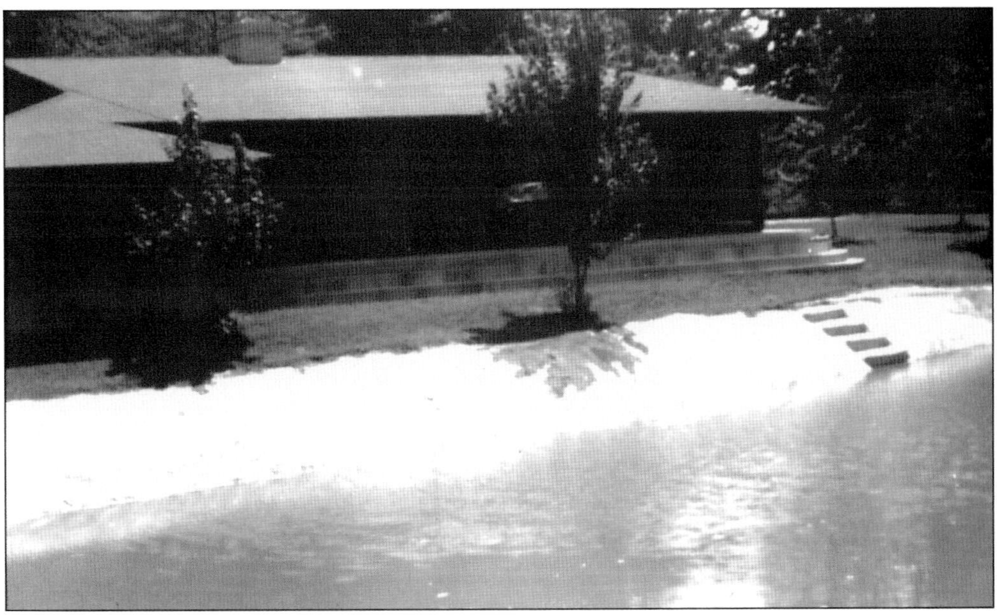

Following the success of *From Here to Eternity*, additional facilities were constructed, including the "Ramada." It had cooking facilities, a dining area, and a large recreation area. Handy Writers Colony members also built a small lake, which has been drained.

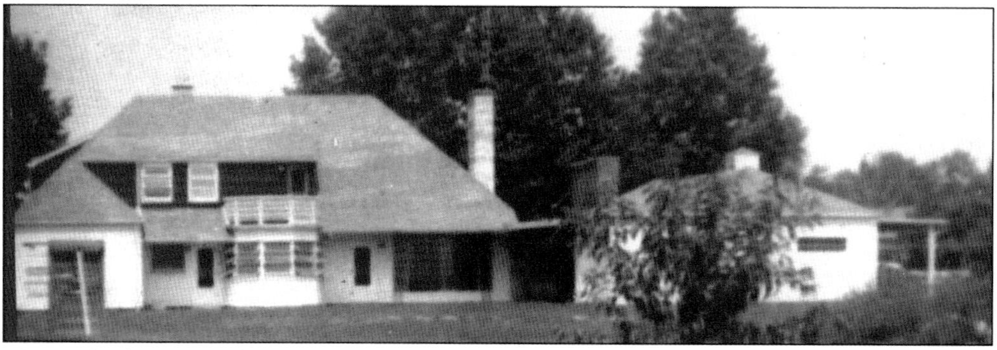

This is the back, or colony, side of James Jones's house, built with some of the proceeds from his blockbuster book *From Here to Eternity* in 1951. Jones left the colony in 1957 after a dispute with Lowney Handy over his marriage to New York model Gloria Mosolino. The house is still a private residence.

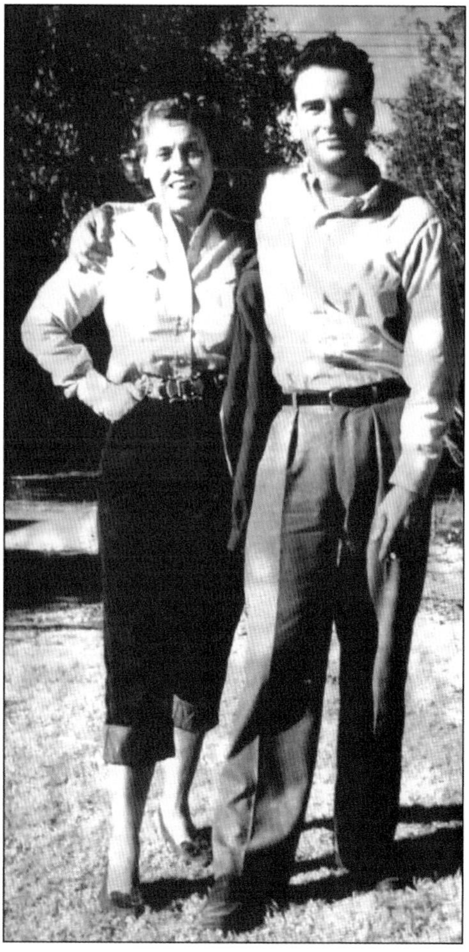

Among the visitors to the colony was Montgomery Clift, who played Prewitt in the motion picture version of *From Here to Eternity*. Another well-known visitor was novelist Norman Mailer. Journalists from such national magazines as *Life* also stopped by from time to time to interview Lowney. After Jones left in 1957, the colony lost its luster. Lowney died alone there in 1963, just a year after husband Harry died.

Seven

RECREATION

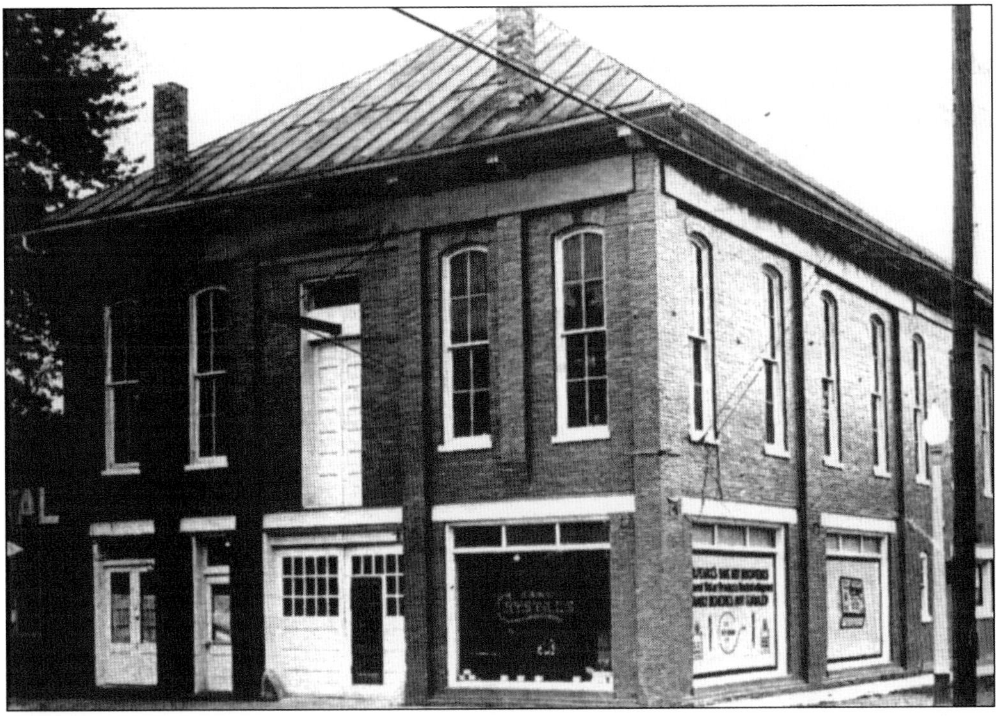

Marshall's Harlan Hall opera house was built by Howard Harlan in 1872 on the site of his livery stable at a cost of $8,000. In building the opera house, he kept the downstairs as a stable. The second floor had space for 700 guests. Harlan had apparently sold the building by 1887. In 1904, the building was purchased by B. F. Johnson, and the entertainment area became known as Johnson Hall.

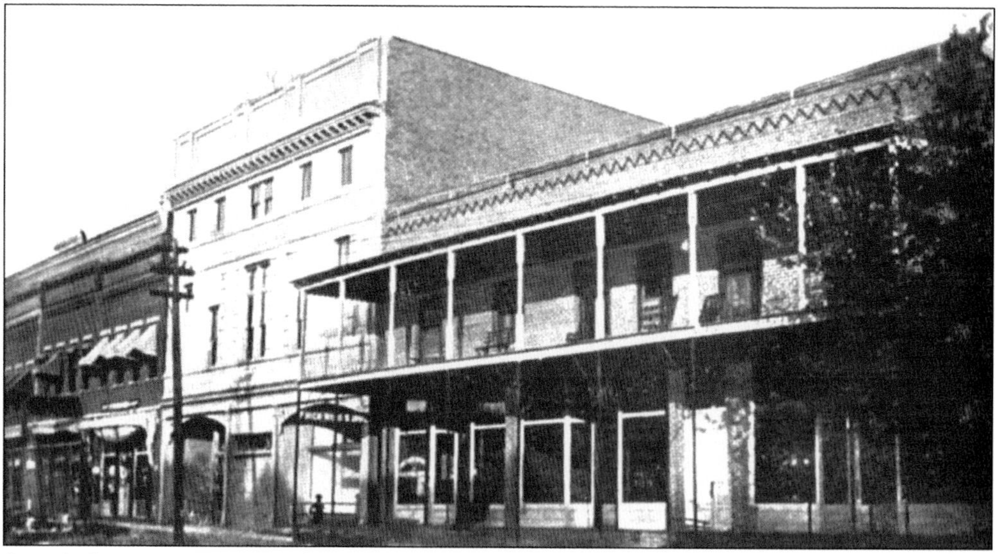

Casey's three-story Hammond Opera House, built in 1906, sat just to the left of the Casey Hotel (later known as the DeLite Hotel) on Cumberland Street. Some of the best performers out of Chicago played at this elegant venue. It was destroyed by fire in 1908. J. V. and W. O. Price built a two-story brick building on this site in 1910. The building was later used as the Lyric Theater, which burned in 1961. Casey City Hall now occupies the site.

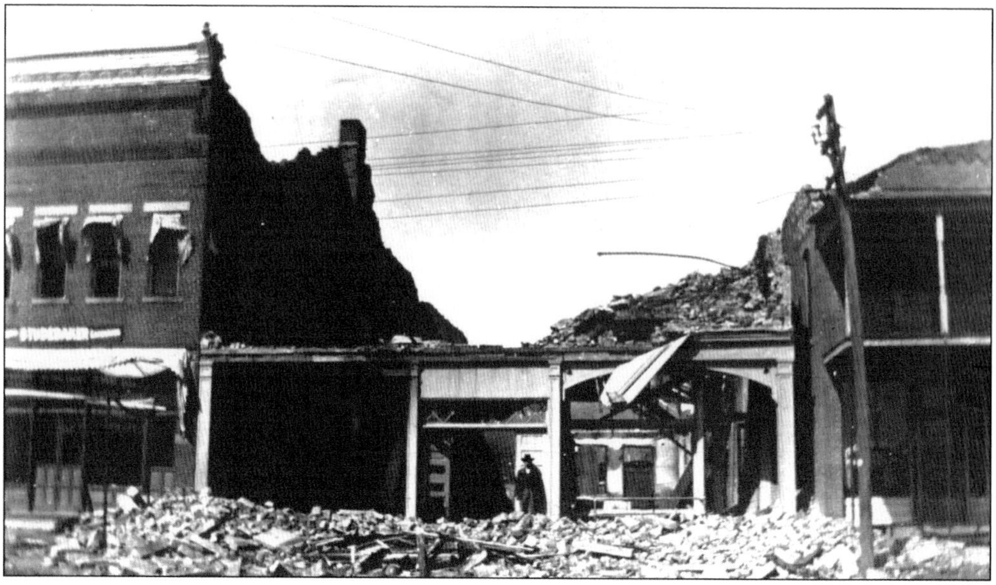

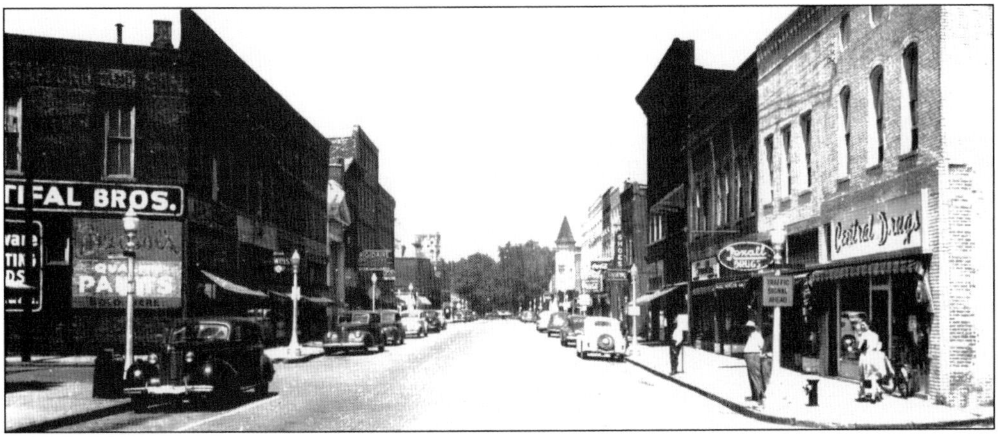

The Casey Opera House was located upstairs in the Sanford and Sons (Stifal Brothers Hardware) building on the east side of Central Street. Performances were conducted as early as 1907. In addition, the opera house also featured wrestling, dancing, and roller-skating. The opera house area has been preserved, and there are still many signs of past activities. Downstairs on the right was the Orpheum Vaudeville Theater, which offered live performances and early movie films. The post office was next door.

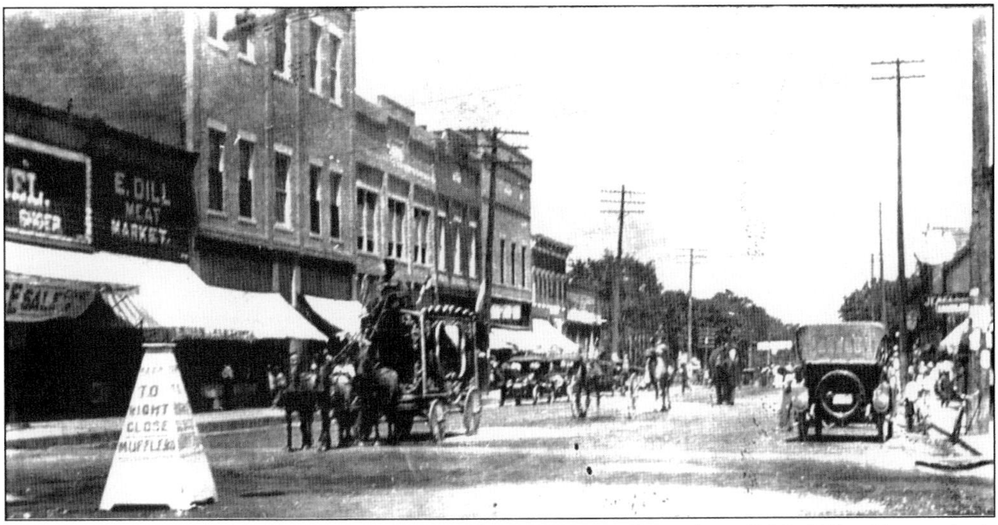

The background structure to this circus parade in Martinsville is the tall IOOF building, which housed the opera house upstairs. To the right, behind the circus wagon, the Mars Theater was built in 1939, closing in 1956.

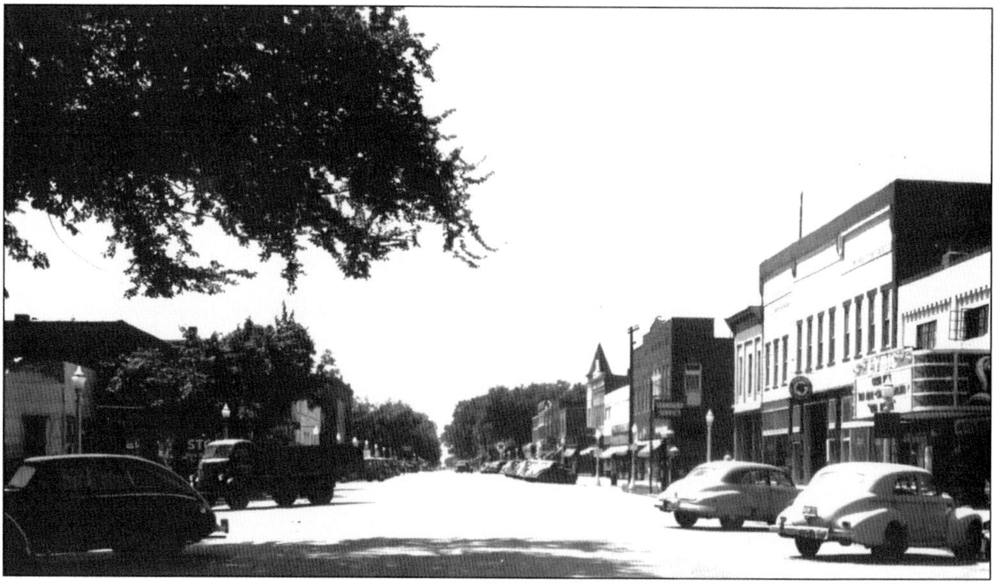

The original Lyric Theater in Casey opened in 1914 with silent films at 8 West Main Street then moved to East Main Street. Talking films made their debut in the 1920s, and the Lyric Theater was expanded in 1935. Air conditioning was added in 1939, among the first in this area. More remodeling was done to the 500-seat theater in 1951. Fire destroyed the Lyric Theater in 1961, and the site is now the city hall parking lot.

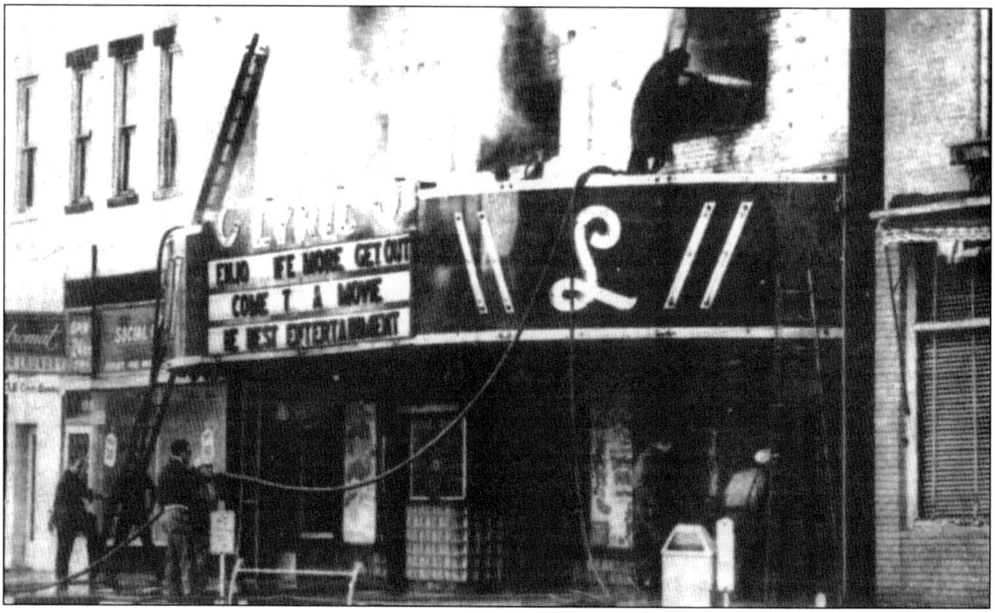

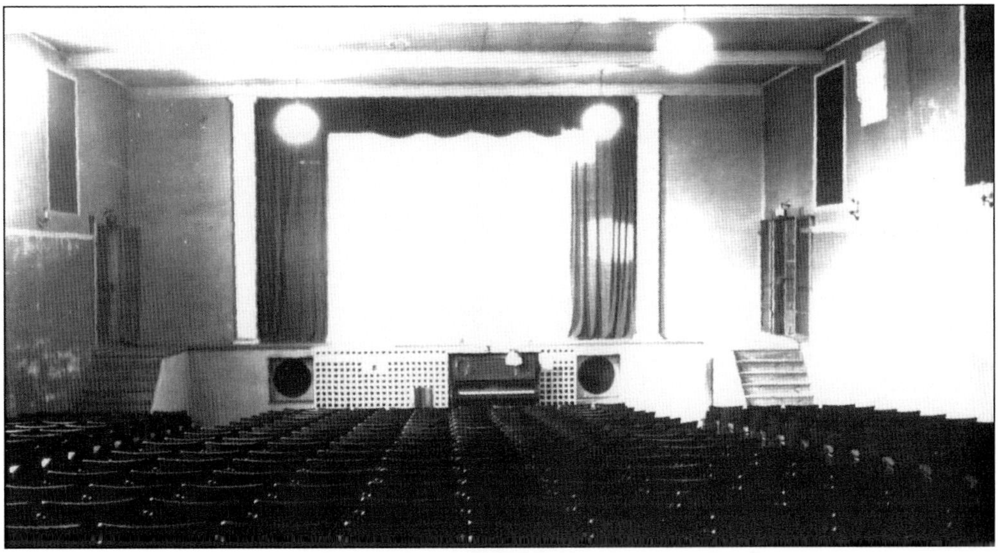

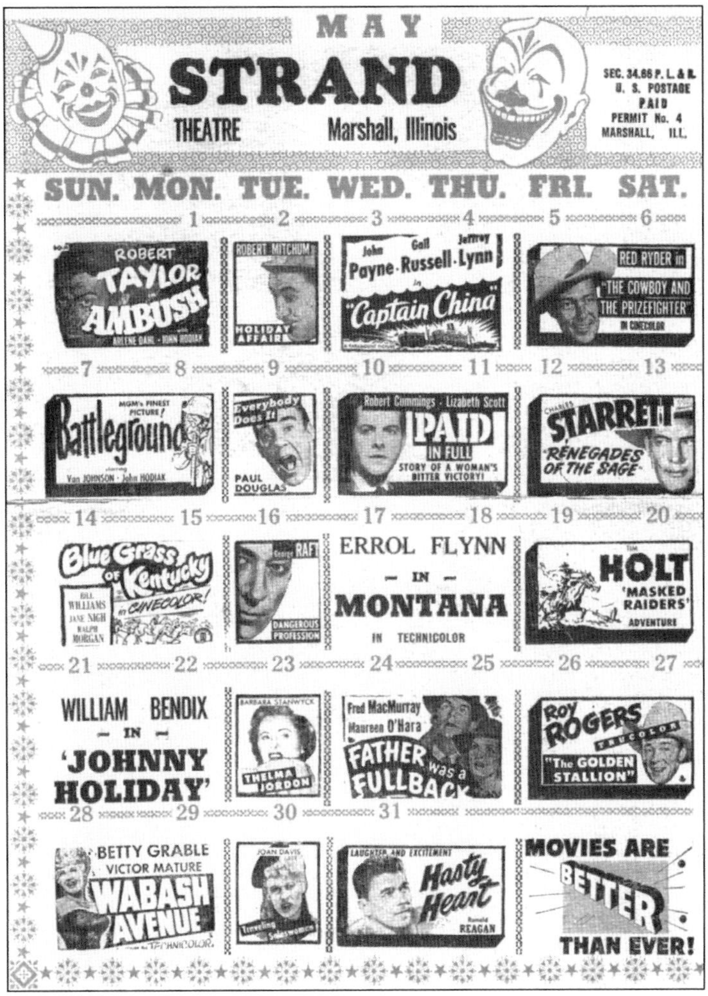

The Pythian Temple, which opened in 1901 on the south side of the square in Marshall, featured a 500-seat "opera house" on the second floor, which became the Strand Theatre in 1943. Live performances, such as the 1909 comic opera *Trial By Jury*, evolved into silent movies, accompanied by the pianos of Helen (Coldren) Moore and Silvia (Millhouse) Ritter, then sound films. This building burned in 1957, destroying the Knights of Pythias facilities and the Strand Theatre, as well as the J. Earl Finney insurance office and Dr. H. E. King's chiropractic office.

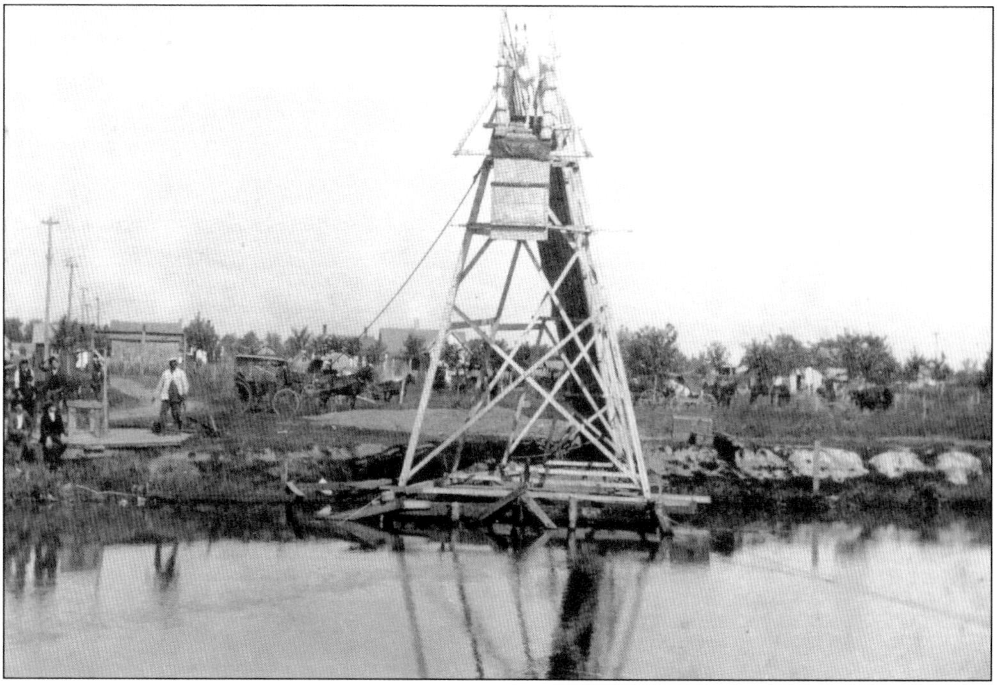

The spectacular opening of Casey's Fairview Park in 1902 featured two white horses leaping from an 80-foot platform into the park's lake. The celebration, staged by the Casey Modern Woodmen, also included a three-day carnival, a woman pulled by her hair over the pond, and trapeze performers. There were 13,000 paid admissions on the first day.

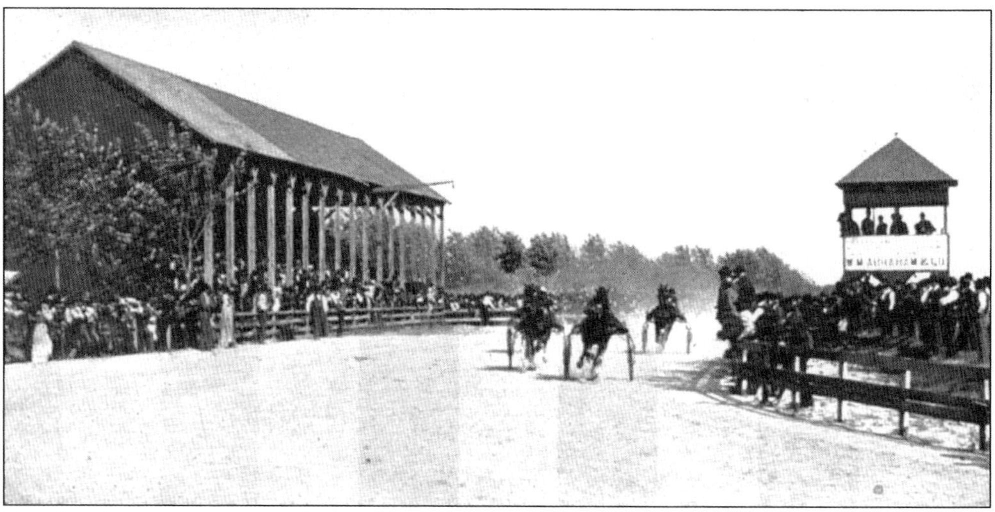

The first horse race at Casey's Fairview Park took place in 1902 and the sport created much excitement over the next 20 years, especially during the oil boom. Nat Lee, probably the biggest horse and mule trader in the area, raced at this track. His groom, Joe Davis, was one of the few Black residents of Casey. Davis' daughter, Elizabeth, was a nurse in Casey from 1908 until 1963.

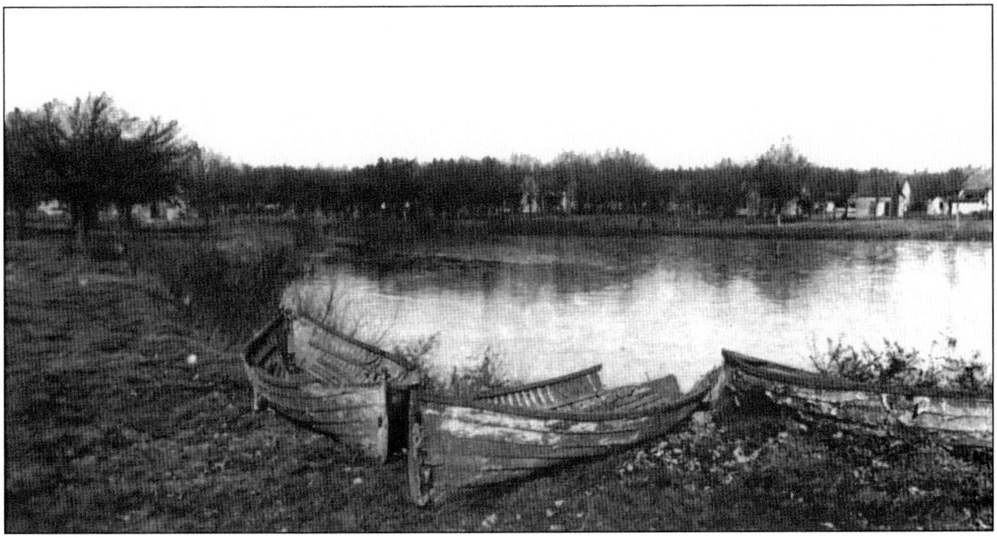

The lake at Casey's Fairview Park has provided recreation since it was dug by mules and dirt scoops around 1895. Additional improvements have been made, including bridge work in 2000 between the two sections of the lake.

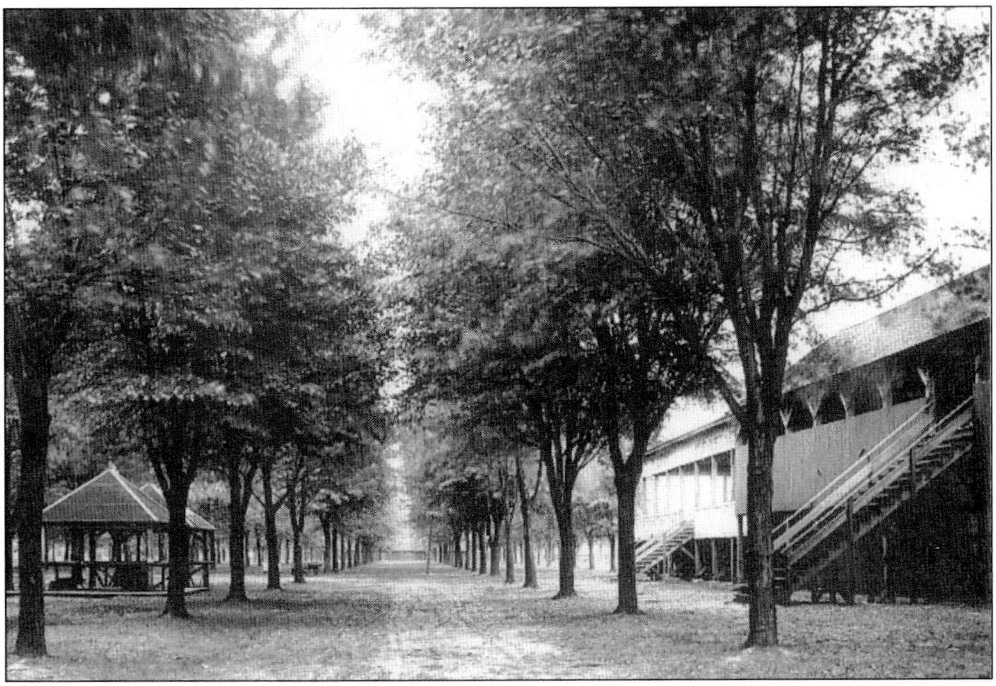

When Fairview Park was laid out in the 1890s on 40 acres of land acquired from Samuel Adkinson, trees were planted in rows and structures carefully planned.

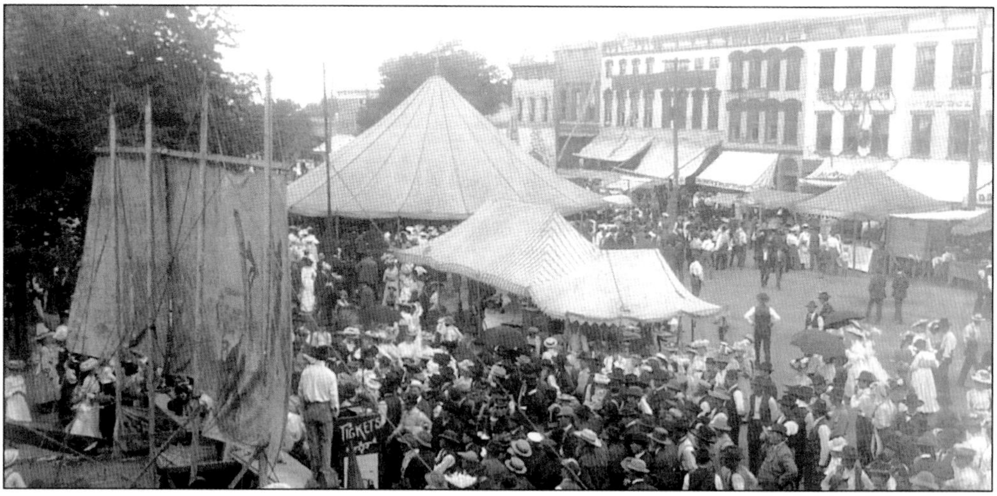

The June 29–July 4, 1903, Royal Carnival Company free show drew thousands to the vacant courthouse square, where the courthouse had burned six months earlier. Dogs and monkeys were among the many attractions.

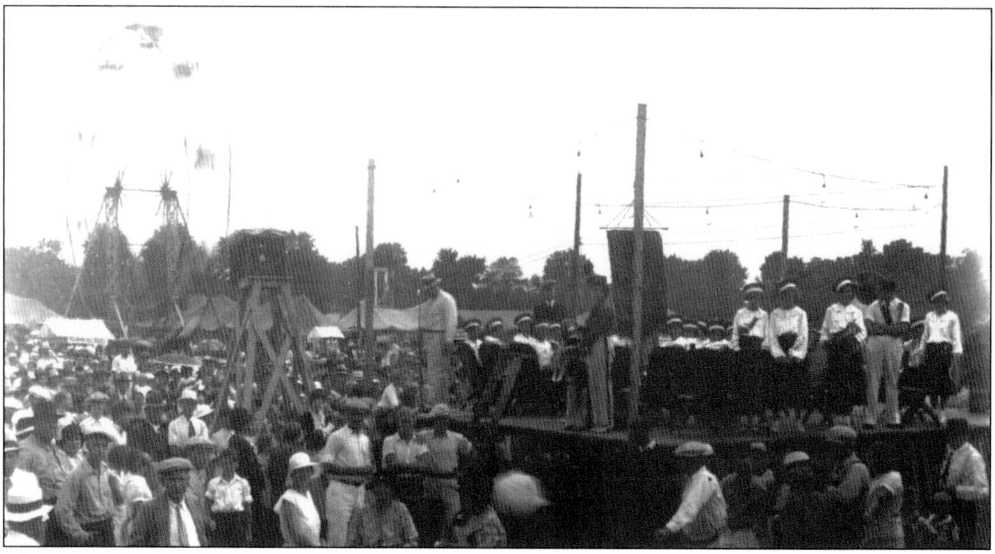

The Ferris wheel was a big attraction at the Clark County Fair in Marshall. The Clark County Fair was originally held in Martinsville, beginning in 1897, but the Martinsville fairgrounds were destroyed by a tornado in 1912 and did not reopen until 1917. It closed again in 1930 during the Great Depression, and there was no fair until 1946 when it was reorganized as the Martinsville Agricultural Fair. The Clark County Fair has been held in Marshall since 1934.

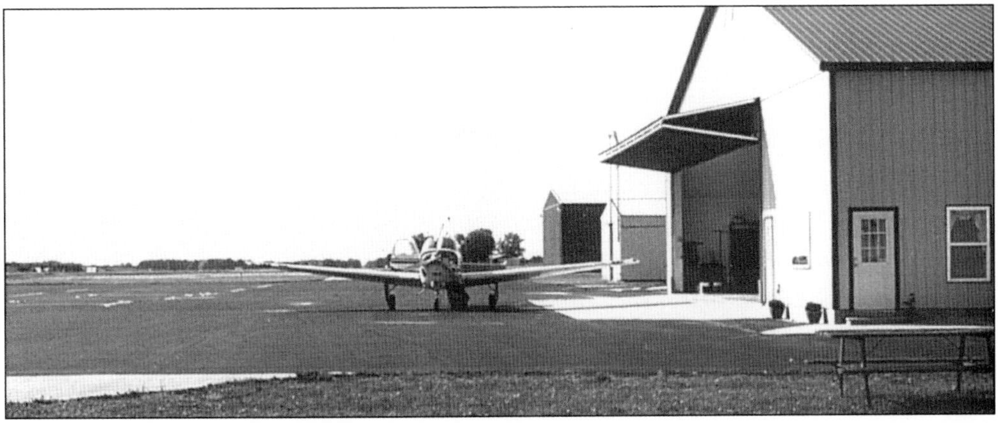

The Casey Airport has served both recreational and business flyers since its organization in 1946. It was essentially the fulfillment of a dream by Kermit Patchett of Martinsville, who set up the airport and ran it successfully for many years, assisted by his wife, Eileen. She tells the full story in her book *Fly-by of Memories*. This airport was not Casey's first, however. That honor goes to the Washington Street Airport, which was sponsored by the Casey Chamber of Commerce and dedicated with much fanfare in 1931. By 1932, however, it had closed.

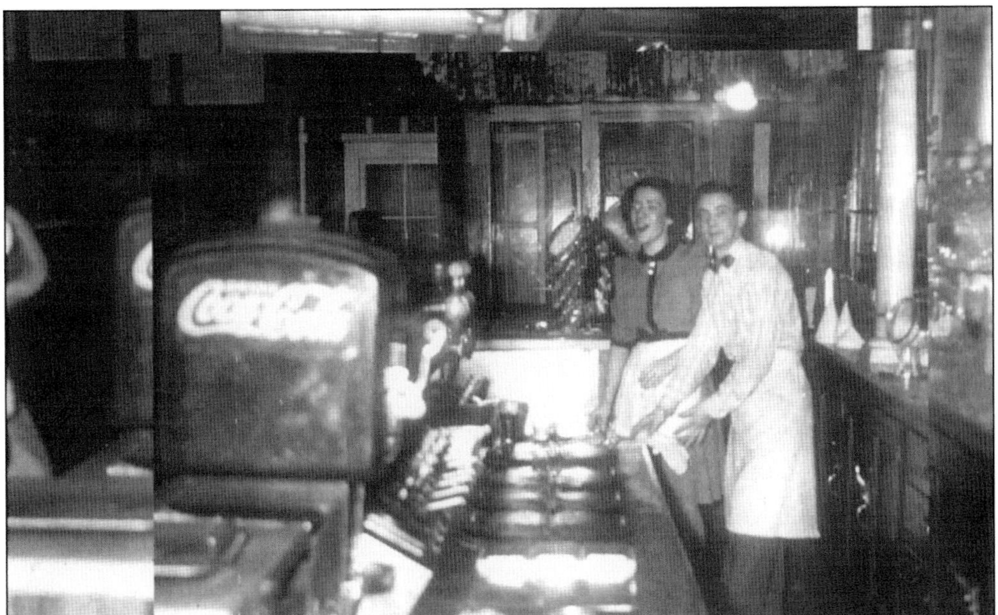

A favorite Marshall hangout was the Candy Kitchen, which was started in 1915 by Tom Koutsoumpas, Nick Borglas, Pete Hilakos, and George Hilakos—"the Greeks." It was bought in 1932 by John Rademaker, then in 1944 by Eamer Haugh and Martha Rademaker Haugh (above), who ran it until its closing in the 1970s.

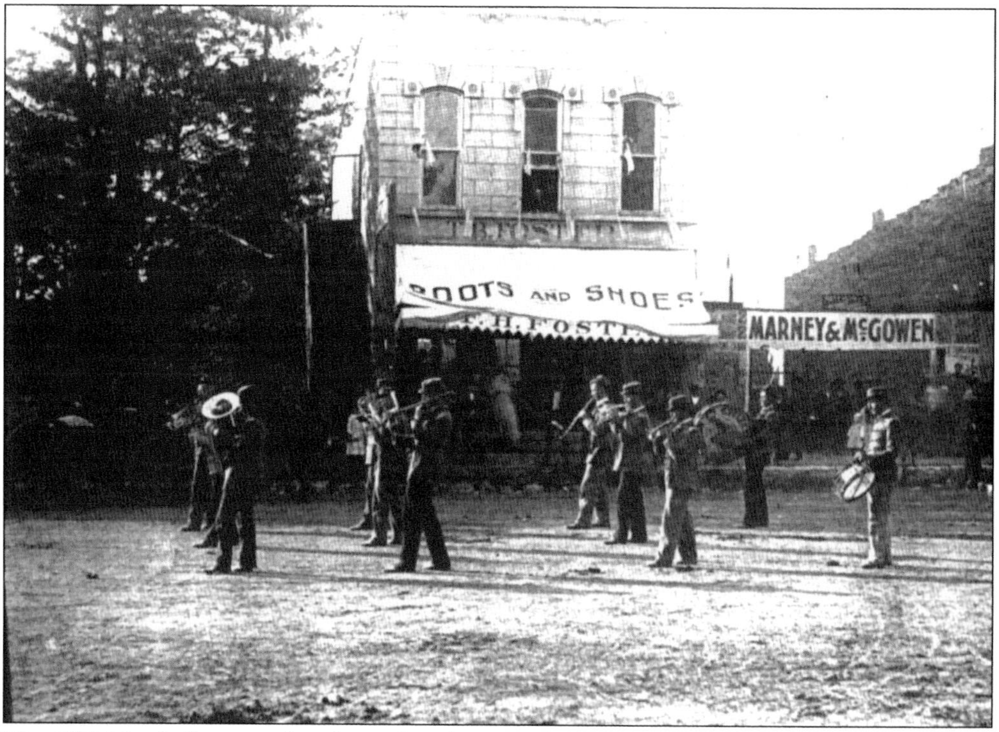

The 1892 Marshall coronet band marches down Archer Avenue between Fifth Street and Sixth Street. The F. H. Foster Boots and Shoes building, behind the band, was later a restaurant, and the vacant area to the right was filled in 1896 with the Odd Fellows IOOF building.

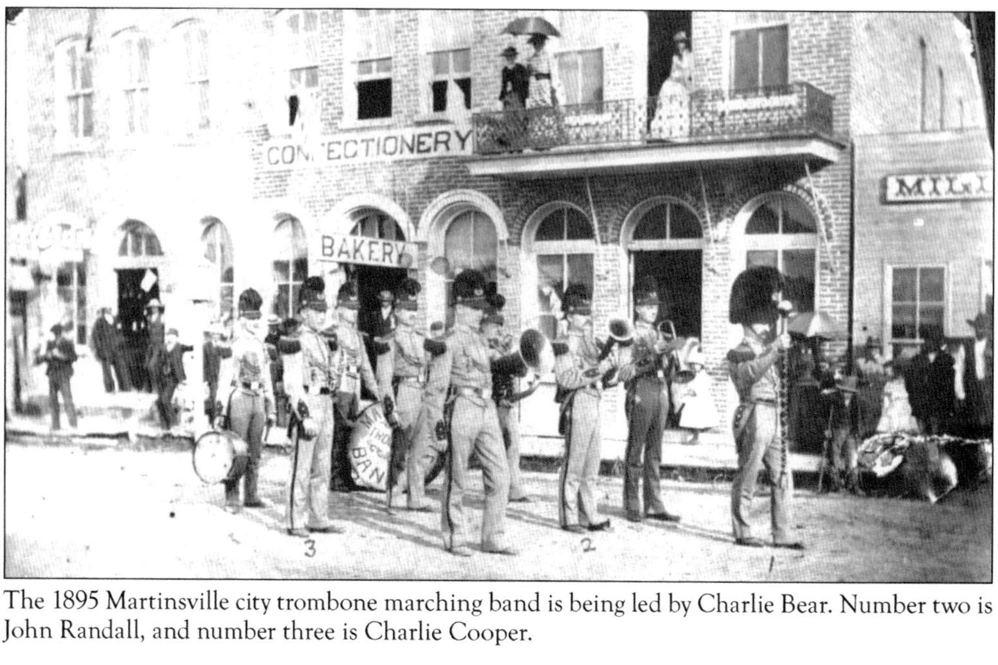

The 1895 Martinsville city trombone marching band is being led by Charlie Bear. Number two is John Randall, and number three is Charlie Cooper.

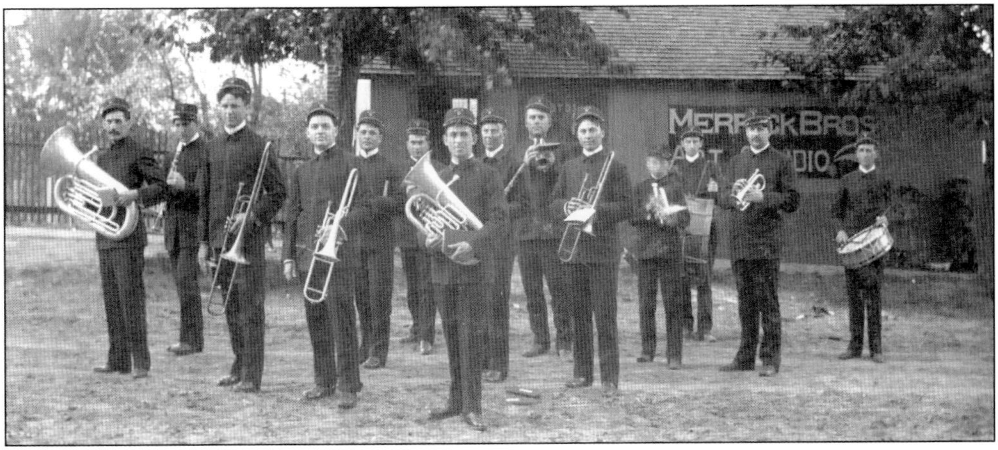

Here is a photograph of the 1903 Westfield band.

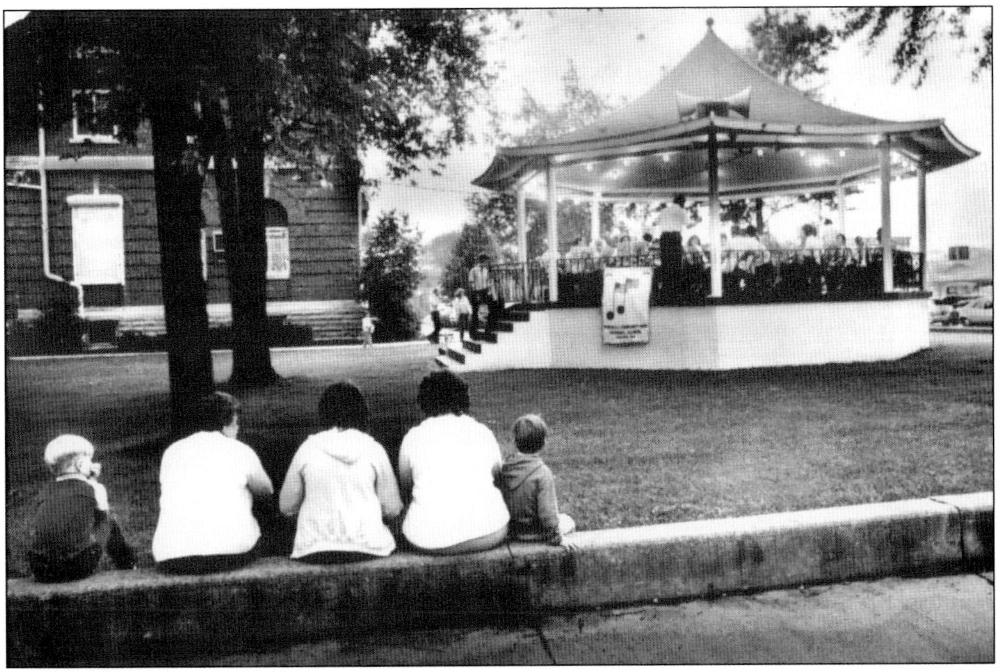

Friday nights on the courthouse grounds in Marshall provide entertainment each summer as the Marshall city band performs. The band has been in existence since 1875 and has been led by director Harold Ellshoff since 1964. The current bandstand was built in 1929.

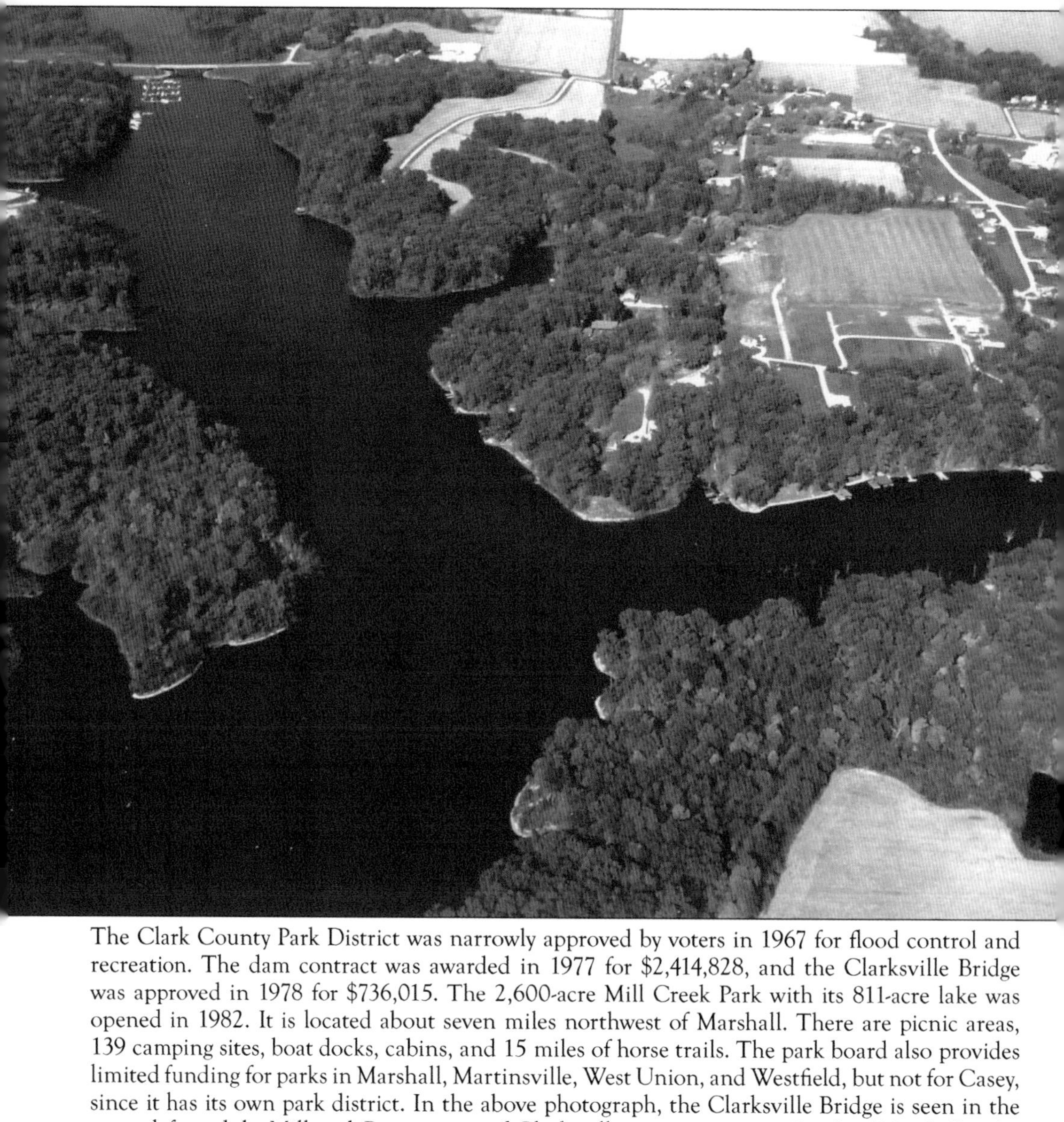

The Clark County Park District was narrowly approved by voters in 1967 for flood control and recreation. The dam contract was awarded in 1977 for $2,414,828, and the Clarksville Bridge was approved in 1978 for $736,015. The 2,600-acre Mill Creek Park with its 811-acre lake was opened in 1982. It is located about seven miles northwest of Marshall. There are picnic areas, 139 camping sites, boat docks, cabins, and 15 miles of horse trails. The park board also provides limited funding for parks in Marshall, Martinsville, West Union, and Westfield, but not for Casey, since it has its own park district. In the above photograph, the Clarksville Bridge is seen in the upper left, and the Millcreek Restaurant and Clarksville are upper center. South of Marshall is the 1,023-acre Lincoln Trail State Park, featuring a 146-acre lake, a restaurant on the water, camping, and picnic areas. The state began acquiring land for Lincoln Trail in 1936, but the park was not opened until 1958. (Courtesy of Pat Rhoads and the Millcreek Restaurant.)

Eight

CHURCHES

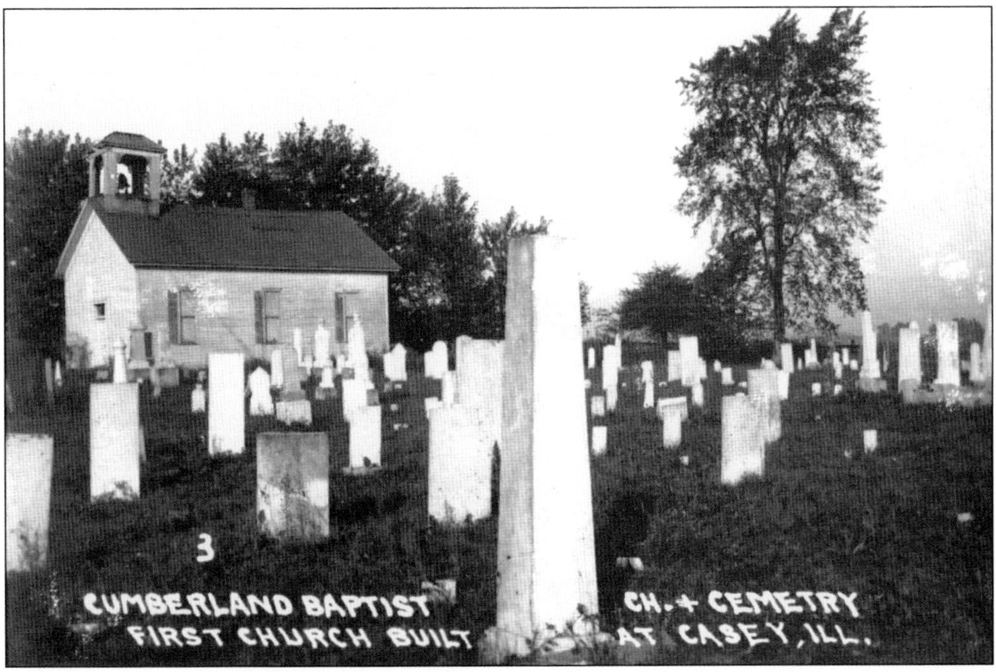

Clark County's first settlers met in private homes to worship, but after a while log churches were built. Eventually the churches were built to last, often constructed of brick. The above photograph shows the old Cumberland Baptist Church along the National Road, just east of downtown Casey. It was the first church in what is now the city of Casey. The congregation disbanded around 1890, and the church building stood until the 1930s.

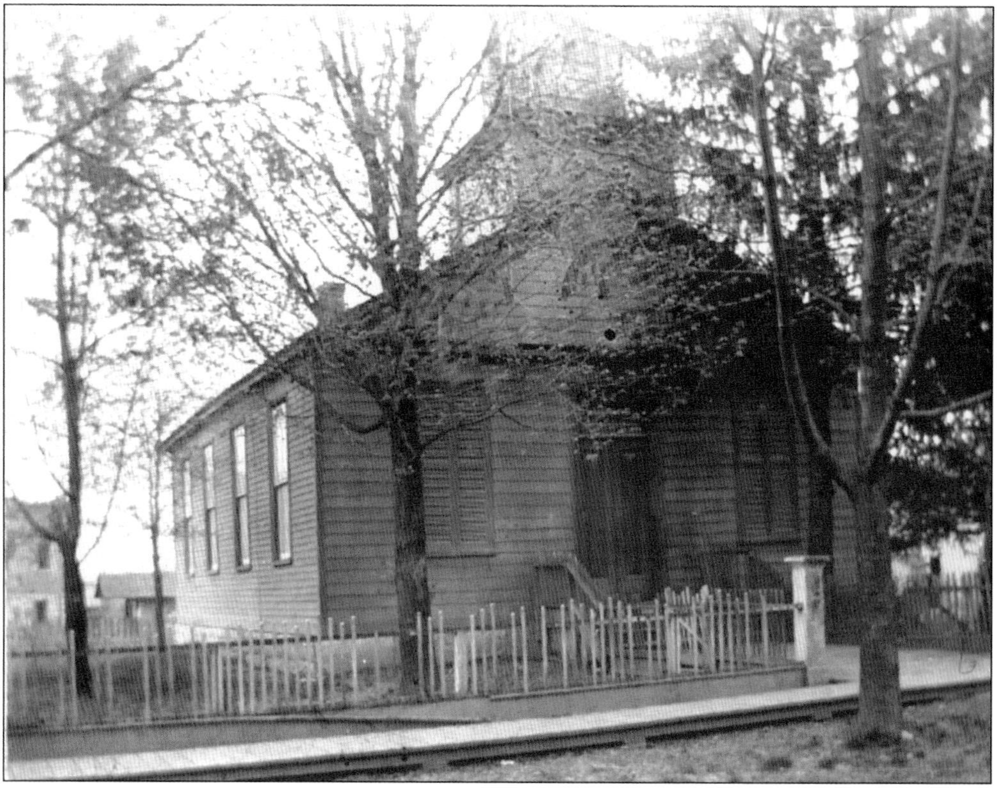

Although the First Congregational Church of Marshall came into existence in 1841, the church building on North Sixth Street was not erected until 1850. It was built on ground donated by Col. William B. Archer. A second church was built on the site in 1892. The current church building (below) was built in 1909 at the same location.

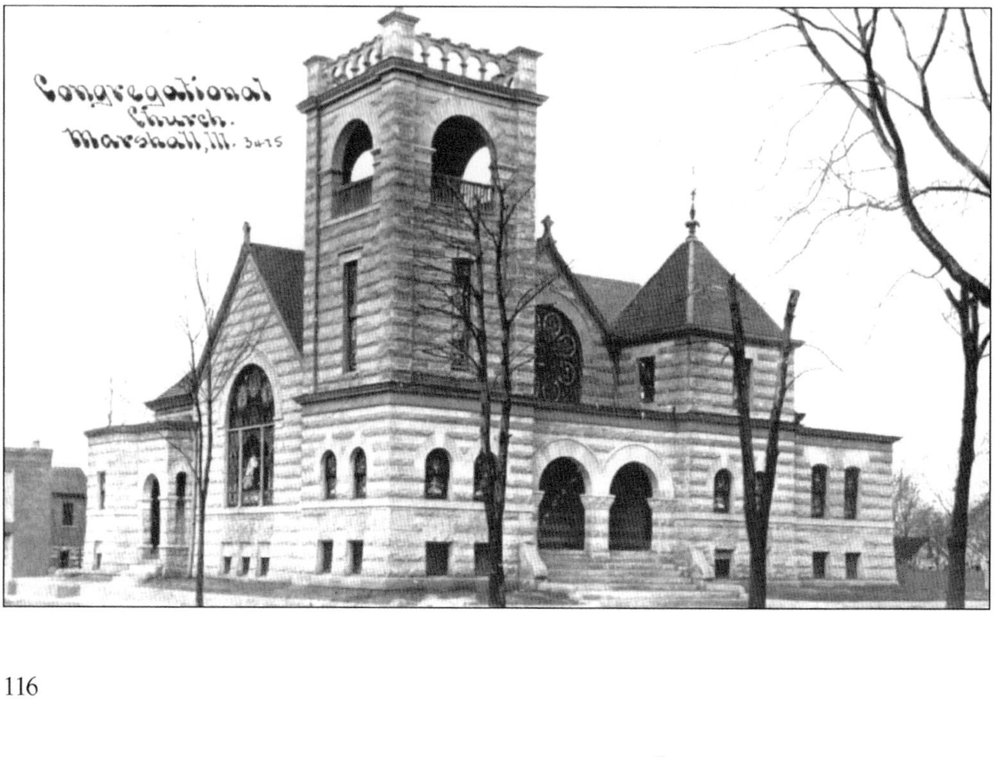

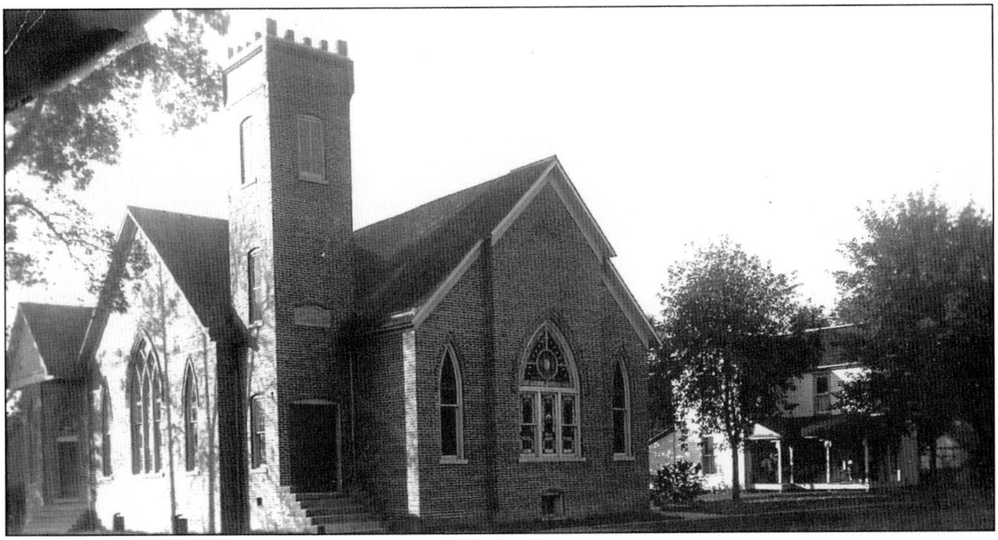

The Martinsville Church of God was organized in 1847, and the first church building was built in 1858. This frame structure was used until the above brick church was built in 1900. The parsonage is to the right. In 1947, the church withdrew from the Church of God organization and became independent under the name of the Martinsville Bible Church. In 1948, Rev. George Nika was named minister, serving in that capacity for 50 years. In 2006, a new church was built on Ridgelawn Road, and the above building is now privately owned.

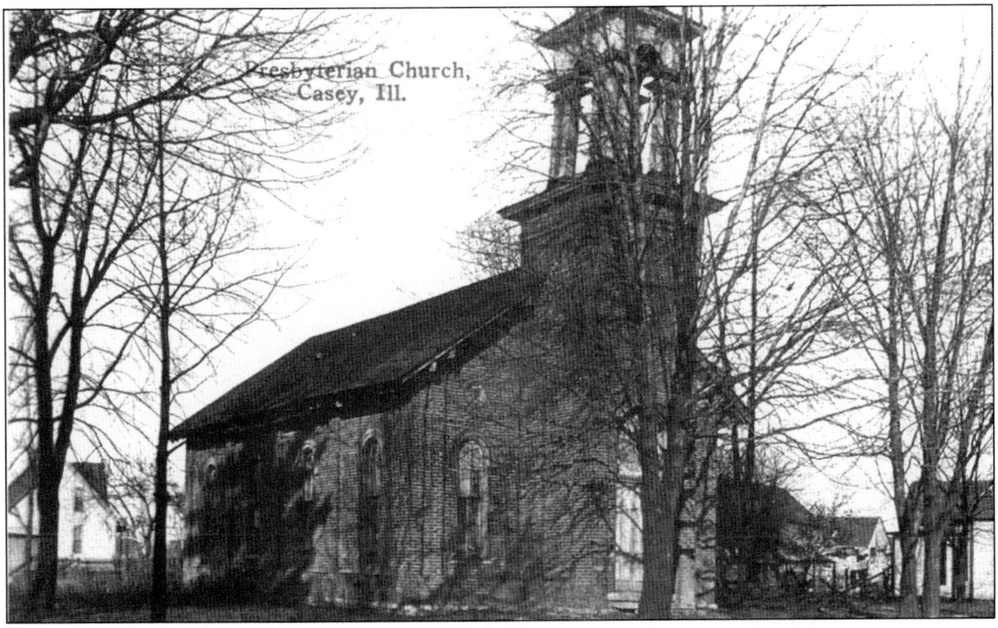

The Casey Presbyterian Church was built in 1873 at the northwest corner of Fifth and Alabama Streets in Casey. It was sold to the Lutheran organization in 1949 and demolished.

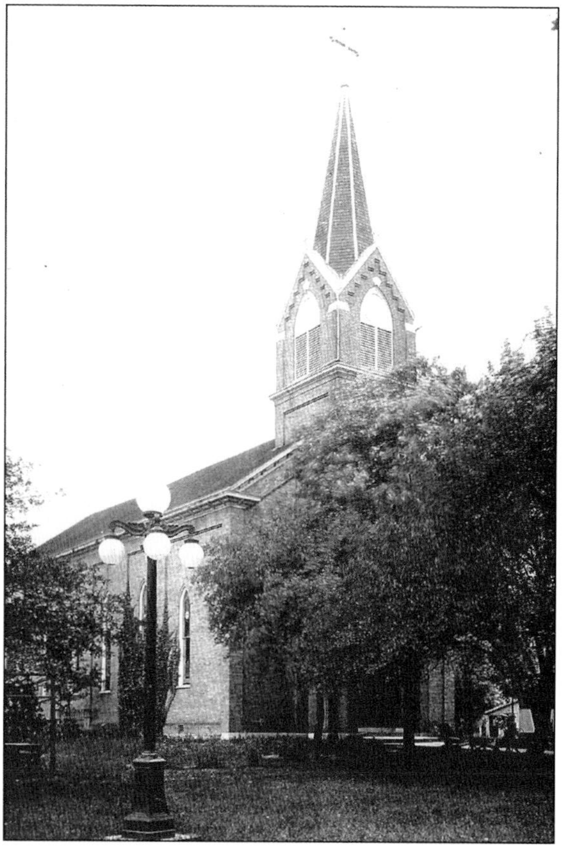

Catholics have been active in Marshall since 1836, and were attended by Father Brady from Vincennes in the early 1800s. Col. William Archer donated land for a Catholic cemetery, and Robert Wilson gave land nearby for a church. The first church was built in 1848–1850, and the present church on South Sixth Street was constructed in 1868. The first rectory was built in 1872, and a new rectory in 1922. A rectory was completed in 1924, but burned in 2001. It was replaced in 2002.

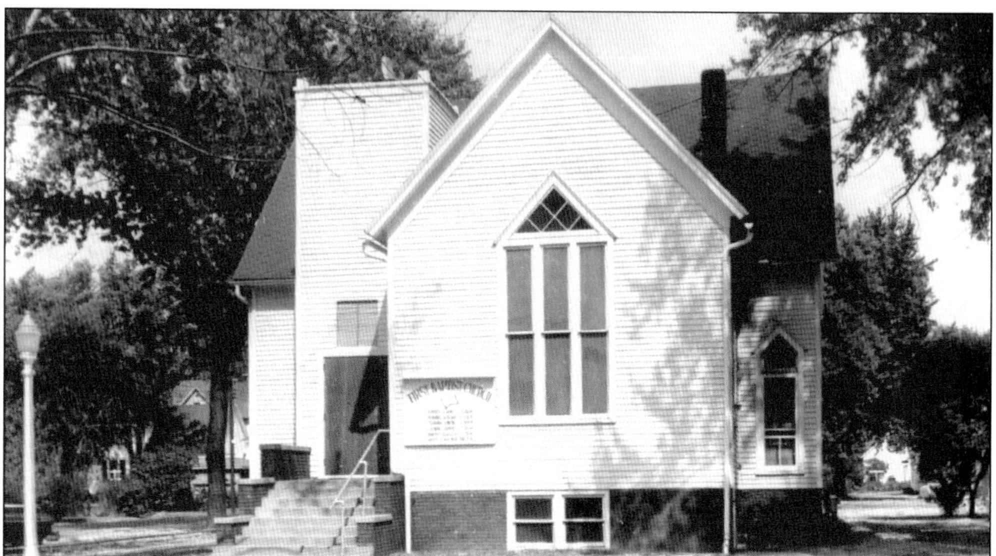

The Casey First Baptist Church was organized in 1893, and the first building erected in 1895 at Northeast First and Alabama Streets. In 1960, the old building was razed and a Bedford stone church took its place. It was expanded through 1976, then again, beginning in 2003.

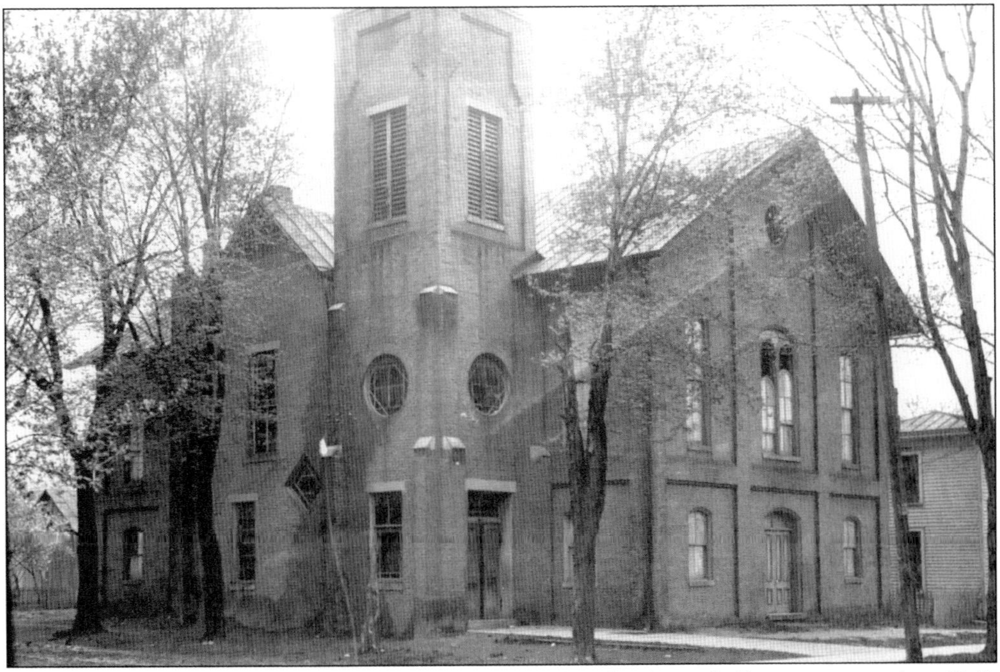

The First United Methodist (Methodist Episcopal) Church of Marshall was organized in 1841, with the first meetings in the frame school of Dean Andrews. The first building, constructed of logs, was completed in 1849 in the 200 block of South Sixth Street. A new building (above), made of brick, was located at the corner of Seventh and Plum streets in 1874. In 1907, this building was torn down, and members met in the courthouse until a third building was constructed of Indiana stone in 1908.

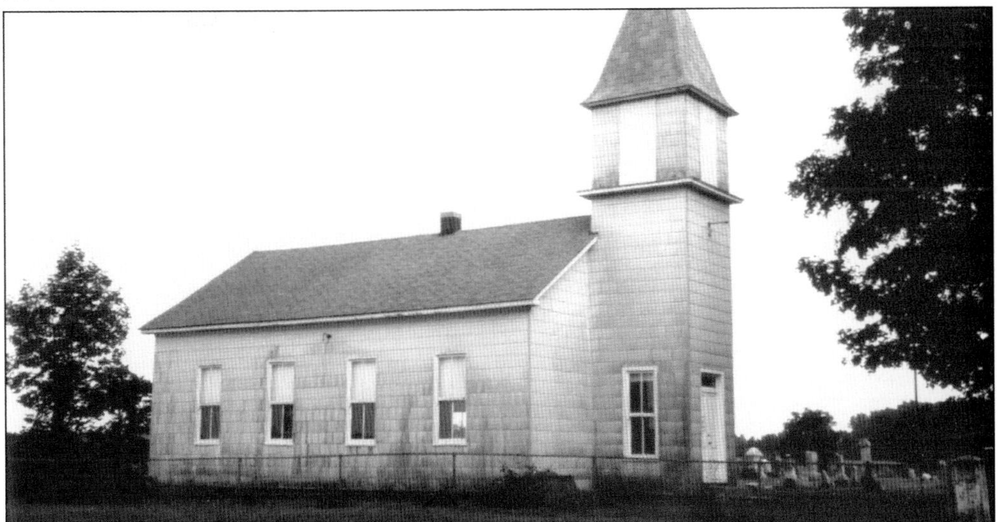

The Green Moss (Dolson Chapel Methodist Church) in Dolson Township, Clark County, is typical of the many country churches in Clark County. The earliest services in the 1850s were held in homes, then at the Green Moss schoolhouse. The current church was erected in 1866. A cemetery is associated with the church, and the will of Ethel Burnside provided funds for maintaining the church and grounds.

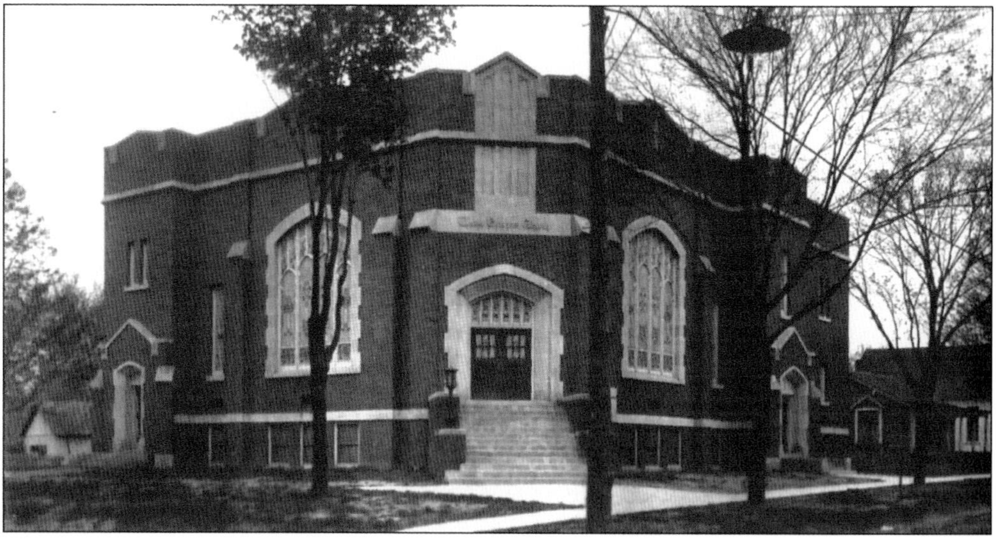

The Westfield United Brethren Church grew out of the Otterbein Chapel in Coles County, which moved to Westfield and built in 1852. Closely connected with Westfield College, the church used a campus building from 1862 until it burned in 1917. A new building of Bedford stone was constructed two blocks north of the campus in 1918. The church merged with the Westfield Methodists in 1969 to become the Westfield United Methodist Church.

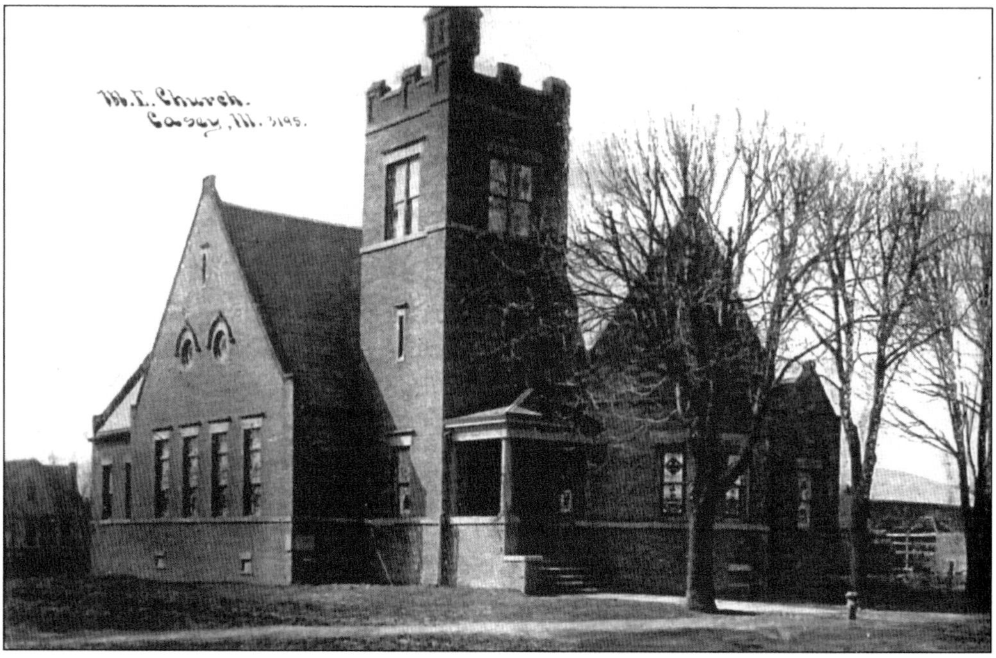

The Casey Methodist Church was organized in 1853, and the first church building constructed in 1856 at 115 East Main Street. In 1894, a two-story frame building was built at Buckeye Avenue and Sixth Street. Four years later, a brick church replaced the frame building. In 1968, the name was changed to the United Methodist Church of Casey. A new church was built in 1976 at 700 North Central Street.

Nine

People and Events

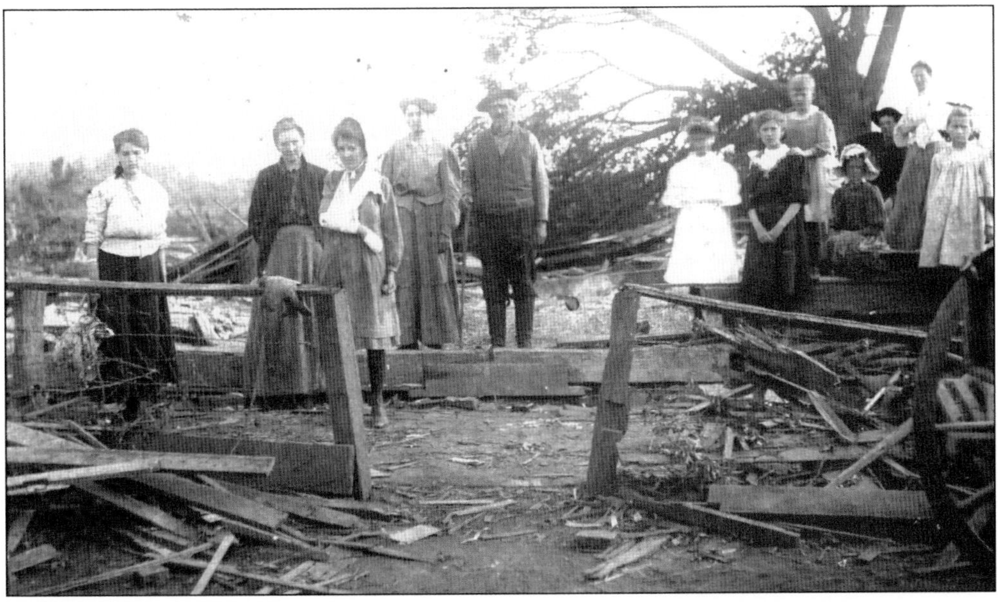

A tornado hit York in 1907, killing two people and destroying two-thirds of the community. Standing in the remains of their home are M. R. Newman, his wife, and daughters. Annabelle was the only one injured. A devastating tornado struck Livingston on May 26, 1917, badly damaging the Livingston Hotel and the home of Til Acorn. In July 1982, a tornado touched down at the Snake Trail campground, destroyed a mobile home, and injured one person.

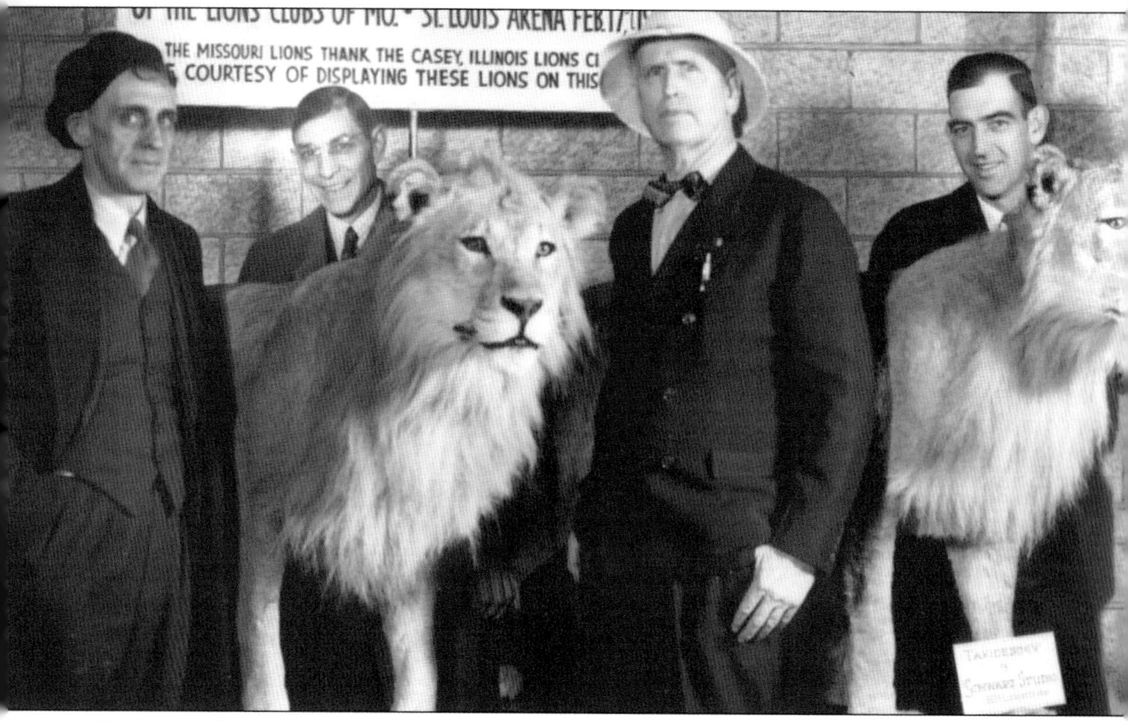

When the Gould Circus came to Casey in 1941, all went well with the traditional parade until one of the animal trucks stalled on the Pennsylvania Railroad track and was struck by the *Spirit of St. Louis*. A male lion, a female lion, and a black bear were thrown from the wreckage. The lioness was mortally wounded, but the male lion and bear roamed the track area, frightening the assembled onlookers. When the male lion moved toward the crowd it was shot by Casey policeman Troy Pulliam (or with his gun by a circus attendant, depending on the source of the information). The circus gave the two dead lions to the Casey Lions club, which had them mounted by a St. Louis taxidermist. One was sold to another Lions club, and the remaining one was alternately exhibited and stored at the Markwell Funeral Home, the Casey library, and Arndt's Dime Store. It was eventually sold to Jim Hutton. Pictured above with the two lions are, left to right, Roy Hutton, Otto Gust, Sid Johnson, and Chief of Police Robert Endres.

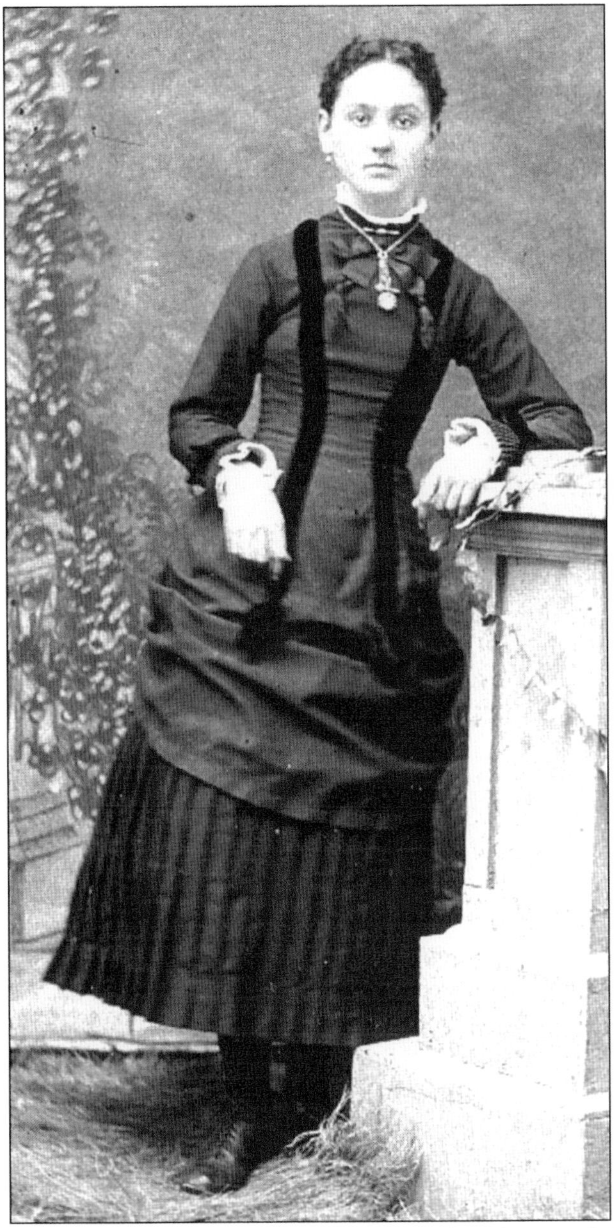

Born in 1869, Casey's Lizzie Johnson sustained a back injury when she was 13. By age 27 she could not lift her head from the pillow, and could move only her hands and forearms, but she accepted her illness as God's will, and looked for some way to help others. She decided to make a crazy quilt and sell it to help girls in Africa. It took six months to painfully finish the small quilt, but no one wanted to buy it. She switched to making bookmarks with verses on them, and sold them for 14 years in every state and 16 foreign countries, earning about $20,000 for missionary work. Bishop Ware of India visited her, was impressed, and took her small quilt. He circled the globe three times telling Lizzie's story, raising $100,000 for missions. After Lizzie died at the age of 40, her younger sister Alice and her father raised an additional $5,000 to erect the Lizzie Memorial Church in India. Lizzie's quilt was given to the United Methodist Church in Casey, where it still hangs.

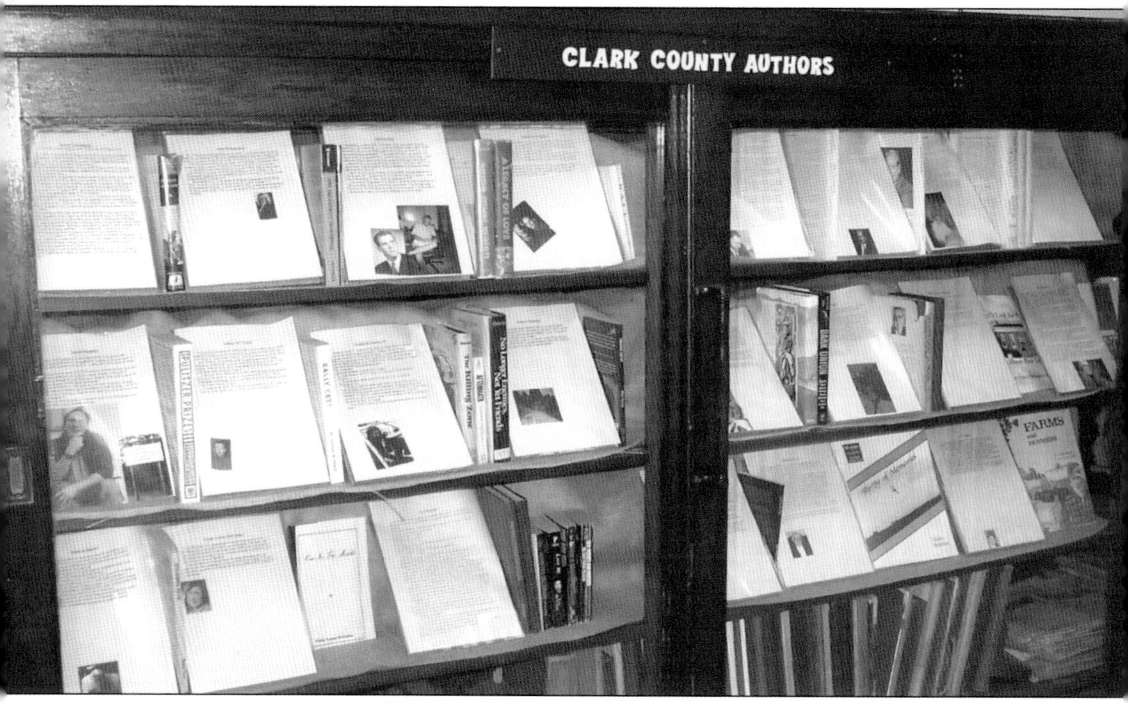

Clark County has produced a number of authors, and the Clark County Historical Society Museum in Marshall features a detailed exhibit which includes the following. Lee Butcher, a 1956 graduate of Marshall High School, authored six non-fiction books and is still writing. While growing up in Marshall, Butcher had a special association with Lowney Turner Handy and James Jones at the Handy Writers Colony. Dwight Connelly, a Martinsville High School graduate, authored two non-fiction books. Mildred Dennis, born in Clarksville, wrote one non-fiction book. Frederick Downs Jr., a 1962 graduate of Marshall High School, penned three non-fiction books about his Vietnam experiences. Joe Fender, born near Westfield, authored four non-fiction books about life in Clark County. Linda Inman, a 1962 graduate of Martinsville High School, authored one non-fiction book, which is extensively illustrated by Linda Miller of rural Martinsville. Rev. Charles Jacobs of Casey wrote a biography of Lizzie Johnson. Butch Martin, a 1956 graduate of Marshall High School, wrote one novel. Joe McCammon of Marshall penned one non-fiction book about Clark County heroes. Vivian McClellan, a 1931 graduate of Marshall High School, authored one non-fiction book about growing up in Marshall.

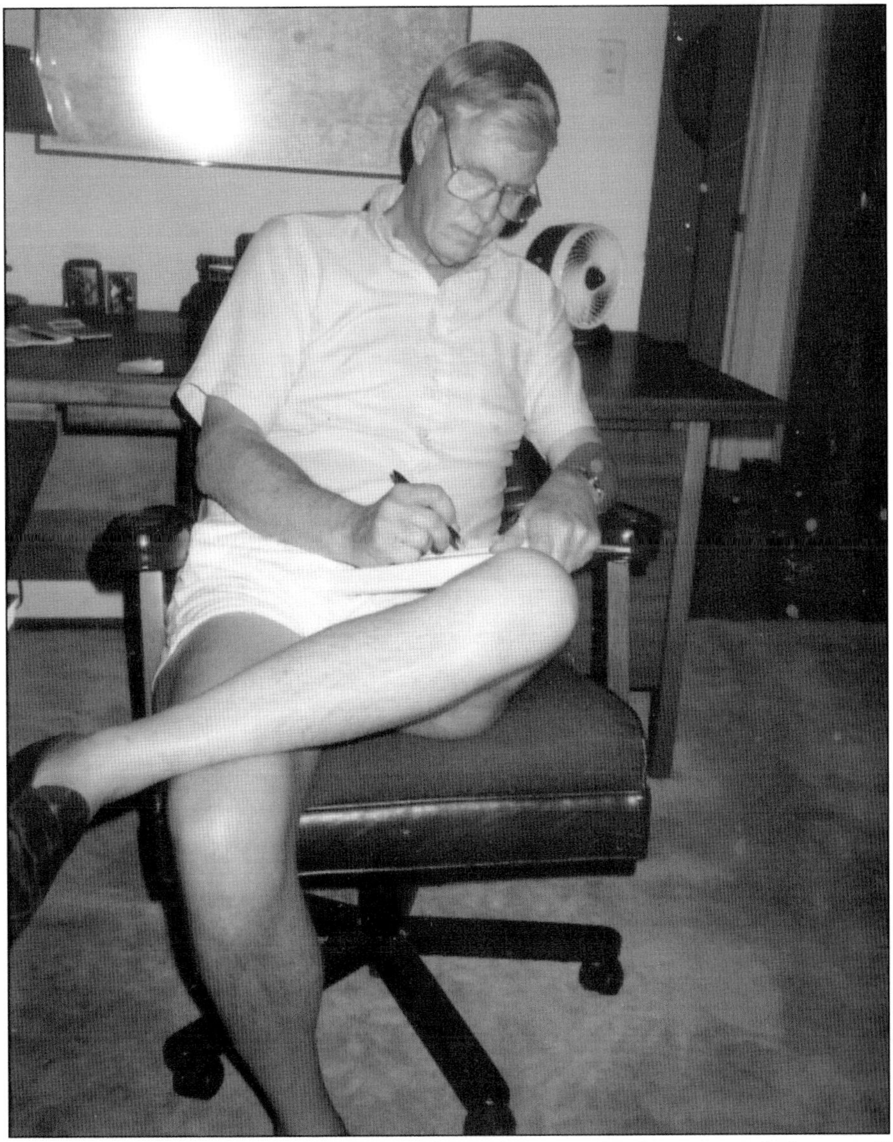

Edwin "Sonny" Daly (above) wrote two novels, working on the first one with Lowney Handy at the writers colony in Marshall while still a student at Marshall High School. Other Clark County authors include Dr. George Mitchell, a 1931 graduate of Marshall High School, who wrote two non-fiction books about his life as a physician; Basil Moore of Marshall authored one book about Lincoln; Ray Neff of Marshall penned two non-fiction books about the Civil War and Lincoln; Eileen Patchett of Casey wrote one non-fiction book about the Casey airport; Cindy and Kirby Pringle of Casey authored two children's books; Dan Reedy, a graduate of Marshall High School, wrote one non-fiction book about growing up in Clark County; Joyce Van Dyke Skinner and Loistel Summerville of Casey joined to write two books about Casey; Don Stephen, a 1963 graduate of Casey High School, authored one non-fiction book about Vietnam; Dr. Mary Emma Thompson, a graduate of Westfield High School, wrote three non-fiction books about post office art; Don Tingley of Marshall authored five non-fiction history books; Jeffrey Veach of Martinsville wrote one book about Clark County in the Civil War; and Edie Wittenmyer of Marshall authored one non-fiction book about horses.

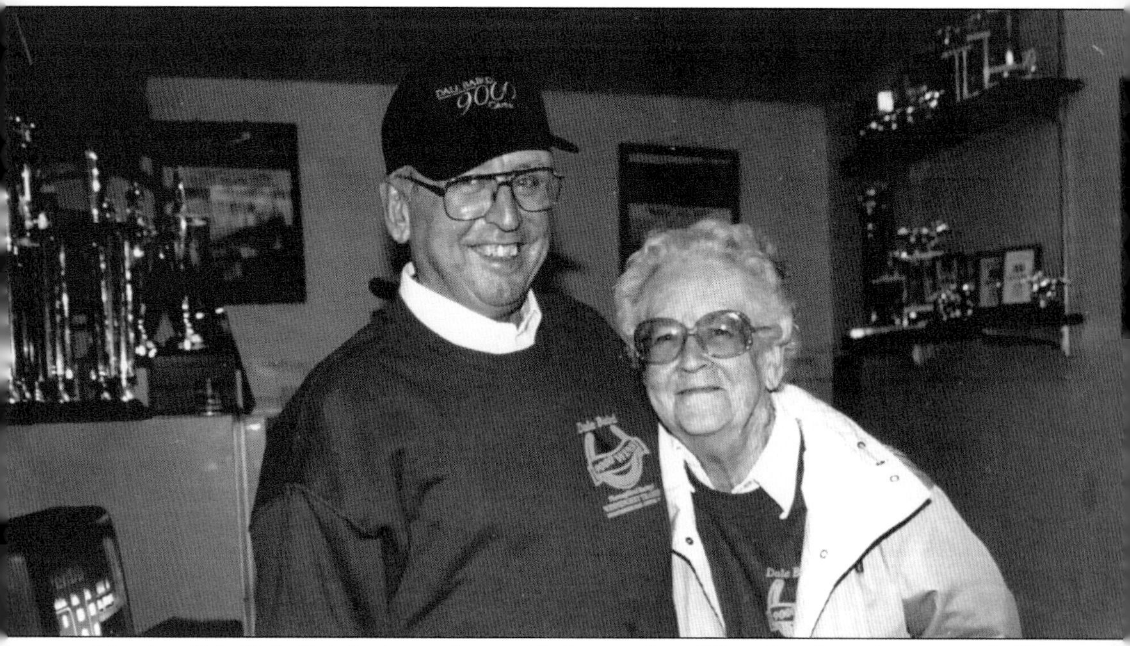

Martinsville's Dale Baird, shown here with his mother, Edna Baird, is the national all-time leading thoroughbred horse trainer, with more than 9,400 victories, most with horses which he owned. He died in a vehicle accident in 2007. Other county natives have also earned national and international recognition. Casey's David Hanners received the Pulitzer Prize in 1989 while writing for the *Dallas Morning News*. West Union's John Strohm was nominated twice for the Pulitzer for his stories about the Soviet Union and China. He was the first non-Canadian to be given Canada's Roland Michener Conservation Award. Strohm died in 1988. Martinsville's Bob Millis, director of the Lowell Observatory, was part of the team which discovered rings around Uranus in 1977. Marshall's Frederick Downs Jr., the author of three books about Vietnam, serves as chief prosthetic and clinical logistics officer at the Veterans Health Administration, managing a nationwide program. He also assists with the search for MIAs in Vietnam.

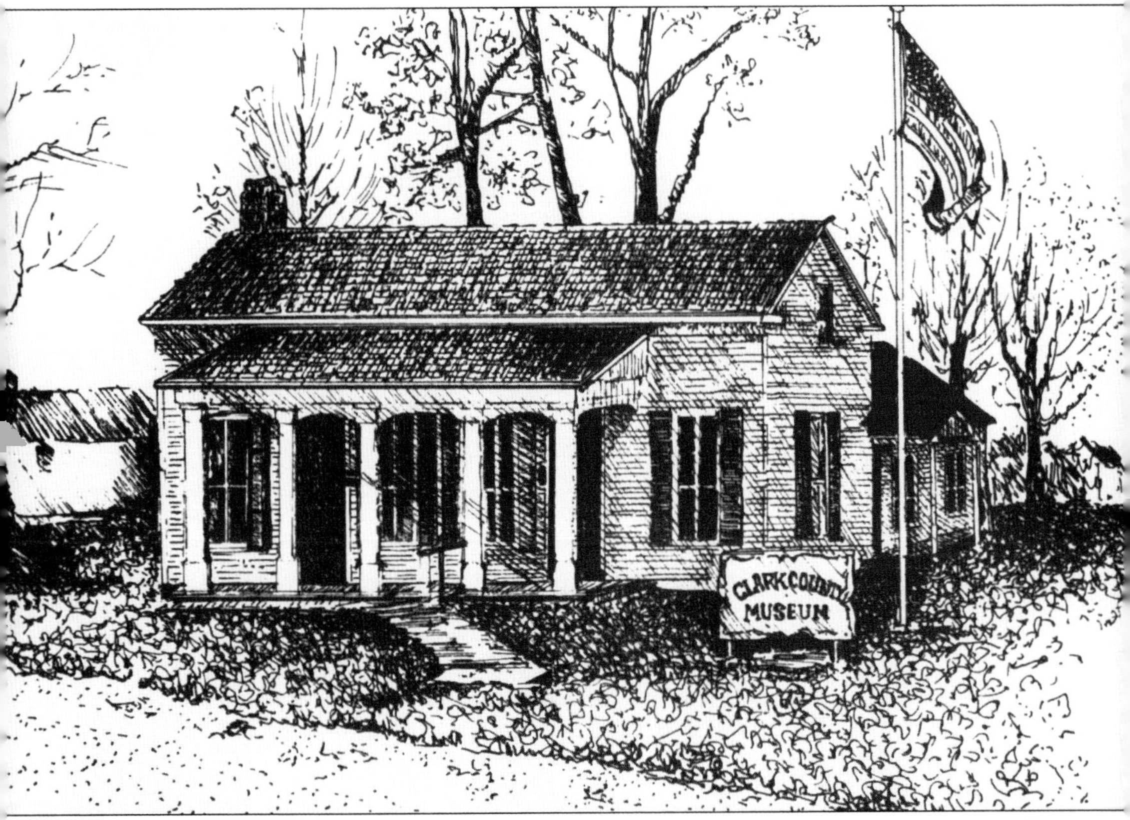

The Clark County Historical Society was founded in 1966 with the late Dr. George Mitchell as its first president. The organization maintains three buildings at Fourth and Maple Streets as museums. The main building was built in 1838 and served as a temporary post office. It was opened as a museum in 1970 and was listed on the National Register of Historic Places in 1982. One of the exhibits in the main building is the desk used by Marshall co-founder Col. William Archer in the early 1800s. Other interesting items include a piano made in Marshall, kitchen chairs made in Marshall, and a desk made by Omer T. Shawler in 1885 from a steamboat wrecked on the Wabash River. A second building is used for special exhibits, and the third building is the Henry Baggs log house which was moved to the museum site and restored. Membership in the Clark County Historical Society is open to everyone with an interest in county history. Donations of items related to Clark County which can be displayed are encouraged. (Drawing by Linda Miller.)

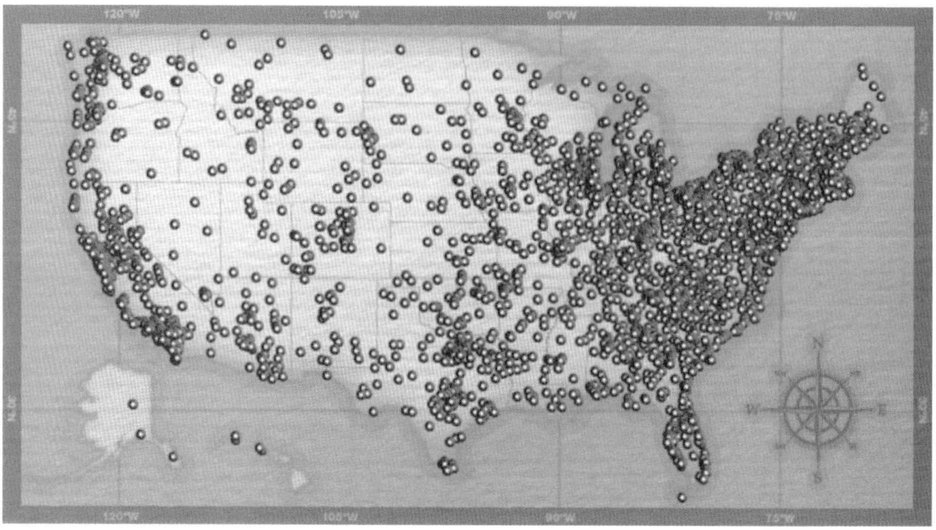